Riding the Wave

Riding the Wave

Designing Your Organization's Architecture for Enduring Success

KEITH MERRON

VAN NOSTRAND REINHOLD
I(T)P A Division of International Thomson Publishing Inc.

New York • Albany • Bonn • Boston • Detroit • London • Madrid • Melbourne
Mexico City • Paris • San Francisco • Singapore • Tokyo • Toronto

Copyright © 1995 by Van Nostrand Reinhold
I(T)P™   A division of International Thomson Publishing Inc.
         The ITP logo is a trademark under license

Printed in the United States of America
For more information, contact:

Van Nostrand Reinhold
115 Fifth Avenue
New York, NY 10003

International Thomson Publishing
   Europe
Berkshire House 168-173
High Holborn
London WC1V 7AA
England

Thomas Nelson Australia
102 Dodds Street
South Melbourne, 3205
Victoria, Australia

Nelson Canada
1120 Birchmount Road
Scarborough, Ontario
Canada M1K 5G4

International Thomson Publishing
   GmbH
Königswinterer Strasse 418
53227 Bonn
Germany

International Thomson Publishing
   Asia
221 Henderson Road #05 10
Henderson Building
Singapore 0315

International Thomson Publishing
   Japan
Hirakawacho Kyowa Building, 3F
2-2-1 Hirakawacho
Chiyoda-ku, 102 Tokyo
Japan

International Thomson Editores
Campos Eliseos 385, Piso 7
Col. Polanco
11560 Mexico D.F. Mexico

1 2 3 4 5 6 7 8 9 10 RRDHB 01 00 99 98 97 96 95 94

Library of Congress Cataloging-in-Publication Data
Merron, Keith.
   Riding the wave : designing your organization's architecture for enduring
success / Keith Merron.
      p.   cm.
   Includes bibliographical references and index.
   ISBN 0-442-01803-7
   1. Organizational change.   I. Title.
HD58.8.M466   1994   94-21084
658.4'063—dc20   CIP

Contents

Preface

We live in a world in which change is so massive, it plagues the minds and hearts of managers and business leaders everywhere. Amidst this, leaders of organizations are constantly looking for ways to manage the growth of their organizations so that they can stay ahead of the pack or, at the very least, not get too far behind. All too often, however, business leaders react to change after it happens. Given the speed of change, *reacting* to it is a sure guarantee for failure. Success in today's business climate goes to those organizations that *anticipate* change and *respond* in a way that poises them for more success in the future.

Picture a series of ocean waves rapidly moving toward the shoreline. These waves are much like the sea of changes that are occurring in today's business climate. These ocean waves are huge and ever present.

Like a swimmer in the ocean who is taken unaware of their presence, businesses that get caught up inside these waves of change are likely to be churned and pummelled by their massive force. The challenge for any organization is to *not fight the waves,* for the organization will surely be swept up in the powerful current. Further, to deny the existence of the waves is to invite them to crash upon the organization. The path of wisdom in today's business climate is to learn how to catch the wave early as it is evolving and surf on top of it, staying ever aware of its presence and power.

While easy to say, this is extraordinarily difficult to do. There are numerous forces that impact our ability to ride the waves of change: our abilities, where we focus our attention, our available technology, and our financial resources, to name a few. Perhaps the greatest impediments to riding the waves of change are the human aspects of the organization. How we design and structure the organization and how we relate to one another determines, to a large extent, whether we either experience an exciting ride on the waves of change, or get crushed by their force. All too often, leaders of companies create structures, systems, and processes that are successful in the short run, but hinder their organization's ability to respond to the waves of future change. Part of the dilemma is that success often directs leaders to develop strong structures, strong cultures, and strong systems that become deeply etched in the organization's fabric. This paradoxically renders the organization slow to change and therefore less effective in the future. In other words, one's present success can sow the seeds for future failure.

This book is intended to help organizations transcend this scenario and create an alternate one. It was born out of the premise that the way we design and lead our organization's architecture has all to do with its future success. For the purposes of this book, the *organization's architecture* refers to the most fundamental elements of the organization that drive the choices people make and how they make them. The organization's architecture includes its vision, strategic direction and strategic goals, its culture, and its structure.

This book is written for leaders who want to "architect" their organization in ways that will make them both adaptable and strong—to lay a foundation for success in riding the waves of change well into the future. It is also based on the premise that strength need not breed rigidity, but that it is possible to create strong organizations that are also quick and nimble. All too often, organizations reach a state of maturity where it is almost impossible to change. They become bloated with bureaucratic systems and policies, and imbued with politics. In such conditions, more energy is spent on maintaining positions of power than on meeting customers' needs and requirements. Few large, mature organizations have the ability to transform, yet they must do so in order to survive in a changing environment.

This book is directed toward leaders of organizations, from small and young organizations to large and mature. For those readers who are leading young organizations, I strongly urge you to start thinking about the future now and how to prepare your organization's architecture for that future. If you wait until things "settle down a bit more," you may become slow-footed and stuck all too soon. For those readers of more mature organizations that are stuck and not growing, you must act now for the next phase of your organization's life is likely to be one of decay and slow demise. And if you act, be prepared to act with courage, for you will likely find significant resistance to change along the way.

Why write a "how to" book on whole systems change? One of the reasons I wrote this book was that while the fields of organizational development and transformation have played a significant role as a catalyst for growth and change, few books are written in these fields that give the reader a clear sense of how to manage the process. They often provide elegant theories and are rich in research and example, but leave the reader guessing how to put these principles and theories into practice. It is the intent of this book to fill this void. It is both a theoretical and a "how-to" book. I feel very strongly that theory is empty without an understanding of how to put that theory into practice. At the same time, actions without the bedrock of values, principles, and theory to guide them are subject to dangerous malpractice and generally not replicable in a wide variety of situations. Put more directly, any practical set of skills has an underlying theory and set of principles. If you follow the principles and you understand the theory, the skills will come much more easily. It is the intent of this book to provide both theory and practice, and to use examples so that the reader is rarely left guessing as to how to proceed.

How this book is organized. The first four chapters of the book explain the steps involved in designing one's organizational architecture and the key principles that underlie the process. The rest of the book gives specific guidance on how to do it, with examples along the way. Specifically, this book begins with an introduction that provides a definition for "organizational architecture," a rationale for the importance of growing one's organizational architecture, and a description of the process. Chapters 2 and 3 explain each of the five elements of an organization's architecture and an example of the implications of mismanagement of the architecture.

Chapter 4 discusses the values and principles needed to effectively design an organization's architecture.

The book proceeds with an overview of the decision-making phases of designing or redesigning an organization's architecture, exploring the reasons behind the phases and the skills required for their effective implementation (Chapters 5–7). The next five chapters focus on the implementation phases. They help leaders facilitate actual changes in your organization. This phase is described in detail, demonstrating how to change each of five key elements of an organization's architecture and how these changes can help you develop your organization as a whole (Chapters 8–12). Chapter 13 describes an example of the inner workings of an organizational architecting effort. The book ends by discussing the importance of evaluating your efforts and explores the critical features and functions of a learning organization, an organization able to continually adapt and grow in the future.

Examples and concrete illustrations are given throughout the book to highlight key principles and to reduce ambiguity and potential confusion. Most of these examples are drawn from actual companies. A few examples are made up to illustrate a point. Even these, however, are generally drawn from my experience or that of others. I have altered some examples slightly so as to maintain the anonymity of the company. I have endeavored, however, to maintain the spirit of the facts and to accurately represent them.

A personal note to the reader. Writing a book that provides clear step-by-step guidance has been an enormous challenge for me. It has required me to answer the question: Given only a limited amount of time to communicate what I think, what would I say? After having written the book, I now have a deeper appreciation for why so few authors explain in detail how to lead whole systems change. The differing possible situations and permutations of these situations are endless. I have done my best to give clear instructions for how to go about designing an organization's architecture, knowing full well that the reader will face numerous situations I did not anticipate, or ever could. For this, the reader will have to fall back on theory and principles for guidance. The principles of how to lead change will endure while the situations themselves will inevitably vary. If, along the path, you find yourself unsure of how to proceed, I urge you to fall back on your own instincts and let your values be your guide. Ultimately, when all is said and done, these are what must endure.

Keith Merron

Novato, California

Acknowledgments

While the writing of this book has been a singularly individual effort, it could not have occurred without the support, guidance, and input from a number of fellow colleagues and friends. I wish to take this opportunity to thank each and every one of them for their kind help and generous insights, all of which made this book a true labor of love.

Thanks first go to Bob Lindsay. His eloquence of speech and writing is only exceeded by the care and time that he took in poring through an early draft and giving me extremely useful feedback. I also wish to thank my colleagues Mike McKeon, Tim Fuller, and Becky Smith whose support and comments on an early draft helped improve it considerably. Much appreciation goes out to my colleagues Jack Knight, Mary Gelinas, Martha Danly Greer, Lion Goodman, and Jeff Heilpern whose comments on early chapters greatly enriched their content. Particular thanks go to Leland Brendsel and David Glenn, who were extremely generous with their time and provided valuable guidance in helping me understand the growth and development of Freddie Mac. Thanks also go to Beth Preiss who helped improve the chapter on Freddie Mac immensely.

Much appreciation goes to Steve Weinstein, President of Logistix, Coleman Andrews, President of WorldCorp, and Steven Cumbie, President of NV Commercial, whose comments and feedback on early chapters did much to ensure the relevance of the book to senior executives.

I wish to thank my editor Jeanne Glasser and her assistant, Dawn Wechsler, who provided valuable support and guidance in the process of developing the book. I also wish to thank Lynne Ciccone for the wonderful work she did in developing the graphics for the book.

I would also like to acknowledge and thank some of the people who have greatly shaped the thinking in this book and my career as a consultant. Warm and deep appreciation goes to Bill Torbert who inspired me to become an organizational consultant early on in my adulthood, and provided me with much needed coaching and guidance; to Chris Argyris, Lee Bolman, and Terry Deal, who stimulated my early thinking as a graduate student and budding consultant; and, most importantly, to Mike McKeon, whose caring guidance, belief in my abilities, and more recent partnership has provided me with far more than I can ever give in return.

Finally, I want to thank my wife, Tina Benson, who endured numerous early morning forays to the computer without ever complaining, who provided enormous encouragement in the writing of this book, and who has never wavered in her belief in my abilities as a consultant and potential as an author. It is to her that this book is dedicated.

1

Introduction

*You cannot step twice into the same river, for other waters are
continually flowing on.*

—Heraclitus

He sat slumped in the soft leathery
chair of his library. Books were strewn about. Piles of
computer printouts like pillars of Greek ruins were rem-
nants of glory past. His computer terminal lay tired
beside him. He was exhausted. He had just spent two
hours responding to a cacophony of questions by re-
porters from all over the computer industry. The hours
seemed like an eternity. "Where did it all go wrong?,"
asked one. "Will you make a comeback?," asked another. "When did you know you were going to go
bankrupt?" "Did you know that sales were going to be
as bad as they were?" "Why didn't you heed the advice
of your Chief Financial Officer?" "How much will you
personally lose as a result?"

The questions haunted him now, relentlessly reminding him of the frustrations of the past year. A

rapid succession of nightmarish images flashed through his brain. The moment he realized the company was in severe trouble. The meeting with his financial consultant. Going over the books time and time again. Is it really this bad? Are the projections that gloomy? Is this really possible? That was a year ago. Since then, the struggle to get back on track. The layoffs. The public relations messages. The news articles. The last-ditch effort to salvage the company. And now, the statement to the press about the bankruptcy.

Until recently, he and his company had led a charmed life, like no other in the history of the modern business world. He was the darling of his industry. The technical genius turned business genius. The brilliant architect of one of the most creative business inventions of the new age. He was William Techbright, the founder of Techbright Electronics.

The company started with a dream: to be the quality company of choice in its industry. At the end of the first year, sales were over $3 million. By the end of the second year, they were well over $40 million. The company, in the span of three years, became one of the fastest growing companies in history. But then the ground fell from beneath him. Sales declined rapidly, and product development slowed to a crawl. Critics argued that his greatest mistake was that, in spite of the hypergrowth the company was experiencing, it was never financially sound. In addition, many said that the company did not anticipate that the market would change as rapidly as it did, nor were they ready for the influx of Japanese companies competing in its market. But underlying this mistake was a more fundamental one: William Techbright had not taken time to thoughtfully architect his organization. It grew, to be sure, but his people were hired hastily to perform duties and carry out responsibilities for which they had little experience. It grew because the company was founded on a good idea, and was at the right place at the right time. The company grew enormously, but it lacked the social structure and business foundation to sustain growth. It grew, but it did not develop from within.[1]

The story of William Techbright's company is not an unusual one. Similar things are happening in companies throughout the country. According to a recent study, less than 30 percent of small businesses formed in the late 1970s survived (with the same owner) for at least eight years.[2] The remainder either failed or underwent significant changes in ownership and focus. While not as dark a view as that of conventional wisdom—which says that only 20 percent of businesses survive for at least five years—most business efforts are far more apt to fail than succeed. This failure is, in part, directly attributable to the fact that *most leaders of businesses focus their efforts on a limited few aspects of the business, to the exclusion of managing the process of growth and change.* It is happening because leaders of businesses don't have the knowledge or understanding of the process of development necessary to expand or grow their business. Successful companies, like Corning Glass, do.

The story of Corning Glass' turnaround in the last few years is a story quite different than that of Techbright Electronics. Born from the hopes and dreams of its president, James R. Houghton, the great-great-grandson of the founder, it is a story of success. This success was built not from riches, but from a strong social foundation, a vision of the future, and a carefully laid plan of execution. It is the story of the process of

---

[1] While the drama of the story is fictitious, the essence of the story of Techbright is true. Some of the facts have been altered slightly and the name changed to protect the anonymity of the company.
[2] Kirchoff, B. *Dynamic Capitalism*, Praeger, 1994.

designing anew one's organizational architecture and the effective management of change.

When Houghton took the reins from his older brother in 1983, the company had just experienced three years of declining profits. In addition, 70 percent of its revenues came from slow-growth business where Corning controlled little of the market share. Building from a vision of establishing an organizational foundation for his company that would endure, Houghton embarked on a six-point plan to develop his company. This plan included:

1. *A Focus on Quality.* To help make his pursuit of quality a reality, Houghton established partnerships with union employees and trained all employees in the tools and techniques of continuous improvement.

2. *Forming Alliances.* As of mid-1991, Corning had established 19 partnerships with other companies to strengthen its technology and expand its markets.

3. *Share Technology.* Rather than reinforce separate efforts at technology advance, as had been the case in the past, technologies were communicated and recycled throughout the organization, thereby leveraging technological advances.

4. *Cooperation with Labor.* Far more than ever before, union members were involved in key decisions, even to the point of having significant roles in the design of plants.

5. *Promoting Diversity.* As a result of its training efforts to spread sensitivity to the need for diversity, more women and black executives than ever have reached top management and attrition among women and blacks is down significantly.

6. *Improve the Community.* Corning became actively involved in efforts to improve the community, including rehabilitating commercial properties and selling them back to the community at market rates.

As a result of these efforts, in 1991 return on equity was 16.3 percent, up from 7.3 percent in 1983. As of 1992, Corning was leading the market in optical fibers and in ceramics for pollution control, and earnings were up considerably from years past.[3]

Although you may not be the owner of a large company like William Techbright, or the president of a large company with a proud corporate history like James Houghton, as a leader of your organization you must care deeply about the success of your company, the organization or unit for which you are responsible, and the people you employ. You undoubtedly feel responsible for finding out how you can best steer your organization's effectiveness in the future. If you are like a growing number of executives and managers, you also feel responsible for finding out how you can best contribute to the overall success and development of your employees in following that course.

As a leader, you have two monumental tasks ahead of you: (1) *how to manage your organization in a way that is most successful right now* (William Techbright did that relatively well); and (2) *how to redesign your organization toward enduring success in the future* (William Techbright did not do this). This book speaks to your second challenge.

---

[3] See *Business Week*, May 13, 1991, pp. 68–76.

WHAT DOES ORGANIZATIONAL ARCHITECTURE MEAN?

The dictionary defines *architecture* as the design and structure of a building. The phrase "architecture of the organization" implies the same, as it relates to the organizational systems, processes, and structures. It is a phrase that is growing in popularity among theorists of organizational behavior and practitioners of organizational development.

In this book I use the phrase "organizational architecture" to denote the design and structure of the organization: those features of the organization that guide human interactions, relationships, decision making, and organizational direction. While this book focuses primarily on the human factors that affect success, they do not exist within a void. Organizations are most successful to the extent that the social design and structure match well with the technical features of the organization. It is through the organization's architecture that the technical features are used to their fullest potential.

Organizational Architecture is a powerful metaphor for describing those features of the organization that represent its foundation and ensure its success in the future. While easy to say, creating a viable organizational architecture is not so easy to do.

The great Loma Prieta earthquake of October 19, 1989, taught everyone living in the San Francisco Bay area a dramatic lesson in the importance of architecture. Architects say that the design of a building and its construction have everything to do with how well that building will withstand a major earthquake. Proper guidelines for designing a building have to do with two factors: the strength of the structure and its flexibility.

The strength of the building refers to the degree to which its elements will not crumble under the enormous force of an earthquake. The flexibility of the building has to do with the degree to which it will flow with the earth's movement and therefore be unaffected by much of the earthquake's shock. If a building is to be both strong and flexible, these properties have to be designed into the building's structure and its foundation by the architect who wants a building that is not only effective now, but will be a monument of strength, beauty, and endurance far into the future.

Exactly the same principles apply to the building of a human organization. Organizations, like buildings, must have a firm foundation in order to grow, change, and prosper, and they must have the flexibility to endure the vast array of challenges they will face during their life cycle. Leaders of organizations are, in effect, responsible for creating the architecture of their respective organizations. They have the responsibility to ensure that their organization is built on a foundation of values, has a clear direction, and is structured in a way that ensures flexibility in the face of environmental challenges and efficiency in the face of stiff competition. By being thoughtful about the critical elements of the design of his or her organization, an effective leader defines the architecture of the organization and significantly increases the likelihood of success for the future.

Few modern business leaders have this focus, however. They put their attention instead on other aspects of running an organization that are perhaps more familiar to them. Most leaders attend to such things as the technology of the organization, the day-to-day problems that plague the firm, or the financial aspects of the company. The latter, in particular, consumes the minds of most business leaders, often to the detriment of the long-term success of their companies.

An example of this came to me recently in the form of my local newspaper, the *San Francisco Chronicle*. The leading article in the Business section of a recent issue revealed in dramatic fashion the "CHRONICLE 100: Northern California's Best Companies." In this article, the newspaper reported the "company of the year," "comeback of the year," "fastest growing company," and in general the "top 100 companies" and their results.[4] What stood out to me was their criteria for determining the "best." It was purely short-term financial results. They used (as do most articles of the kind) the following criteria to determine the winners: return on equity, change in annual net income, one-year percentage increase in sales, and total return to shareholders.

Most people would not take issue with this definition of "best," yet ironically, an article on page 3 of the same Business section reports that "31 Companies Fell Off List—Including Last Year's Winner." Being the best sure is a fleeting experience.

Defining and measuring business success based purely on short-term financial results reinforces a paradigm that is a key cause of our business system's slow decline. As a result of our focus on short-term financial results, we get just that—*short-term* success. Some leaders of organizations take the short-term view so far they think that by manipulating some aspects of the organization's finances, or by cutting costs through downsizing, they can change the organization. A recent "Laborforce 2000" study of over 400 companies, for example, pointed out that when asked their reasons for downsizing, most companies listed the need to contain

---

[4] *San Francisco Chronicle*, April 19, 1993, p. D1.

costs, improve profitability, improve efficiency, and counter growing competition.[5] Yet downsizing, while sometimes necessary, in the long run does none of these things. In a recent story on the morale crisis in U.S. business, *Fortune* magazine reported that half of the 275 major companies studied felt that their cost-cutting programs and restructuring had not achieved their objectives. In another study of 1,005 corporations, *Fortune* reported that most senior executives felt that their companies' efforts at downsizing and restructuring had missed their mark. Fewer than half met their cost-reduction targets, only 32 percent raised their profits to an acceptable level, and just 21 percent improved return on investment to any appreciable degree.[6]

Moreover, downsizing often does more harm than good. Four out of ten of the companies in the above Laborforce 2000 study reported that downsizing had some severe negative consequences. Sixty-one percent of the companies that downsized experienced lower morale, 41 percent reported the need for significant re-training as a result of the downsizing, over a third used more temporary workers and more overtime, 30 percent had increased retiree health care costs, and 20 percent said they lost the wrong people. All of these factors affect the long-term viability of the company.[7]

In contrast to the all too prevalent myopia, the best companies are those that sustain results over long periods of time. To be the best requires a commitment to long-term financial viability as well as long-term satisfaction of customers and employees. An organization's

---

[5] *Building the Competitive Workforce: Investing in Human Capital for Corporate Success.* John Wiley & Sons, New York, 1993, Mirvis, P., ed., pg. 68.
[6] Fischer, A. "Morale crisis." *Fortune*, November 18, 1991, pp. 70–80.
[7] *Building the Competitive Workforce: Investing in Human Capital for Corporate Success.* John Wiley & Sons, New York, 1993, Mirvis, P., ed., pg. 75.

effectiveness is determined by its architectural design and the effective execution of that design. If an organization does not have a firm foundation of values, strong pillars built from trust between people, a shared sense of direction, and the flexibility to respond rapidly to changing conditions, regardless of what the leader does to affect finances, the organization will eventually crumble and fall.

THE FOCUS OF THE ARCHITECTING EFFORT

The phrase "architecting the organization" has to do with development—preparing the organization for its future success. If you were to ask a number of leaders or managers what they are doing to help their organization develop, they would probably say things like:

I'm looking into cutting manufacturing costs of our Chemico product. It's margins just are not high enough.

I'm sending my people to be trained in object-oriented software. It's the new wave of the field.

I'm building the new product line. It will increase the company's market share and stretch us into a whole new and potentially lucrative market.

We're getting together next week for our yearly strategic planning day. It helps us renew our goals, explore new opportunities, and get to know one another better.

I'm meeting with my managers in the next few weeks to go over how we can improve the production process. There are still a few kinks in it that need working out.

While each of the above activities are potentially valuable in their own right, they all reflect the notion that if I just do what I'm doing a little better, then my organization will be successful. These are important changes, but they are not *development*. They represent a change in *degree*, but not in *kind*. Good leaders and managers should be exploring ways to improve their production, to monitor their processes, and to cut costs toward greater productivity. This is the function of management, at least in the traditional sense of the term. However, none of these activities fundamentally impact the architecture of the organization and truly develop it for enduring success.

For years, managers and organizational consultants have been speaking about the idea of development as if it were assumed that we all know what it means. To many, development means growth and change for the better. To others it may mean better able to meet customers' needs. Still others think of development in terms of bigger, stronger, wiser, smarter. To ask the question "what does development mean?" seems absurd these days because it is a term we have all grown accustomed to and its meaning seems intuitively clear. But while the *idea* of development may be all too obvious, our intuitive grasp of the term does little to help us know what "better" actually looks like, whether our efforts to help our organizations develop really do the job, or to explore effective ways to move from where we are to where we want to be.

For the purposes of this book, development means *to create in one's own organization a greater capacity to anticipate and respond to future needs and solve future problems.* This represents a significant positive shift in the organization's ability to do business. When an organization develops, it becomes more adaptable, more integrated, more skilled at doing its work, and more satisfying for its members. Development is not *business as usual;* it has to do with designing the organization's architecture to ensure its success in the future.

This distinction between solving immediate problems and preparing the organization for future success needs to be on the minds of all leaders, particularly in a highly changing world. Unless your organization has the capacity to grow and develop, it will not be able to stay up with the competition, and it will slowly but surely become obsolete. Let's look at some examples of one organization's experience.

In one part of the XYZ organization a group of middle managers of the product development division is going through a strategic planning session. The group's director has organized this meeting as part of a six month effort to sow the seeds for organizational change that he believes will be needed in the coming years. The effort, thus far, has included three afternoon meetings discussing changes in the industry that are underway, a two-hour presentation by a futurist regarding projected changes in society, and an open discussion among top management regarding expected changes in the company over the next three years. Now, the middle managers are assimilating the information and are discussing the implications of these industry changes on their own product development group. The discussions have focused primarily on the future: what products the company will need to produce, and what new tools and methods will be needed to create those products.

In another part of the organization the head of a manufacturing unit is putting the final touches on its plans for reorganizing their production process. Four months before, a massive study of the entire manufacturing process had been completed, highlighting the consequences of an inefficient assembly line process and how the constant repetition of many of the subassembly processes led to high turnover, absenteeism, and low quality output. As a result of these studies, the leader invited the input of a cross-section of employees and developed plans for changes in the overall manufacturing system. Now, each unit is taking those rough plans, exploring the implications for its area, and reporting back to the leadership on ways the plan will affect their group, both positively and negatively. A buzz of both excitement and trepidation is heard throughout the plant as all groups are undergoing this study over the next two weeks. Whatever the outcome, people are sure things will be different, and hopefully better.

In a third part of the organization, a newly hired V.P. of Marketing has a vision of how she would like her unit to be working more productively. She has just replaced the previous V.P. who, although recruited from a competing company with a reputation for stellar marketing ideas, was later discovered to be callous and insensitive. The new V.P. explains her vision to her management team and asks them for their reactions. Responding to her initiative, each manager offers clear and well-thought-out suggestions for how these new ideas can be implemented in their own business units. Underlying their suggestions is a quiet sense of excitement. They are experiencing for the first time an opportunity to affect change in their own department, and to be freed of the oppressive management style of the previous V.P. of Marketing.

While each of these scenes are quite different in their focus and function, they have one significant thing in common. They are all efforts to help the organization, or a part of it, revitalize itself. Each of these managers examines the effectiveness of the process by which business gets done, explores a more effective way of doing business, and infuses new energy into the organization. Each in their own way is exploring a feature of the architecture of their organization and creating new designs intended to increase the likelihood of future success. Moreover, they are each occurring in an organization that is actively pursuing ways of strengthening the organization as a whole by reinforcing their newly created values, and by looking at ways to function more effectively as a whole system.

WHY DESIGN YOUR ORGANIZATION'S ARCHITECTURE?

Managers in the 1990s are seeing the dawn of a new age. As chronicled by such authors as John Naisbitt (*Megatrends*, 1988)[8] and Daniel Bell (*The Coming of Post-Industrial Society*, 1973),[9] we live at a turning point in the history of our society. Just as preindustrial America gave way to an industrial society in the late 1800s, our highly bureaucratized industrial society in the late 1900s is now giving way to a "postindustrial" society. The primacy of machinery and large-scale production is being replaced by rapid growth in technology, an increase in accessibility of information, a heightened consciousness of the population, and a shift from an emphasis on products to services. Alvin Toffler termed these changes *"The Third Wave."*[10]

These changes are like no other we have experienced in our lifetime. They are so fundamental they affect all organizations in both the public and private sectors. Recent studies identify the following significant trends and changes presently shaping the future of business in our society:

---

[8] Naisbitt, J. *Megatrends*, Warner Books, New York, 1988.
[9] Bell, D. *The Coming of Post-Industrial Society*, Basic Books, New York, 1973.
[10] Toffler, A. *The Third Wave*, William Morrow, New York, 1980.

1. *Movement From Goods to Services.* While the need to develop products efficiently and effectively was the *modus operandi* of business in the past, the need to provide effective service is the hallmark of successful businesses today and will be in the future. Moreover, our economy is now more service-based than product-based, a trend that is likely to continue into the foreseeable future.

2. *Increasing Global Competition.* The U.S. no longer can claim dominance in most major industrial markets. Japan and Germany have a significant edge over the U.S. in many key markets. Korea is rapidly gaining ground. In general, there are an increasing number of legitimate competitors emerging from other countries, forever threatening our former dominance. Global competition is further heightened by increased communication and distribution capabilities that have forever changed the face of business. Fierce global competition is further exacerbated by the fact that in today's society, the supply of most products and services exceeds the demand.

3. *Population Growth and Dwindling Resources.* Our natural resources are rapidly dwindling, giving rise to significant concerns about the future well being of our society. This, coupled with population growth, is now the number one threat to planetary survival.

4. *Shift From Financial Capital to Human and Information Capital.* Key strategic resources are shifting from financial capital in an industrial society to human capital in an information-based society. Computers and related technological advances have forever shifted the balance of power to those with information and knowledge at their fingertips and to those that can effectively mobilize their organization quickly and in a focused manner.

5. *Changing Organizational Models.* The traditional hierarchical/bureaucratic model of organizations is rapidly giving way to new models of more effective and more fluid organizational structures. These include network-based organizations, organizations that are organized around self-managed teams, and other uniquely designed systems. These alternative models, coupled with growing pressures to cut costs, have led to a reduction in the ranks of middle management. In addition, we are experiencing changes in the patterns of corporate ownership, leading to greater opportunities for workers to invest in and shape their financial destiny.

6. *Diversification Within the Workforce.* The workforce is becoming increasingly diverse. White males have for a long time been in the majority in business. This is no longer the case. Changes in the makeup of the workforce—including gender, race, country of origin, education level, and age distribution—are creating a workforce significantly different from that of the past. This, coupled with changing family relationships, is forcing businesses to adapt to many diverse needs. Progressive organizations are doing more than adjusting to these changing workforce demographics. They are welcoming diversity and seeing it as a way to heighten their effectiveness and creativity.

7. *Increased Customer Expectations.* Customers have far more choices now than ever before. Their expectations have risen as has the ability of organizations to respond to consumers' ever-changing needs. The successful organizations of today and tomorrow will be those that respond more quickly and more effectively to their customers' needs, and who anticipate their changing needs with new products and services.

8. *Rapidly Changing Technology.* Technological advances have forever changed the business landscape. These technological advances are being created at an ever-increasing rate. This rate of change threatens existing positions, investments, and strategic plans and calls for the leadership of modern businesses to be both visionary in focus and technologically savvy in execution. In addition, increasing availability and sophistication of information technology calls for the flattening of organizational structures as many mid-management-related responsibilities are more easily managed by computers.

These changes, and many more like them, mark the beginning of an era where change is no longer an event to respond to and stability is the norm. *Now, change occurs so frequently that stability is unusual and change is the norm.*

Not only are changes occurring more frequently, but they are happening at an ever-increasing rate. For example, the number of technological advances in the past 45 years is greater than the number of all of the technological advances in the history of humankind. That is extraordinary!

In addition to rapid technological change, our ability to integrate new technology into our daily lives is speeding up. Whereas it took almost 50 years for the automobile to be in widespread use, it took the personal computer only six to seven years. (Figure 1–1).[11]

---

[11] Adapted from Schon, D. *Beyond the Stable State*, W.W. Norton & Company, New York, 1971, p. 24. I have added the latter example. In this case, I am dating the first commercially viable personal computer as the one built by Apple in the mid 1970s. Arguably, the personal computer has been around for many years prior to the modern version we are most accustomed to.

Time taken for invention to be in widespread use	
Steam Engine	150-200 years
Automobile	40 - 50 years
Vacuum Tube	25-30 years
Television	about 20 years
Transistor	about 15 years
Personal Computer	about 7 years

Figure 1-1. Invention to widespread use.

In spite of these changes, we have an enormous ability to ignore the changes around us. We ignore them, we rationalize them, or we simply deny their very existence, all of which leads to the ultimate demise of our organizations. These acts of denial and ignorance are also perhaps the single greatest cause of the slow, steady decline of U.S. leadership in world markets. Described in a recent book by Ian Mitroff (1987),[12] one executive called it *The Glacier Effect.* Here is how he put it:

> I think most businesses today are the prisoners of
> what I call "the glacier effect." If you look at a glacier
> at any moment in time, it appears to be sitting still.
> You know in your head that it's constantly creeping
> along but it's doing it so slowly that at any point in
> time you can't see its movement. Thus, it's always
> possible to say that the glacier and all that it
> represents really doesn't affect me. I think this is how
> the vast majority of U.S. businesses have reacted to
> all the changes taking place around them. They've

[12] Quoted from a top executive of major entertainment firm in Mitroff, I. *Business Not as Usual*, Jossey-Bass, San Francisco, 1987, pp. 2–3.

either denied their existence altogether or they've pretended that they were occurring so slowly that they didn't have to take them into account, or that they had plenty of time to adjust to change. For instance, at any point in time, the U.S. auto companies could deny that radical changes were occurring in the car-buying tastes of the American public or in the quality of the cars being produced by the Japanese. Believing that this was so, they not only denied that the glacier was moving at all, but stronger still, they denied its very existence. One day they awoke to find that the glacier was not only bearing down on them in their own backyard, but that it had actually rolled over and flattened them during the night when they were asleep feeling very fat, comfortable, and cozy.

The inability to detect and respond to changing conditions in the global marketplace has led Robert Reich, U.S. Secretary of Labor and one of the leading analysts of our economy, to say that "by almost any standards, the quality of management is declining. Theories abound to explain this decline. What remains evident is that the U.S. has not changed with the times. Countries with lesser resources have leap frogged us."[13] This condition must not remain, for if it does, our lifestyle will be in severe peril.

With all the changes in our society comes a great deal of uncertainty. In the wake of a new business climate, few of us know what will happen or how best to proceed. For example, the health care industry faces significant uncertainty about the future. Rising health care costs have made the present system untenable, yet the

---

[13] Reich, R. *The Work of Nations*, Vintage Books, New York, 1991, pp. 117–118.

solution remains in doubt. Moreover, the source of the funding for that care is at present quite uncertain. The insurance and banking industries are also undergoing massive changes. They are rapidly merging from separate entities into a giant diversified financial services industry. Utility companies, which have existed in a highly regulated environment, are experiencing the prospect of competition as they have never faced before. And companies in high technology industries have no idea which technologies will win out in the 21st century. In short, the world has shifted dramatically and few industries are protected from having to face the implications of massive change.

Given the tendency of most people to focus on the present, most organizations are not prepared to meet the challenges of postindustrial society. Thus, while some organizations continue to grow and expand in size, few develop the infrastructure (the systems, management skills, and human resources policies) to adapt well in this period of uncertainty and change. Those that architect their organizations to respond rapidly to external changes will be the winners of the future. Those that do not will stagnate and die.

In a fascinating article on the subject, David Nadler and Michael Tushman[14] posed the challenge of organizations in today's business climate this way. In looking at the factors that affect change, they suggest that the ability to manage radical change is far more critical to an organization's success than ever before. They pose four alternative ways of looking at change, based on the confluence of two separate, yet related, forces. On the one hand, they distinguish between two types of ap-

---

[14] Nadler, D., and Tushman, M. "Beyond the Charismatic Leader: Leadership and Organizational Change," in *California Management Review*, 1990, Vol. 32, No. 2, pp. 77–97.

proaches to change: (1) anticipating change in the environment and proactively responding versus (2) reacting to changes that have already occurred in the environment. On the other hand, they distinguish between two types of environmental change: incremental versus frame-breaking change. Frame-breaking change represents a change that is a fundamental or discontinuous departure from the past. When you combine these dynamics, four possible alternative change methodologies emerge (Figure 1–2).

Adaptations or incremental changes in response to environmental change is what is often considered the mark of a successful organization. While this may have

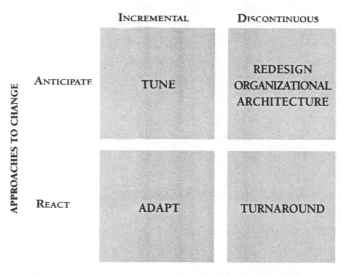

DEGREE OF ENVIRONMENTAL CHANGE

	INCREMENTAL	DISCONTINUOUS
ANTICIPATE	TUNE	REDESIGN ORGANIZATIONAL ARCHITECTURE
REACT	ADAPT	TURNAROUND

APPROACHES TO CHANGE

Figure 1-2. Approaches to organizational change. (*Source:* Adapted from Nadler, D., and Tushman, M., "Beyond the Charismatic Leader: Leadership and Organizational Change," in *California Management Review*, 1990, Vol. 32, No. 2, p. 80. Copyright 1990 by the Regents of the University of California. By permission of the Regents.

been true in the past, in a world that is changing rapidly, adaptation will lead to rapid failure. It is too slow. Fine-tuning the organization, on the other hand, is appropriate in conditions where changes in the environment are relatively slow. Fine-tuning in reaction to major environmental changes, however, will likely force an organization to fail rather quickly. In such situations, the organization will have to face a turnaround situation just to survive.

Anticipating major environmental change and poising the organization for success in such an environment is what redesigning an organization's architecture is all about. It is, without a doubt, the greatest insurance for long-term success in today's rapidly changing, highly competitive environment.

Not surprisingly, research shows that executives who anticipate change and orchestrate a redesign effort are far more effective in leading their companies and their companies are far more successful in the long run.[15] At the same time, such visionary executives are the exception. In a recent study of cases where significant redesign efforts occurred, only 6 out of 40 CEOs initiated frame-breaking change within their own company. The rest were initiated by a new CEO.[16] In retrospect, this is not surprising. Most leaders wait until change is forced on them. Then it is often too late, for it usually takes many years to successfully lead a redesign effort, particularly in large companies.

Perhaps the greatest challenge to managers today is to create an organizational architecture that is increas-

---

[15] Tushman, M. L., Newman, W. H., and Romanelli, E. "Convergence and Upheaval: Managing the Unsteady Pace of Organizational Evolution." *California Management Review*, 1986, Vol. 29, No. 1, p. 41.
[16] *Ibid.*, p. 42.

ingly anticipating change, responsive and effective. Such a challenge represents a major departure from leadership of the past. Fifty years ago, business leaders could put their primary focus on the typical functions of management such as controlling, directing, or evaluating and be successful. This is no longer the case. Indeed the term *management* itself is outdated. It comes from the Latin word "manus," which literally means "hand." The original "managers" were people who handled horses. It strikes me as prophetic that the original models of managers were horse trainers. Such a "crack the whip" model has long since outlived its purpose, yet many in positions of organizational responsibility hold on to that image even to this day.

Leaders and managers in today's business world can no longer continue to lead in the ways that worked well in the past. Einstein once said that "we cannot solve today's problems with the same thinking that created them." In other words, our present problems are created by our present and past thinking patterns. Our tendency to focus on immediate financial returns to the exclusion of long-term viability, to focus on production efficiency and to lose sight of customer satisfaction, to split the functions of our businesses up into small parts and to lose sight of our ability to work together have conspired to cause much of today's business problems. These approaches, while successful in the past, have produced a system of business management that needs an overhaul. As a result of such thinking:

- U.S. manufacturing productivity has been flat compared to years past.
- In 1970, over 95 percent of all radios sold in the world were made in the U.S. By 1985, the proportion was less than 5 percent.

- In 1955, the Big Three car makers in the U.S. had almost 100 percent of market share in the U.S. and almost 75 percent in the world. The figures are now roughly 65 percent and 30 percent respectively.
- As of 1993, our government debt exceeds $4 trillion and has almost quadrupled in the past 10 years.

These facts are causing many business leaders to question the approaches they have taken in the past and seek alternatives. While heady in its implications, being concerned about changes in business and in society is not just the stuff of the corporate boardroom. These changes filter down to affect leaders and managers at every level. As a leader of your organization you may have experienced the result of an organization not adapting to changes in time. Let's look at a few examples.

Chris Beatty is the cofounder and president of a 120-person marketing research company. Until recently, he has been able to successfully operate by taking a hands-on approach to all of the operations within the company. Unexpectedly, however, business is growing in the company's major areas of industry expertise to the point where the company will likely have to double in size in the next two years to keep up with growing demand. Clearly, he will not be able to directly control the company as he has in the past and at the same time provide leadership to explore new market avenues. At present he has a number of questions in mind: Do I reorganize? If so, how do I go about it? Where should I put my greatest energy? Into maintaining effective research? Into exploring and capitalizing on the new avenues for the business? Into both? How do my own career goals fit with the growth of my company? I want to retire in the next three or four years, yet no one is prepared to take over the reigns. What do I do? His answers to all these questions, as well as some unantici-pated ones, will profoundly affect the success of the growth and development of the business.

Sally Johnson just took over the reins of a 400-person department in a *Fortune* 100 company. Her department is responsible for designing and developing the top-selling product line for the company. Upon taking over the position, however, she discovered that all was not well. People made technical product commitments they couldn't keep, there were crippling conflicts and dis-agreements among her immediate staff, and product development was lagging severely behind schedule. It was clear that changes needed to be made, but what changes? Where to begin? What were the causes of the problems? If changes are made, will they be the right ones? Like Chris, Sally faces a significant challenge: How to help her organization grow and develop in a way that ensures its ongoing success.

John Billerica has been getting pressure from the Human Resources Department to do something about the high attrition rate in his area. His product services department of 150 has experienced a turnover rate aver-aging 32 percent per year for the past two years, twice as much as any other department throughout the com-pany. Some say it is due to low pay. Others say it is John's management style—overly authoritative and overly controlling. Still others say it is the nature of the business, always dealing with customer problems, never seeing the light of day. But John suspects much more. He is convinced that each of these factors has some validity (although he questions whether his style really has anything to do with it) but that people are being attracted to positions in other organizations that are doing more innovative work, projects that make his organization pale in comparison. He believes that as a result morale is low, there is evidence of dissension, people do not seem to be working very hard, and there is little discipline in handling customer complaints. The question in his mind is: What is causing the attrition and what can he do about it?

Each of these managers faces the ultimate challenge of a leader in any organization throughout the world. How do I make my organization better than it is now? How do I prepare my organization to make the changes it needs to grow in an ever-changing, ever more competitive market? How do I design the most effective organizational architecture?

Without a clear model for how to proceed, most managers fumble in their attempt to improve their organization's functioning. Some, for example, make significant changes without understanding their changing business environment. As a result, they spend enormous amounts of money with little payoff. Others don't know how to begin, so they make a few cosmetic changes, believing that something needs to be done and often wind up making the situation worse than it was before. Others make short-term tactical changes without looking at the long-term strategic needs of their customers or the organization as a whole. Some communicate the changes they want in ways that are so vague and unclear that the organization "freezes" from uncertainty, or people go off in all different directions. Still others make changes that are indeed massive, like completely restructuring the organization, but irrelevant given that the structure of the organization was not what was impeding progress.

Mistakes like these stem from two different possibilities: (1) the leader or manager has an incomplete understanding of the implications of an organization's architecture on its overall performance, or (2) the leader or manager has an incomplete understanding of how to design the architecture of his or her organization. This book addresses both of these problems in a step-by-step manner.

THE FIVE-PHASE PROCESS OF DESIGNING AN ORGANIZATION'S ARCHITECTURE

The aim of any architectural design effort is to increase the organization's overall ability to do business. A good design affects the process of work, it impacts the organization's strategic direction, it influences the way people interact with one another, and it changes the nature of people's roles and responsibilities. Each successful organizational design effort, no matter how large in magnitude or how long in time, needs to go through five successive phases. Moreover, these phases affect five major areas of a leader's responsibilities. They represent a comprehensive, complete, and powerful approach to designing any organizational architecture at any given point in time.[17]

Phase One: Communicating the Need. Once you as a leader decide to undergo an organizational architecture redesign effort, the first step is to effectively communicate the need for change to others whose acceptance is critical for the success of the change process. This requires that you (1) find the right time to discuss the problems (or opportunities) that lead you to think a development effort is needed, (2) gain acceptance from key people in the organization to the point that they feel motivated to work with you in redesigning the organization, and (3) decide on how to proceed. The key

---

[17] These phases are also consistent with the steps that most effective organization development consultants follow in their work as described by Block, P. *Flawless Consulting*, Learning Concepts, Austin, Texas, 1981.

in this phase is to create conditions where people in the organization sense its future is at stake and feel a strong need to help the organization grow in addressing the future.

Phase Two: Analysis of the Organization. The next step is to begin an analysis of your organization. This analysis helps you understand the present state of the organization and the internal changes needed to prepare for success in the future. Depending on the magnitude of the need for internal change, the analysis phase can be quite comprehensive or quite narrowly focused. Whatever the case, the analysis phase requires the organization to gather data and analyze the cause(s) of present problems or an understanding of what changes will be needed to become successful in the future. This analysis needs to be complete and compelling, demonstrating the areas that need to be redesigned in order to increase the organization's future well being.

Phase Three: Decision Making. Once the analysis is complete, the ideas and suggestions derived need to be communicated to the organization and decisions made regarding how to proceed. The analysis should be shared with all employees in the organization in various levels of detail, depending on the importance of their commitment to the overall organizational design effort. The decisions on how to proceed with the organizational architecting effort then get made by a select group of people who will be responsible for the overall process. This group is typically the top management team. Sometimes, however, it includes representatives from all levels in the organization, thereby ensuring the greatest sensitivity to the concerns of all people throughout the organization. The decisions need to reflect an understanding of where the organization is, where you want it to be, and how you will get from here to there. How you will get from here to there, and the design changes that are needed, represent the plans for the new organizational architecture.

Phase Four: Implementation. All organizational architecting efforts require change in any or all of the following areas of concern for a manager:

- the organization's vision for the future
- the organization's culture
- the organization's strategic direction
- the organization's strategic goals
- the organization's structure

These five areas represent key aspects of the organization's architecture, whether it be a three person start-up, or a $30 billion company (see Figure 1–3). (Architects work on small buildings as well as huge skyscrapers, but the same fundamental principles apply.) All of these elements need to be working effectively for the organization to be healthy as a whole. In addition, they need to be working in harmony with one another. The strategic direction and goals should flow naturally from the vision and need to be designed in a way that reinforces and is a direct reflection of the organization's culture, which in turn should clarify the kind of structure needed. The architectural integrity of the organization is ensured when changes are made in ways that create alignment and consistency among these elements.

In this book, these five elements of an organization's architecture are described in a particular order to reflect the degree to which they influence one another and to which they endure over time. Defining or clarifying your vision, for example, must come first. It should be the most solid feature of your organization's founda-

Figure 1-3. The five elements of an organization's architecture.

tion. While other things may change, the vision must endure over time. The same is true for your organization's culture. Like the personality of an individual, culture tends to be deeply etched in the organizations social fabric. As such, it is both difficult to change and relatively enduring. While it is impossible to be precise, both the vision and the culture for most organizations may have a 15- to 50-year life span. Your organization's strategic direction needs to be relatively stable, yet it must change as the environment and your vision change. Hence its life span may need to be in the 5- to 15-year range. The strategic goals and structure of the organization must be the most fluid, as they are the

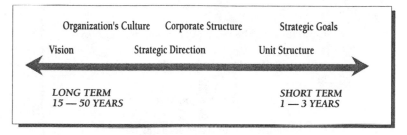

Figure 1-4. The relative stability of different elements of an organization's architecture.

primary means by which you achieve your aims and adapt to variations in the environment. Perhaps 1 to 10 years is appropriate (see Figure 1–4).

Phase Five: Evaluation. Once the changes are complete, the organization needs to evaluate its efforts. Were we successful in making the changes? Did the changes produce the outcomes intended? Were there unintended outcomes that now need to be addressed? This evaluation is sometimes an end and sometimes a beginning. It marks the completion of the initial development effort and evaluates its effectiveness. But it also may be a new beginning in that the evaluation may discover new areas to be looked at that were not considered before. The evaluation, if successful, allows the organization to test the success of the architecting effort, celebrate its efforts, and pave the way for new architecting efforts in the future. (See Figure 1–5 for a view of the total design process.)

ARCHITECTING CHECKLIST

1. A long-term view of the organization's success is critical for an organizational architecting effort to be viable.

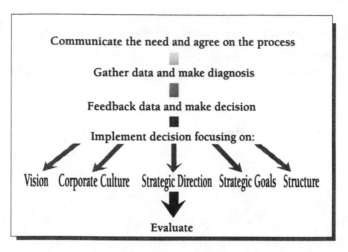

Figure 1-5. An overview of the architecting process.

2. The business environment is rapidly changing, making the ability to anticipate change and direct one's efforts to that change as the most critical factor in an organization's enduring success.

3. Effectively designing an organization's architecture does not represent small incremental improvements in the organization. Rather, it is a fundamental shift in the quality and nature of the organization as a whole.

4. There are five key phases in an architecting effort: communicate the need, analyze the organization, make decisions to change, implement those decisions, and evaluate the results.

5. The five elements of an organization's architecture represent an integrated whole. To successfully redesign the organization's architecture requires examination and potential change in all five elements.

2

The Five Elements of an Organization's Architecture[1]

In working as an organizational consultant over the past 15 years, one fascinating phenomenon keeps emerging time after time among my efforts to help organizations grow and change. Relatively few people leading such efforts seem to appreciate the dynamics associated with managing large systems change. Due to a lack of understanding or perhaps out of personal discomfort, many consultants and business leaders shy away from addressing the human elements of managing change. Inevitably, they underestimate the time and effort needed to accomplish the change

[1] Many of the ideas in this chapter were expressed by the author in an earlier article published in *Quality Progress* magazine titled, "Creating TQM Organizations: Setting the Proper Direction Makes All the Difference," Vol. 27, No. 1, January 1994, pp. 51–54.

process. As a result, most efforts to grow or change the organization fall well short of their initial aspirations.

Some of the difficulties that companies are having in implementing total quality management efforts, for example, have much to do with this shortcoming. The field of TQM has its primary roots in the traditions of statistical process control, quality control, and group problem solving (quality circles). These disciplines primarily focus on the rigorous application of data collection and logical analysis to help make better business decisions. Historically, however, the primary mode for instituting a TQM change has been the teaching of valuable and simple tools and techniques of problem solving and process improvement throughout the organization. Teaching people how to use these tools is important, but that is the easy part. Even more difficult is getting people to utilize the tools and techniques, as well as the philosophy that underlies them. This requires that the tools and principles be rewarded and reinforced throughout the whole system of the organization. That is where the weaker TQM efforts stop and, as a result, the change effort is not complete. I would argue that the greatest challenge of all in instituting a TQM effort is in getting the people, all of the people, moving in the same direction.

Perhaps the three biggest reasons why organizational change efforts fall short of the mark are (1) the internal politics that lead people to be narrow in focus, (2) the conflicts between people that arrest decision making, and (3) the dogmatic and counterproductive attitudes that people hold. These features of organizational life are the toughest to change because they are etched so deeply in the fabric of our organizations and our society. Changing the culture of an organization is a huge and difficult task. Yet that is exactly what managers and leaders engaging in system-wide change efforts need to do.

This chapter focuses on the critical challenge of managing the process of whole systems change. An organizational system is whole to the extent that it is both relatively autonomous and self-sustaining. I use the term "relatively" intentionally, for in practice no system is separate. It interacts with other systems. Organizations interact with other organizations in their industry, with vendors, and with customers. Therefore, systems exist within larger systems and are never fully separate. They can be—and often are—relatively autonomous, however.

In this chapter I explain in depth the five key elements of an organization's architecture. These are the things a leader of an organizational architecture design effort needs to focus on in order to ensure the organization is moving in the right direction. These elements form not only the basis for an organization's architecture, but describe a way of thinking that can leverage the organization's ability to manage change effectively.

HOW WE THINK ABOUT WORK

In physics, work is defined as the product of force times the distance in which the force moves. In other words, it is the result of energy aimed in a particular direction. We learned this in high school and were taught ways of measuring and increasing work done by increasing the expenditure of energy. Unfortunately, we are also taught the same idea in organizations, without any alternative approach to heightening our work efforts. In business, and in our society in general, most of us believe that the principal way to heighten productivity in organizations is by applying more energy or effort.

- "Put your nose to the grindstone"
- "He's a hard worker"
- "No pain, no gain"
- "You've got to tough it out"

These platitudes are so commonplace in our businesses they are seldom called into question. Even the great inventor, Thomas Edison, upheld the hard work norm as he defined innovation as "1 percent inspiration and 99 percent perspiration."

While in the short run working harder may sometimes produce greater results, in the long run, organizations that are set up only along these principles are doomed to failure. Their sights are set on only half of the work equation. Given the existing strong work ethic in our society, the challenge in most of our organizations is not in applying more effort, but in providing the proper direction for that effort to be applied. Having discovered the proper direction, the leadership challenge is to create alignment among people to move in that direction. Alignment in this case means three things: (1) people agreeing on the direction; (2) people being committed to that direction, and (3) people actually working in that direction. Organizations that understand and abide by this principle are vastly more productive than their sweat-producing counterparts.

Animals understand the principle of alignment extremely well. Witness how geese fly. They typically fly in a V-shaped pattern to take advantage of the principle of drafting. Like a runner or bicyclist who expends less energy by following closely the person in front, or a car that uses less fuel to go the same speed by following a truck, geese align themselves to move more efficiently.

Let's look at this phenomenon more closely.

WHAT ORGANIZATIONS OFTEN LOOK LIKE

The model in Figure 2–1 below depicts what often occurs in organizations, projects, or organized group efforts. In many situations where people get together, the direction of organizational energy often looks something like this.[2]

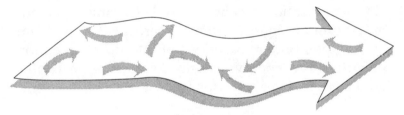

Figure 2-1. Organizational misalignment.

The arrows within represent the direction of people's energy—often dispersed and conflicting, while the larger arrow represents the direction of the organization —unclear, wobbly, and diffuse. I call this condition *misalignment*. In most organizations, people are somewhat unclear on why they do their work, and how their efforts fit into the overall scheme of things. They have some sense of the strategy by which the organization is

---

[2] See Kiefer, C. and Stroh, P. "A New Paradigm for Developing Organizations," *Transforming Work*, John Adams, ed., Mills River Press, Alexandria, Virginia, 1984, for a fuller explanation of organization alignment.

going to achieve its goals, although rarely is that strategy discussed. They sometimes know their own part of the overall strategy, but not that of others. And although their own goals may be clear, they are often in conflict with others' goals. Such conditions result in the organization operating much like materials that are known as resistors. The electrons in a resistor move around a lot, but in all different directions. Energy does not flow well in a resistor.

Unfortunately, people in organizations are often unaware of organizational misalignment, so when conflicts arise, they perceive an intention to sabotage, they view the behavior of others as counterproductive, or they see others as just plain stupid.

In organizations characterized by misalignment, applying more energy often exacerbates the problem. For example, under conditions of internal competition, applying more energy actually heightens the conflict and tension between groups (see Figure 2–2).

Figure 2-2. Conflicts and competition exacerbated.

Early on in my career as a consultant, I had the opportunity to see examples of misalignment all too clearly. Several years prior to my consulting for a particular company, the management had set up a competition between two separate project teams in two separate geographic locations. Their task was to create the fastest, most powerful, state-of-the-art product in their industry. The winner of the competition would have its product brought to market, and garner all the associated accolades, while the loser would have nothing other than the deflating experience of going down in defeat. After eighteen months of hard work, one project team completed their project and came out with an extraordinary product. It won the competition, and its product was marketed, widely touted, and acknowledged in the industry as the next breakthrough in technology.

Unaware of what had happened seven years before, I was brought in to work with the losing group. When I arrived, I found an organization that for years had a revolving door of leadership, had extraordinary turnover (over 25 percent) per year, and continued to do mediocre work. When I asked them how they saw themselves as an organization, they said they felt defeated, had no support from their corporate home office, and felt that they were like a "farm team" (the baseball vernacular for minor league). Prior to the big event of seven years before, they were considered a classy organization, and were set up to do exciting, cutting-edge research and development for the overall organization. Now, for seven years, they had been operating with extremely low productivity and even worse morale. Given the size of this group (over 150 employees) you can imagine what the cost of internal competition in this company had been.

Applying more energy in misaligned organizations also results in more lost causes (Figure 2–3). Witness the number of projects that get nowhere in organizations. For example, one company I worked with underwent a multimillion dollar effort to create a new personal computer. After over three years of developing the product, the project was put on the back

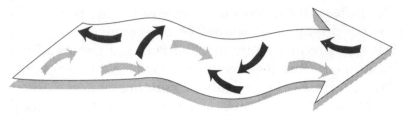

Figure 2-3. Efforts that are not consistent with the overall direction—lost causes.

burner, never to be revived. After working with the project team to help them manage some strong internal conflicts, it became apparent that there was little real commitment for the project by the leadership of the organization as a whole. (The project had been kept alive by the head of R&D, without the blessing of the company's Executive Committee.) As a result of the misalignment, tens of millions of dollars were lost to wasted effort.

Not only is effort lost to internal misalignment, but also to misalignment between the company and customers as well. It has been estimated that at one computer company, for example, tens of millions of dollars were lost on the creation of a highly sophisticated, state-of-the-art personal computer that was not in alignment with customers' needs.

More effort under conditions of misalignment also increases burnout and worker sabotage. Even Japanese management, often extolled as a model of effectiveness, is facing problems due to the overworking of employees. It is not unusual for the average worker in a Japanese company to work six days a week, year round. While it is true that Japan has gained a competitive edge due to hard work, it is not without a price. Many workers, particularly in the younger generation, are feeling resentment toward their companies and toward their culture in general. Their frustration is due to lack of opportunities for self expression and for lack of balance in their lives.

THE FIVE ELEMENTS OF AN ORGANIZATION'S ARCHITECTURE

While working harder to increase productivity is the norm in our society, a few companies are beginning to see that working harder under conditions of misalignment is damaging to the overall vitality and productivity of the organization. Instead, these companies are refocusing their energy to ensure they are moving in the proper direction, driven by the needs of their present and potential customers. Key to proper direction is alignment among five elements of organizational life. These elements form the organization's architecture (see Figure 2–4).

Vision is the leadership's view of the organization in the future, including its *purpose, mission,* and *values.* This involves projecting the organization into the future and envisioning that future in all its full-blown glory. The *purpose* has to do with why the organization is in existence. The *mission* of the organization is the overarching set of goals the organization will focus on in the next two to five years to increase its success. *Values* are the principles the organization holds as most critical to guide people's actions and behaviors.

Of all the features of a *vision,* "purpose" is the most misunderstood. The *purpose* is the organization's reason for being in the business and for providing the services or products they do. An excellent example of a purpose statement is that of Merck, a leader in the pharmaceuti-

Figure 2-4. The five elements of an organization's architecture.

cal industry and one of the most successful and well-respected companies in the United States. Their stated purpose is:

> We are in the business of preserving and improving human life. All of our actions must be measured by our success in achieving this. . . .[3]

Note how far-reaching and ambitious Merck's purpose is. Such is the nature of purpose; it is an overriding

---

[3] Quoted in Collins, J. and Porras, J. "Organizational Vision and Visionary Organizations," *California Management Review*, Vol. 34, No. 1, 1991.

reason for an organization's existence. When the purpose is big, so too are the organization's ambitions. That is why most successful companies achieve so much. They are driven to success by a deep commitment to a higher purpose.

The organization's overriding purpose relates to and drives what most companies refer to as *mission*. Interestingly, most organizations are not clear on their purpose, and they confuse purpose with their mission or with their objectives. One way I have come to know this is a simple exercise I often do with clients. Early on in some of my consulting work, I often ask my clients: "What are the key things you need people to understand and support in order to be effective as an organization?" The key term here is *effective*. They often answer such things as:

- the objectives
- how we are organized or structured
- our policies and procedures
- our strategies
- the direction we are going
- who is responsible for what
- our new technology

Nine times out of ten, however, they will fail to say "the *purpose* of the organization." I then point out that I think one thing is missing on the list, namely your *purpose*. Inevitably, one of the members of the client team will react quickly and ask: "How is that different from objectives?" My answer is simple—to me *objectives* are the measurable outcomes the organization wants to produce in a particular time frame. *Purpose,* on the other hand, refers to why the organization is in business in the first place.

This purpose directly affects one's motivation to work, as well as the degree to which one works well with others. When I ask people in an organization what their purpose is, they will, more often than not, say "to make money." This is a personal goal, not the purpose of the organizations (except perhaps the U.S. Mint). To make money, more often than not, is an objective; a necessary one to stay in business, but an objective nonetheless. The question of purpose is: Why make money in *this* business? One can make money in a lot of businesses. Why *this* business?

The answer to this question is truly critical, for when an organization's purpose is clear, it can withstand great difficulty, persevere in spite of enormous obstacles, and attain enormous achievements. Without a sense of purpose, both people and organizations often feel empty or lost.

Culture. An organization's culture refers to the norms, rules, and guidelines for behavior that are designed to support how people work together. The culture is what makes an organization more than boxes on an organizational chart. Organizations have built values, norms, and expectations that over time influence the decisions people make and the way they interact. While culture is an outcome of all the above, it is also a generator. In other words, our organization's culture also determines and shapes to a large extent the choices people in organizations make about their purpose, objectives, strategy, and structure.

Strategic Direction. Strategic direction is the degree to which the organization has a clear sense of the environment it is in and has an overall plan for managing in that environment. While vision tells you where to aim, the strategic direction tells you the pathway. Included in an organization's strategic direction is its core competence,[4] its competitive strategy,[5] and the forces that drive the organization.[6] The strategic direction of the organization says: given X assumptions about the trends and changes in our business environment, this is the direction we need to take in order to succeed and thrive.

✠ *Strategic Objectives.* The strategic objectives of the organization are the specific things it wants to accomplish in a given period of time. Effective strategic objectives have embedded in them clear measures. Examples are: "over the next two years our market share will grow by 5 percent," or "in the next three years we will increase our customer satisfaction rating from 7.3 to 9.5." Strategic objectives are specific, concrete, time bound, and measurable aims of the organization.

By definition, strategic objectives are more short term than the strategic direction. Strategic direction provides the map while strategic objectives pinpoint the milestones. They tell the organization exactly what it intends to accomplish, by when, and how it will be measured.

✠ *Structure.* The structure refers to how the organization is organized: who reports to whom, the boundaries in the organization, and people's roles and responsibilities. When things go wrong, the first thing managers often think to do is to change the structure. While the structure of the organization may have something to do with an organization's productivity, it is but one of

---

[4] Prahalad, C and Hamel, G. "The Core Competence of the Corporation," *Harvard Business Review,* May-June 1990, pp. 79–91.
[5] See Porter, Michael, *Competitive Strategy,* Free Press, New York, 1986, for an excellent view of this subject.
[6] See Michel, R., *The Strategist CEO: How Visionary Executives Build Organizations,* Greenwood Press, Westport, Conn., 1988, for an excellent discussion of this concept.

many other factors. Yet it is often the easiest to think about conceptually because it is concrete—right there on the organization chart. Unfortunately, what ails most organizations cuts much deeper than the organization's structure, and so efforts to improve organizations by changing their structure often fall flat. A lot of time and energy is wasted from the overused tendency to reorganize in the face of difficulty.

Nevertheless, the structure of an organization does have a lot to do with its success, particularly in terms of the ability to mobilize forces and accomplish tasks. Structures can either aid or impede progress, depending on the organization's strategy and its key tasks. If designed well, the proper structure can go far in giving an organization its competitive edge.

Taken together, these five elements form the foundation and design of the organization, and perhaps more than any other factors determine its future success. When the elements are right, and when they work together, the organization is poised well for success, now and in the foreseeable future.

This idea of working together is not just some empty platitude about organizational success, it is the *key* to success. Now more than ever before must we understand that organizations are systems. When one part of the system or one element in the system does not integrate well with another, the possibility for success is highly impaired. For example, what might happen if you want your organization to be highly responsive to customers needs, yet you organized it to maximize the division of labor, rather than customer "response-ability." You would not likely to be successful. Alternatively, if your strategic direction focuses on enhanced utilization of new technology, yet your culture is one that is averse to risk, then your ability to rapidly exploit new technology will be limited.

As simple as it may seem, few leaders of organizations effectively see their organizations as systems and, as a result, send communications or lead initiatives that are doomed to fail. Their failure is not from lack of commitment, but from not understanding how these five elements of the organization's architecture impact one another and the future success of the organization as a whole.

In a recent and highly provocative book on the subject, John Kotter and James Heskett demonstrated convincingly that the most successful organizations are characterized by three key qualities: (1) their cultures are highly adaptive—able to respond quickly in a changing environment; (2) their cultures are strong— there exists a strong shared identity among people in the organization; and (3) the culture of the company and its strategy are well matched and are appropriate to the external environment. In other words, they are well architected.[7]

These features of an organization's architecture are not just things that happen, they are things that leaders of organizations intentionally (or unintentionally) create.

When people are clear on each of these features of organizational life in their organization and in their work, and when they are fully committed to them, the organization is far more productive, and employees are far more satisfied. Everyone's contribution to the overall company is clear, and everyone feels the direct re-

---

[7] Kotter, J. and Heskett J., *Corporate Culture and Performance*, The Free Press, New York, 1992.

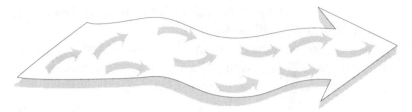

Figure 2-5. Organizational alignment

sults of their efforts. The consequence of such an organization looks something like the following (Figure 2–5).

The expense of organizational alignment is much like the energy that moves in materials that act as conductors. In a conductor, the electrons move quite rapidly and in the same direction. Hence, in a conductor, energy moves quickly.

Alignment is particularly critical in an environment of ambiguity and constant change. Most organizations in such conditions respond with multiple initiatives and in multiple directions. As a result, organizational confusion ensues. The challenge is not to respond in a diffuse and unfocused manner, but to create a condition in the organization of clarity, alignment, and commitment to a shared direction. Such a condition differentiates successful organizations from those that perpetually struggle.

One such organization I have worked with claims that due to their strong alignment, meetings are three to four times more efficient than ever before. When asked about the organization now versus before the architecting effort, many report that they are far and away more successful, and they work together far more effectively. *Such is the aim of the organizational architecting process. It is to produce quantum leaps in the quality, viability, and vitality of the organization in a way that endures over long periods of time.* While perhaps lofty in its aims, this is not without precedent as more and more organizations throughout the world are seeking and finding radical and effective alternatives to tried and no longer true methods.

Designing an effective organizational architecture is not just an interesting concept, it must be the guiding force behind organizations. Without it, more effort only means more frustrations, wasted efforts, and greater internal conflict. With it, the organization has the possibility of having an enormous competitive advantage as well as greater satisfaction for all the employees.

How to Create the Need for Redesigning an Organizational Architecture

Creating an organization's architecture almost always must start from the top. It is difficult to get an organization pulling together and moving in the same direction when the leadership of the organization is fractured or locked in internal conflict. Hence, it is the responsibility of the organization's leadership to design its architecture and provide the direction for the future. To successfully craft an organization's direction, the organization must achieve alignment among each of the five elements of its architecture. This involves what I call the Three C's:

Clarity

Congruence

Commitment

To create alignment around an organization's architecture, all members of the leadership team must *clearly* understand what each of the five elements of their organization's architecture mean. In addition, all the members must agree on the five elements and the five elements must be consistent with one another. This results in *congruence*. It doesn't work, for example, to have a strategy and structure that is dependent on teamwork and a culture that reinforces internal competition. Finally, each member of the leadership team must be completely *committed* to the organization's architecture in order to implement its design.

An exercise: Take some time to reflect on the degree to which your organization's leadership team is aligned around your organization's architecture. To do this, get the leaders of your organization together and ask them to independently rate the organization on each of the above elements of its architecture: vision, culture, strategic direction, strategic goals, and structure (including roles and responsibilities). Use a scale of one to seven, where one means no alignment and seven means full alignment. The key question to ask in this meeting is: How clear are the members of our organization on the vision, culture, strategic direction, etc., and to what extent are people committed to this architecture?

After rating the organization independently, ask each leader to communicate with the others what their ratings are and why they give the organization the ratings they did. More often than not, the ratings will either vary considerably (which tells you there is little shared understanding of the organization—a useful discovery in itself), or the ratings will likely be low. If the rates are high, and the group is not collectively denying the truth, then alignment is probably not a key problem for your organization at this point in time. One way of testing the assumptions of the leadership is to ask others, particularly at lower levels to grade the organization. Often their perception is that the leaders of the company disagree or are not committed to the same direction. This naturally leads to confusion for the rest of the organization and also a lack of commitment.

When the rating for organizational alignment is low, or when there is a gap between the leadership's perceptions and the rest of the organization, it tells the leadership that it has not done a good a job of identifying, communicating, and/or reinforcing the critical features of the organization's direction and creating a condition of organizational alignment.

In addition to being in alignment, of course, the organization must also have the right architecture. The architecture needs to match well the demands of the environment. Organizations that don't change their architecture in response to or in anticipation of changes in the environment are doomed to failure. The next chapter highlights such a problem in the form of Wang Labs, a company that was extraordinarily successful, but did not grow and develop to meet changing market demands. It is for these reasons that leading and creating anew the organization's architecture is exactly the responsibility of the leadership of the organization. Someone's got to have their hand on the tiller, and if it is not you and the other members of the leadership team, then who is it?

ARCHITECTING CHECKLIST

1. One key to an organization's success is the degree to which there is alignment among all of the elements of an organization's architecture.

2. The process of redesigning an organization's architecture represents a whole systems approach to growth and change that has a greater chance of yielding success than piecemeal approaches.

3. The five key elements of an organization's architecture are its vision, culture, strategic direction, strategic goals, and structure.

4. The beginning point in designing an organization's architecture is *vision*.

3

The Consequences of Mismanaging the Organizational Architecture

The toughest business obstacle to overcome is success.
—Malcolm Forbes

What do Xerox, Pan Am Airlines, General Motors, and U.S. Steel have in common? They are all companies that, at one time or another, had the largest individual market share of any company in their industry. If you were a betting person, you would say they were a safe investment, as safe as any. Yet they all lost huge amounts of market share. Xerox had 80 percent of the world copier market share at one time. Now, after many years of massive change, it has less than 20 percent. Pam Am was the leader in the airline industry for decades. It is now defunct. GM and the other U.S. auto manufacturers have been losing market share steadily to the Japanese auto makers for almost two decades. U.S. Steel is but a shell of its former self.[1]

How do companies die when once they were great? To understand this question, one must understand the dynamics of the life cycle of a business enterprise and how the mismanagement of an organization's architecture speeds up its ultimate demise. To understand this more fully, let's briefly look at one small chapter in the well-known story of GM.

GM, up until about ten years ago, had long been admired as one of the strongest, most financially sound companies in the history of Western society. Yet they let their past success get in the way of present and future success. Twenty years ago, at the height of their success, they held 44.5 percent of the U.S. automobile market. Now, GM holds only 30 percent.[2] If you were to ask GM what would account for their decline, they might blame it on forces outside their control like unfair trade barriers, exploitation of labor, the economy, and so on. But the greater truth lies within their own doors. They let their own perception of invulnerability affect their decision making. Management decided they didn't need to significantly develop their company's architecture. James O'Toole, in a revealing analysis of GM, asserted that the company managed itself in the mid to late 1970s based on the following assumptions:

- GM is in the business of making money, not cars.
- Cars are primarily status symbols; style is more important than quality.

---

[1] I am indebted to my colleague, Mat Juechter, CEO of ARC International, a leading international consulting firm in the area of organization transformation, who I heard tell this story to a group of clients and who graciously gave permission to use it in this book.
[2] *USA Today*, October 28, 1993, pg. 5B.

- The U.S. market is isolated from the rest of the world and will never be penetrated.
- Workers do not have an important impact on product quality.
- Strict centralized financial controls are the secret to good management.
- Energy will always be cheap and abundant.
- Consumer, environmental, and other social concerns are unimportant to the American public.[3]

Until very recently, GM felt so good about these assumptions that, in spite of data to the contrary, they held steadfast to their beliefs. Why not? These were the assumptions on which Alfred Sloan had built one of the most successful industrial giants in history.[4] Yet time, and two decades of experience, have proven these assumptions faulty.

Many of the Japanese car manufacturers operate under a fundamentally different and more accurate set of assumptions—that a company is in business to serve customers, that workers are the primary source of innovation, that an organization is a system and teamwork is the key to success, that fuel resources are becoming increasingly scarce, and that automobile owners care deeply about quality and reliability. As a result, while GM has been steadily losing world market share, Japanese car manufacturers increased their market share in world motor vehicle production from 1 percent to 28 percent between the years of 1955 to 1988.[5]

The same unwillingness to look at significant patterns or trends affecting their industry has been hap-

---

[3] Adapted from O'Toole, J. *Vanguard Management: Redesigning the Corporate Future*, Doubleday, New York, 1985, pp. 55–56.
[4] Sloan, A. *My Years with General Motors*, Doubleday Anchor, New York, 1972.
[5] Womack, J., Jones, D., and Roos, D. *The Machine That Changed the World: The Story of Lean Production*, Harper Perennial, New York, 1990, p. 69.

pening at Sears Roebuck and at IBM. Long respected as market leaders, their market presence has gradually eroded as competitors have either seized a growing market or have adapted more quickly. In his autobiography, Sam Walton, founder of Wal-Mart, put it this way: "One reason Sears fell so far off the pace is that they wouldn't admit for the longest time that Wal-Mart and Kmart were their real competition. They ignored both of us, and we both blew right by them."[6] Why? Because of their corporate attitude. Donald Katz, author of a book about Sears, describes their mentality as "caretakers," more focused on maintaining what they have than on growing and exploring new opportunities.[7] As a result, in 1992, Sears lost $3 billion in their merchandising group alone while Kmart and Wal-Mart combined earned almost $3 billion in that same time period.

IBM has had different problems. Their size and bureaucracy has made them slow to change. Said one of IBM's business partners recently, "trying to get action out of IBM is like swimming through giant pools of peanut butter."[8] To protect their investment in mainframe computers, for example, IBM has been slow to promote new technology in smaller computers. They got into the personal computer market rather late, taking a long time to exploit the RISC microprocessor they invented in 1974.

The inability of organizations to learn, adapt, and change is not just something that GM, Sears, and IBM have faced alone in the United States. The corporate graveyard is packed with companies who, in their collective arrogance, felt they did not need to question the

---

[6] Walton, S. *Sam Walton: Made in America*, Doubleday, New York, 1992.

[7] Katz, D R. *The Big Store*, Penguin Books, New York, 1987.

[8] Loomis, C. J., "Dinosaurs." *Fortune*, May 3, 1993, p. 41.

fundamental assumptions upon which their architecture was built. To understand this dynamic more fully, this chapter provides a detailed understanding of how organizations grow and die, using Wang Labs as an example.

THE RISE AND FALL OF WANG LABS

The announcement that Wang Labs filed for bankruptcy on August 18, 1992, came as no surprise to insiders in the computer industry. There were ample signals over the previous three years to suggest that all was not well. Cited by many as one of the fastest growing, most successful companies of its time, Wang Labs will also likely go down in history as one of the fastest to decline. From this unfortunate compressed time frame, much can be learned to help guide the process of architecting organizations and to prevent making the kinds of mistakes that Wang Labs made that led to its ultimate downfall.

PREDICTABLE PHASES IN AN ORGANIZATION'S LIFE CYCLE

To understand how Wang Labs and other companies decline or die a predictable death, we will select key points during its organizational life cycle. The underlying principles of this cycle are based on the universal patterns of growth that occur in all organisms, as described in George Land's fascinating 1974 book *Grow or Die: The Unifying Principles of Transformation*,[9] as well as

---

[9] Land, G. *Grow or Die: The Unifying Principles of Transformation*, Creative Education Foundation, Buffalo, New York, 1974.

exciting new research on stages of organizational growth and development.[10] The model below (Figure 3–1) depicts four key phases in a company's life cycle, each with its own unique challenges.

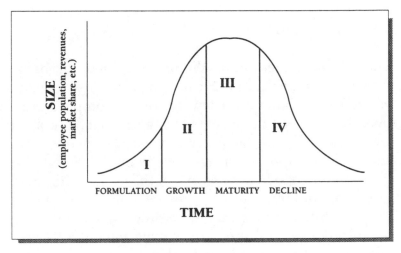

Figure 3-1. The life cycle of organizations.

PHASE ONE: FORMULATION

All organizations, public and private alike, have as their greatest initial challenge to formulate themselves. During this formulation phase, an organization must do three things in order to survive: (1) it must discover and articulate its sense of purpose and mission; (2) it must acquire the necessary financial support to sustain itself during what is likely to be a rocky period of limited early revenues or customer demand; and (3) it must

---

[10] See Torbert, W. *Managing the Corporate Dream: Restructuring for long term success*, Dow Jones-Irwin, Homewood, Ill., 1987, for example.

attract its initial customers and successfully deliver services or products to them.

The formulation phase of an organization's life cycle is one that requires enormous energy and dedication on the part of the founders in order to achieve success. It is not unheard of for organizational members to work extraordinary hours, and to feel as if their whole life is dedicated to the organization. During the formulation phase, members of the organization often experience a strong sense of mission, feeling that they are part of an exciting and meaningful cause. At the same time, there is often a strong sense of angst during this phase, for the organization often lacks the financial foundation to sustain itself. This sense of purpose, then, is critical for survival during periods of trepidation, lack of demand for the organization's products or services, and long hours of hard work.

One leader of a start-up company summed up the typical feeling of formulation-phase organizations recently by saying to a prospective employee: "once you start work here, we own your soul." While hopefully an overstatement, this is often what it feels like for the founder of the organization and its members.

During this phase of the organization's life, the most critical features of the architecture are its vision and strategic direction. This means the leadership of the organization must have a clear sense of the market to which the organization's products or services are aimed, an excellent product or service to meet that market, and a clear sense of how to position the product or service in order to best leverage it. As in all phases, but in particular during this phase, the structure of the organization must necessarily be fluid and adaptable. For this purpose, a less hierarchical, flatter structure works best. At this point, the culture of the organization is just emerging. It is, in many ways, the optimal time to establish a strong organizational culture, for it is the easiest time to influence people's behavior. The organization has little history to pull people in one way or another. Hence, establishing clear values and operating principles early on can establish a strong cultural foundation for the future.

Wang Labs 1951–1976: The Formative Years.[11] Wang Labs had a strong beginning as a result of the charismatic leadership of its founder, Dr. An Wang, a Chinese citizen who moved to the United States in 1945 to conduct research and make his mark in the new field of computers. His earliest and most notable invention was magnetic core memory, which significantly improved the access time and size of the information storage capability of the computer. In 1951, An Wang officially launched Wang Laboratories, Inc., with a vision for building products based on magnetic core memory and developing new and exciting products in the high-technology arena. During this formulation period, the company grew slowly until it produced its first major product in 1964: a new and powerful desktop calculator. As is the case with many companies in their formulation stage, Wang Labs introduced this new product almost prematurely and its overall fate stood in precarious balance.

The story told internally at Wang was that the company had introduced the new desktop calculator during a major trade show with much hoopla and fanfare. However, not all the technology was ready, and the first prototype still had huge unsolved problems at the time of the trade show. The company brought the prototype to the show nonetheless, holding it together

---

[11] I had the privilege of being employed at Wang Labs for three years from 1985–1988. It is from this experience, and conversations with fellow employees, that the description and analysis of Wang Labs is derived.

with little more than rubber bands and chewing gum. They put the product on a table with a tablecloth that covered and disguised a bunch of wires below the table. Unbeknownst to observers of the product, behind a screen hid a handful of Wang developers who manipulated the product by hand, using these wires as people tested and examined the calculator. This created the impression that the product was in full working order, whereas, without the help of the people behind the screen, the calculator was completely unusable. As fate would have it, the ruse worked, and the product was launched with extraordinary success.

This product spurred huge growth, enabling the company to go public in 1967 at $12.50 per share. By the close of the first day's trading, the stock was at $40.50 per share.

Much of Wang Lab's early success was due directly to An Wang's entrepreneurial approach to business and his technical brilliance. Dr. Wang produced numerous patents in the early years and collected around him highly talented scientists and product developers. This was a no-holds-barred period in the company's history, and the only limiting factor was the employees' imagination. Dr. Wang led the company in the early days with compassion and a vision to contribute something of enduring value to the world. He offered much throughout his career, through inventions and through his philanthropy. Dr. Wang was admired and revered during the early days of the company, and considered by many to be both a brilliant scientist and a great leader. This latter assessment would later be deemed as premature as the company grew in size.

In 1976, Wang Labs revolutionized the office environment with the introduction of the first commercially viable word processor. By being a product leader in a market aching to be discovered, Wang Labs literally created a market, and sales soared. Indeed, the word-processing product was so successful that, for all intents and purposes, the company became a one-product company. For many years the name Wang was synonymous with word processing.

By the end of this period in Wang's history, the company had a great product, a vision for the future, a strategy focused around the word processor, a structure that was fluid and growing, and a culture focused on product innovation. This culture produced an extraordinary product, whose successful introduction marked the company's shift from the formulation phase to the growth phase. All of these factors strongly suggest that Dr. Wang did a lot of things right with regard to the organization's architecture. Wang Labs was a success in large part because they had created a strategy and a structure that matched the needs of the company at the time. Moreover, it produced a product that hit the market at just the right time, literally creating a whole new market for word processing that would eventually make the typewriter almost obsolete.

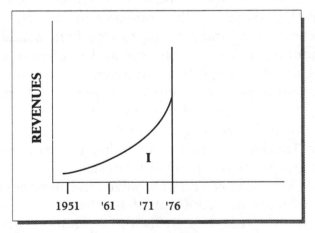

Figure 3-2. Wang Labs' formative years.

PHASE 2: GROWTH

Once they have established themselves in a new market, and have begun to deliver products or services to that market, organizations have the opportunity to enter into a growth phase. To grow successfully, an organization must develop concurrently in a number of potential areas. If the market it identifies is attracted to its products or services, then the organization must develop its ability to meet that market demand. If the customer base does not grow, but remains stable, then the organization must develop its ability to improve its products or services, or else competition will rapidly squeeze the organization out of the marketplace.

If the organization continues to succeed and grow, people in growth organizations often feel overwhelmed. This is due to the myriad of challenges facing them to sustain growth, as well as the demands on their time to produce products or offer services. At the same time, if successful, people in growing organizations often feel they can do no wrong. The growing demand for their products and services tell them they are doing something right. The resulting sense of omnipotence is often a sweet elixir, yet at the same time can mask underlying problems—problems that will likely surface later, and sometimes too late.

To be successful during the growth phase, an organization can no longer just focus on producing a great product, or on defining or understanding a new market. Now the focus of the organizational architecture needs to be more on the quality of the organization, on creating structures and processes that are best able to deliver. As was true in the case of Wang Labs, the organization must now understand the forces that led to its success and to reproduce them.

Wang Labs 1976–1985: The Growth Years. By all outward appearances, Wang Labs was extremely successful during its growth phase, but beneath the surface lurked significant problems. Wang Labs grew from 3000 employees in 1976 to a high of 31,500 employees in 1985. As is true of most rapidly growing organizations, the company was making a lot of money, and was enjoying the flush of success associated with having made its mark. This was an exciting time: people were getting promoted rapidly, being challenged, and there was a fair bit of room in which to take risks and make mistakes. Growing demand allowed for these mistakes, mistakes that later proved to be very costly.

This feeling of excitement is typical of people in a high-growth company and was never truer than at Wang Labs, as evidenced by a report in the August 19th, 1992, edition of the *Wall Street Journal*.[12] According to the authors, An Wang "once toured the United Nations building, and a secretarial pool broke into applause as he passed by. 'I am the secretaries' friend,' Dr. Wang used to explain, 'I have freed them from the typewriter.' " From this strong sense of mission, the company's reputation grew, but to some extent its reputation exceeded its capabilities.

During their growth, Wang Labs began to exhibit signs of poor organizational management. They ignored signals that their product strategy was suspect, for example, and they disregarded key decisions by competitors. One problem for Wang Labs during its growth phase was that its word-processing software was built on minicomputer hardware. This hardware platform was ideal in the early days because it was smaller and cheaper than mainframe computers, and

---

[12] *Wall Street Journal*, August 19, 1992, p. 1.

ideal for office applications. However, personal computers came to the forefront in the early 1980s. PCs were significantly less expensive than minicomputers. When connected together in networks, they had much of the same capability as minis, yet with greater flexibility. Hence, in a span of only five years, the PC technology leapfrogged the need for word processors on the minicomputer, and rendered the Wang Word Processor essentially obsolete.

Wang Labs could have seen this coming in the late 1970s and early 1980s, but chose to ignore the warning signs. Rather than build new products based on a PC platform, it enhanced its current products instead. This strategy was in direct contrast to its earlier position of being a product innovator. Now the company was beginning to stagnate technologically. In effect, Wang Labs became confused about the source of its success. As a company, it thought its success was in word processing on the minicomputer and focused on refining this product. Its real success, however, was due to defining a new market and seizing that market with an innovative product.

In addition, Wang Labs also kept its software proprietary, meaning that its computers could not easily be connected to computers made by other companies, or use software running on different operating systems. Computer users had been shying away from proprietary machines for years, not wanting to be limited in technology. Yet Wang Labs failed to heed this trend. Along came IBM in 1981, which introduced the IBM PC with an operating system that welcomed other players onto the playing field. As a result, in four or five years, Wang Labs' technology was rendered obsolete. Some insiders at Wang could see it coming, but their voices were a cry in the wilderness. Said one former Wang employee in a 1992 newspaper article, "they were feeling

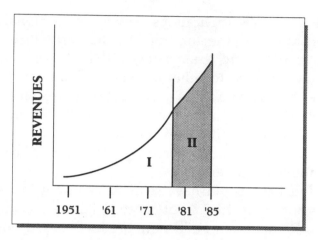

Figure 3-3. Wang Labs' growth years.

so flushed with success from the early days, there was a disregard to what was happening in the industry."[13]

In spite of the signs that all was not well, the company continued to grow, mining new opportunities for its word-processing products. In 1984, total revenue hit $2.1 billion, and Wang Labs enjoyed its last strong year of profitability, earning $210 million. In 1988 total revenue hit $3 billion, marking an almost unprecedented period of rapid growth in U.S. corporate history.

The Absence of Strong Leadership at Wang. The kind of leadership necessary to lead effectively during the growth phase of a company is no longer charismatic leadership, for the growing product demand will often sustain excitement. Rather, a strong organizational leader is critical. The effective leader of the growth stage is one who understands the business and can generate the proper infrastructure to support that business. This is a period where a strong organizational leader can

---

[13] *San Francisco Chronicle,* August 19, 1992, p. B-2.

counterbalance the organization's tendency to feel om-
nipotent, and can create the proper organizational architecture to help the organization move into the next
phase of the organization's life cycle.

This is where Dr. Wang ultimately fell short in his
abilities. He had no prior experience in leading a large
company, and his leadership continued to focus on
product development rather than on changes in market
demand. Most of the new product ideas were internally
generated by product developers. As is true in many
high-technology companies, their ideas were often not
responsive to changing market demands. Hundreds of
millions of dollars, for example, were poured into ill-
fated attempts to create a small minicomputer for the
engineering and technical market, further enhance-
ments of the original Wang Word Processor, and a "me-
too" IBM clone. All of these separate efforts were led
by bright scientists with little shared focus.

Recognizing the need for stronger leadership, Dr.
Wang looked to others, but even his new choices
proved ineffectual. During the 1980s there were four
different company presidents, including Dr. Wang himself. Each showed some promise, yet they were not
enough to counterbalance the company's tendency to
ignore key signs that its strategy and culture were not
poised well for future success.

An example of the difficulty was the experience of
the first president of Wang Labs after An Wang, John
Cunningham. Prior to being named president, Cunningham was the highly successful head of sales at
Wang Labs. He was seen by many as the best candidate
to lead a growing company, having had previous experience at other companies in key leadership positions.
In addition, his market-driven focus was a welcome
new approach to the company's growth. Unfortunately, Cunningham and Dr. Wang often did not see

eye to eye in many areas, not to mention their clear cultural differences. While Dr. Wang was product driven in his orientation, Cunningham was market driven. Dr. Wang was also strongly influenced by his Chinese traditions and hired many people with a Chinese heritage. Among some Americans in the company, these were quietly referred to as the Chinese Mafia, alluding to the stronghold that the Chinese expatriates had in running the company and to the resentment that ensued. (It should be noted that Wang Labs does not hold the corner on cultural favoritism. Many, if not most companies, suffer from a tendency on the part of leaders to consciously or unconsciously hire in their own image and thereby limit diversity.)

The clash of views about how to lead the company proved insurmountable for Cunningham, who resigned in July of 1985.

PHASE THREE: MATURITY

In principle, every organization reaches a phase of maturity or a significant plateau. In reality, few organizations reach their full potential and sustain their performance over long periods of time. Even fewer effectively rearchitect themselves. More often than not, organizations don't respond effectively to competition, and/or they don't renew themselves by developing the capacity to learn, and hence to grow to full maturity.

The quality of organizations at the mature phase is often business as usual. Mature organizations are typically stable, having mapped out their market and secured their position. In such organizations, members often experience a level of security far greater than in earlier phases. Many organizations at this phase of their life cycle often have clear human resource policies, relatively productive technical systems, and typically strong cash reserves able to sustain them through long and difficult times.

Organizations that reach mature phases also tend to be slow to move. They have built up such an entrenched infrastructure and an accepted way of doing things that change is often difficult. Interestingly, mature organizations often attract people who welcome stability, and who thereby reinforce the organization's own inability to grow and change.

There are three critical challenges in redesigning mature organizations: developing the proper level of bureaucracy necessary to sustain a mature organization; achieving higher levels of performance; and renewing or regenerating the organization by developing new markets, new products, or new services. Wang Labs did none of these well.

Wang Labs 1985–1988: The Mature Years. Wang Labs had little chance to experience what it is like to be a mature organization. As soon as it reached its pinnacle of financial success, it went into rapid decline. To many people in the organization, this was the equivalent of a sky diving free fall, without the parachute. Perhaps the only identifiable period of relative maturity was from 1985–1988. During this period, sales grew from $2.3 billion to $3 billion on the strength of its large customer base; by 1988, its net income was minimal.

During this phase, in the only significant attempt to break outside of the word-processing, single-product mold, Wang entered into and began defining a new business arena called "document image processing." This technology uses scanners to create electronic images of documents, which, when translated into computer code, can be manipulated and stored electronically for later retrieval. Unlike word processing, which experienced almost immediate success,

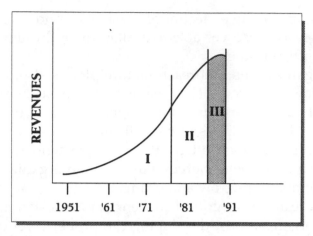

Figure 3-4. Wang Labs' mature years.

however, image processing has only recently taken off as a commercially viable product after almost ten years of development. Unfortunately, Wang Labs bet the bank on this new technology, but did not have the resources necessary to endure a slow growth period of formulating a new product and creating a new market. Had the market opened up more quickly, or if Wang had sufficient resources, the product might have become a major source of income. Instead, by the late 1980s, the market had not yet come to full fruition, and the company's fortunes continued to decline.

To Wang's credit, like many organizations seeking corporate renewal, upper management decided a few years ago that it badly needed to focus its resources. In order to accomplish this, it hired an outside strategic consulting firm. This firm was instrumental in helping Wang focus its corporate energy on the image-processing market. Typical of many mature companies, however, the solution chosen to cure Wang's ills was strategically focused, but did not include a full examination of its organizational architecture. The organization, by this time, was imbued with bureaucracy, and it had lost its original ability to be innovative. Hence, the emphasis on strategic change came too little, too late.

The fundamental architectural problems that Wang Labs faced was how to redesign an existing organizational culture that did not know how to manage its size well and how to respond to changing market demands. This Achilles heel should have been overcome many years earlier in order to effectively exploit new markets and new technology.

The Leadership Drought Continues. The kind of leadership needed for the mature phase of the organization is visionary leadership—leadership that successfully challenges the status quo and seeks to explore new frontiers. There are plenty of people in mature organizations able to manage the organization and provide the proper level of bureaucracy. Few people, however, have the foresight to envision new opportunities, and the strength of character necessary to challenge a mature organization to continually grow anew. Even fewer have the knowledge of organizational dynamics able to manage the difficult process of rearchitecting an already mature company. In the case of Wang Labs, the fourth president of Wang Labs, Rick Miller, might have been such a leader as he made numerous attempts to salvage the company, but he never really had a chance. Miller was brought in to turn the company around, but found the company in rapid decline, with dwindling resources, and a customer base ready to bolt at the first opportunity to invest in new technology. By the time Miller was hired in 1989, Dr. Wang was already drawing up petitions to file for bankruptcy protection. Creating a new organizational architecture that prepared the organization for maturity in a rapidly changing market was needed years before, and Wang Labs never effectively demonstrated this capability.

Without the ability to rearchitect itself, in 1989 the company experienced the loss of over $400 million dollars. Soon thereafter, Miller made a bold and futile attempt to save the hemorrhaging company. He carved an alliance with IBM to sell Wang software on IBM computers.

PHASE FOUR: DECLINE AND DECAY

One of the consequences of the second law of thermodynamics is that all physical systems have an irreversible tendency toward eventual disorganization and decay. The science of physics refers to this tendency as "entropy." Human organizations, no less than physical systems, are inevitably bound to experience increasing entropy and eventual death. While inevitable, this fourth phase can be put off considerably (and, in principle, indefinitely) if the organization properly masters the first three phases. If and when it doesn't, however, organizational decay sets in and corporate death ensues. Such was the case at Wang Labs. In July of 1990, the firm's losses exceeded $700 million and by mid-1992, more than 19,000 workers had been laid off in a three-year period. Finally, on August 18, 1992, Wang Labs filed for Chapter 11 bankruptcy protection, marking the low point for what had previously been a corporate giant in the computer industry.

Wang Labs 1988–1992: A Chapter in Wang Labs is Closed. The last few years have been a particularly difficult period at Wang Labs. The ghosts of past successes and of lost opportunities lurked in the walls and rafters of its corporate confines. For five years the specter of layoffs loomed large and the sadness associated with losing one's fellow employees cast a giant shadow on this once great institution.

Ironically, most companies in the growth phase, by being initially successful, sow the seeds of their own future demise. In their collective arrogance, many organizations get caught up in the excitement of making a lot of money and fail to learn from their mistakes. Inevitably they die an early death. This, I believe, is what happened to Wang Labs, where they built their reputation on only one product, and held on to this mainstay product until it was too late.

While the premise of this chapter is that Wang Labs did not design its architecture well through many critical periods, there is also much that is positive to say about the company. In many respects, it was a leader in its field. During its rise to fortune, few companies treated their employees better, and few people were as generous in supporting community causes as Dr. An Wang. During its heyday, people in the organization were proud to be a part of Wang Labs, and it was seen by many people as one of the most desirable places to work.

It is too early to write the eulogy of Wang Labs for, although it is a shell of its former self, Wang Labs continues to have the possibility of rising out of the ashes to experience rebirth. The company has recently appointed a new CEO and experienced an infusion of capital from its primary investors in order to focus its efforts on the image-processing system and in software development, with hopes that it will become a financially viable company in the future. This strategy, while not likely to produce the extraordinary results of the past, does show promise. Indeed, as of the writing of this book, it is attempting to emerge from Chapter 11.

LESSONS FROM WANG LABS

The story of the demise of Wang Labs is both tragic and instructive. All companies face the same challenges that Wang Labs faced. Many of them prematurely succumb to the same kind of misjudgments, misguided assumptions, and false expectations that were part of the cause of Wang Labs' eventual demise.

The story of Wang Labs is compelling, for it tells us how critical it is to remain adaptable as a company. Too often companies believe that the reason why they are successful is because they have a great product or service. They assume it is in the brilliance of their people or in their advanced technology. While all these factors may be present, it is a strategic mistake to assume that these factors will ensure future viability. These factors are all subject to change themselves, and it is almost certain that another company will seize the market that someone else's innovation has initially created.

The only sustainable competitive advantage in today's marketplace is the ability to remain ever adaptable to changing market conditions—to design and redesign the organizational architecture. The managers at Silicon Graphics understand this extremely well, as they have carved a strategy out of learning, growing, and adapting as a company. As a result, they have become one of the most successful companies in the country. I believe the primary reason monoliths such as IBM, Digital Equipment Corporation, General Motors, Wang Labs, U.S. Steel, and countless others are suffering today is their inability to remain flexible and customer-focused in today's rapidly changing marketplace.

"Grow or die" used to mean grow in size. Now, nothing can be further from the truth. In today's marketplace, "grow or die" means to grow in one's abilities to adapt, develop, and change. It means to continually examine the quality and viability of the organization's architecture and be willing to design anew. Perhaps the phrase "grow or die" has always meant that. We were just too myopic to see it in the first place.

ARCHITECTING CHECKLIST

1. Contrary to popular belief, the greatest predictor of future performance is not past performance. In many cases, past successes can produce organizations that are entrenched and unadaptable to change.

2. Size alone no longer guarantees success. If anything, it is a major impediment to flexibility and adaptability.

3. Organizations go through natural phases during their life cycle. Each phase brings with it a unique set of challenges. Each phase requires a different organizational architecture for success.

4. Most successful organizations, like Wang Labs, are unable to recreate their success for they hold on to the past, and do not focus on redesigning their architecture for the future.

4

The Three Principles of Architecting Change

We have to believe in free will. We have no choice.

—Isaac Bashevis Singer

Affecting any kind of change in an organization, let alone the kind of profound change that is the subject of this book, is difficult at best. At worst, it is almost impossible, for whatever condition the organization is in now, its present condition has been determined by a set of forces that, taken together, have conspired to keep the organization at its present level of functioning. Like the Hydra of Greek mythology, you fix one problem, and another will likely spring up in its place.

Numerous books on the subject of managing change have been written to help us understand how to do it well.[1] While much has been written and researched on the subject, we still have a great deal to learn about how to manage the dynamics of change in such a way that it produces enduring positive results in the overall performance of the company and in the well-being of its members. This book takes much of what has already been researched and applies it to a specific feature of the change process, that of strengthening the organization's architecture. The process described in this book is not for all organizations, however. It is only for those organizations that are relatively healthy and are ready to apply their efforts to enhance what is already a relatively strong foundation. Let me explain.

---

[1] See for example:

(a) McCaskey, Michael B. *The Executive Challenge: Managing Change and Ambiguity*, Pitman Publishing Inc., Marshfield, Mass., 1982.
This book describes the environment that most organizations face, one that requires the ability to manage change.

(b) Hickman, Craig R. and Silva, Michael A. *Creating Excellence: Managing Corporate Culture, Strategy, and Change in the New Age*, NAL Books, New York, 1984. This book came out on the heels of the success of the book, *In Search of Excellence*. It describes the process of change, the principles of change, and the skills that are required.

(c) Beer, Michael, Eisenstat, Russell, and Spector, Bert. *The Critical Path to Corporate Renewal*, Harvard Business School Press, Cambridge, Mass., 1990.
This is an excellent book based on solid research on the dynamics of managing large-systems change. It challenges the notion that large-scale change must be top down, and points to specific areas to focus on in managing the process of change.

(d) Beckhard, Richard, and Pritchard, W. *Changing the Essence: The Art of Creating and Leading Fundamental Change in Organizations*, Jossey-Bass Publishers, San Francisco, 1992.
The principal author of this book, Richard Beckhard, is one of the founders and leading figures in the discipline of organizational development. His ideas are time-tested and universally accepted among practitioners in the field. This book offers an excellent overview of the critical features of managing the process of organizational change.

(e) Nadler, David, et al. *Organizational Architecture: Designs for Changing Organizations*, Jossey-Bass Publishers, San Francisco, 1992.
This book provides a nice conceptual overview of the value of architecture as a metaphor for organizational design, and it identifies a number of different ways of thinking about organizations and designing them for better performance.

I recently picked up the book *The Road Less Traveled* by Scott Peck and was impressed by the distinction he made between people who are neurotic and people who have what is commonly known in the field of psychology as a character disorder. Neurotic people, Peck points out, are people who have emotional problems, and who tend to blame themselves a lot for their condition in life. They often feel they are at fault for not managing their lives better, tend to be self-effacing at the very least, and self-rejecting at the very most. Their self-questioning nature makes them easy to work with in psychotherapy because they are open to learning, and tend to be self-reflective, sometimes overly so.

People with character disorders, on the other hand, tend to blame the world for their feelings and their unsatisfactory lives. "I'm fine," says the person with a character disorder, "it's the world that is at fault." In contrast to neurotics, who takes too much responsibility for the condition of their lives, people with character disorder take no responsibility. As a result, they are extremely difficult to work with in psychotherapy because they tend to be closed off to learning.[2]

It struck me as I was reading Peck's book that there is an organizational analog to the above distinction. Most organizations have what I would consider typical neuroses. They are imbued with politics; they have counterproductive competition; people don't communicate well with each other; they are rigid by nature; and they have internal conflicts that are not managed well. Although it will likely be difficult, these kinds of organizations have the capacity for change as long as people within them, particularly the leadership, are committed

---

[2] Peck, S. *The Road Less Traveled*, Simon & Schuster, New York, 1978.

to growth, learning, and organizational self-reflection.[3] Some organizations, however, have what is analogous to a severe character disorder. They are fraught with denial, there is significant back-stabbing, and even severe dishonesty. In such organizations, it is very difficult to architect change because the environment is so dysfunctional it precludes the possibility for accurate self-analysis and planned change. In such organizations, a consultant is usually necessary to help address the unhealthy dynamics, or the climate is unlikely to change for the better. Even with a good consultant, it will be extremely difficult.

Most organizations, be they neurotic or healthy, are generally able to change, and to some extent their people are open to challenging their present way of operating, particularly if they are convinced that changing will help them succeed in the future. For such organizations the process of change and its dynamics are relatively predicable. We have learned over the years a great deal about how to effectively manage change and how to create conditions for heightened performance over time. It is for these more healthy or "neurotic" organizations that the principles described in this chapter are appropriate.

THE THREE PRINCIPLES, IN BRIEF

I believe that while this book is a cookbook of sorts (in that it provides some clear and detailed recipes for how to redesign an organization's architecture), without a

---

[3] See Shapiro, E. *How Corporate Truths Become Competitive Traps*, John Wiley & Sons, New York, 1991, for an interesting analysis of typical organizational neuroses, or what the author calls "traps."

clear set of principles to guide one's actions, all the skills in the world will not work, for they will be based on faulty assumptions or faulty motivations. As you continue to read through this book, please take particular note of how the principles described below play themselves out in each of the phases of the organizational architecting process. These principles are your guides for how to manage sticky situations, and how to behave when you are not sure of what it is best to do.

In creating a new organizational architecture, or in any effort to change an organization, three principles are critical. They are:

- full and accurate information
- free choice
- commitment[4]

Full and accurate information as a principle says that no matter what direction the organization takes, the changes must be made based on full and valid information. Valid information is information based on data that are collected in the service of truth. This means that the effective leader collects data, not to prove that he or she is right, but rather to discover the best direction for the organization to take.

Free choice says that people are ultimately responsible and the masters of their own lives. The more we design organizations consistent with people's ability to make responsible and informed decisions, the more likely we will have an organization of people dedicated to a shared cause.

---

[4] See Argyris, Chris, *Intervention Theory and Method*, Addison-Wesley, Reading, Mass., 1970, for an early piece of work demonstrating the importance of these three principles.

Commitment as a principle for organizational architecture says that no matter what architecture you create, you must have the commitment of a critical mass of your organization's members to the direction of the organization and its architecture in order to implement it. Without a full commitment, the effort to grow or redesign the new architecture will probably not be successful.

These three principles—*full and accurate information, free choice,* and *commitment*—are not just a philosophical argument for effective change. They have proven themselves time and time again to be critical features of an effective organizational change process. Without applying these principles, the effort will likely fail. Applying these principles does not guarantee success, but increases one's chances immensely. Let's look more in depth into each.

FULL AND ACCURATE INFORMATION

Organizations rarely operate on the basis of full and accurate information. Most people don't want to be accurately informed. To be accurately informed is to have access to data that may not necessarily substantiate one's own beliefs. That access is threatening. So what we often do is encourage having only some information, and to discourage having other information. The result is that we make decisions and solve problems on the basis of partial or faulty information. It's no wonder that so many mistakes get made.

Witness, for example, the Bay of Pigs fiasco in Cuba in 1960. At the time, President Kennedy and his key advisors approved an invasion by CIA-organized Cuban exiles at the Bay of Pigs, with the ultimate aim of overthrowing the government of Fidel Castro. The outcome was that some 1200 prisoners were captured by Castro's forces and were later ransomed back to the U.S. government for $53 million in food and drugs. What occurred remains to this day one of the most graphic and unfortunate examples of poor decision making in political history. Why did the advisory group fail? According to Janis (1967), the President and his key advisers approved of the Bay of Pigs invasion plan on the basis of six assumptions, each of which was based on incomplete or inaccurate information.

Assumption no. 1: No one will believe that the United States was responsible for the invasion of Cuba. Most people will believe the CIA cover story.
   Fact: During the weeks preceding the invasion, it became increasingly apparent that the cover story would not work. A week before the invasion, President Kennedy complained, "I can't believe what I'm reading! Castro doesn't need agents over here. All he has to do is read our papers."

Assumption no. 2: The Cuban air force is so ineffective that it can be knocked out completely just before the invasion begins.
   Fact: The supposedly ineffective Cuban air force shot down half of the American B-26s attempting to protect the invaders and repeatedly bombed the ground troops as they arrived on shore.

Assumption no. 3: The 1400 men in the brigade of Cuban exiles have high morale and are willing to carry out the invasion without any support from U.S. troops.
   Fact: One month before the invasion, when the policy-making group in Washington was being assured about the magnificent morale of the exile

brigade, the men were actually bitterly
discontented and beginning to revolt.

Assumption no. 4: Castro's army is so weak that the
small Cuban exile brigade will be able to establish a
well-protected beachhead.
   Fact: Assurances of the weakness of Castro's army
   happened to be directly contrary to reports of
   Castro's military strength by experts in the U.S.
   State Department and in the British Intelligence
   Service.

Assumption no. 5: The invasion by the Cuban exile
brigade will touch off sabotage by the Cuban
underground and armed uprisings behind the lines
will effectively support the invaders and probably
lead to the toppling of the Castro regime.
   Fact: An earlier, carefully conducted poll showed
   that the overwhelming majority of Cubans
   supported the Castro regime.

Assumption no. 6: If the Cuban exile brigade does not
succeed in its prime military objective, the men can
retreat to a nearby mountain range and reinforce the
guerrilla units holding out against the Castro regime.
   Fact: Plans were changed just before the invasion
   so that the invaders were 80 miles away from the
   mountain range, too far away to take advantage of
   its protection.[5]

Thus, all six assumptions that were the basis of the
invasion were faulty, and all six were perpetuated by

---

[5] Adapted from Janus, Irving, *Victims of Groupthink*, Houghton Mifflin Company, Boston, 1967.

an overly optimistic advisory group, so wishful in their thinking about the likelihood of success of the operation that they ignored pertinent information to the contrary. Had the advisory group taken the time to access and utilize full information, they would have questioned far more severely the wisdom of the invasion before undertaking it.

Leaders of businesses, no less than political leaders, have to make decisions with only partial information. Ironically, the people who need to have the information the most are often the least well-informed. In the case of upper management, rarely are they aware of critical problems lower down in the organization. In fact, the higher up in the organization one is, the more shielded one can be from key information. This situation is due to two conspiring dynamics. On the one hand, leaders of organizations often behave in ways that send signals to others below them that they just don't want to know about problems. They "kill the messenger," or send messages like "just handle it," both of which send a loud and clear signal: "don't inform me." At the same time, people often don't bring information to the attention of top management because they sense that it is unimportant, or they fear that they will be blamed for the problem they have reported.

The problem of the lack of full and accurate information at the top is endemic in organizations. In one organization, for example, a quality expert once asked a cross-section of people in a large factory to list all the significant problems known to each of them. Of the total number listed, 74 percent of these were known to their supervisors, even fewer to mid-management, and only 4 percent of the problems listed were known to top management. In other words, most of the causes of defects, excess costs, delays, and other problems were

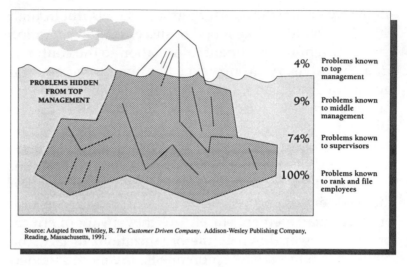

Figure 4-1. The iceberg of ignorance.

hidden from top management. This situation became known as the iceberg of ignorance (see Figure 4–1).[6]

Not only is top management often shielded from critical information, information often does not filter downward as well. Many organizations, for example, have an unwritten policy of sharing information on a "need to know" basis. Still others will not share critical financial information for fear it will get in the wrong hands. I consulted to one such company a couple of years ago that exemplified this attitude. The company is a privately held company that at the time had a strong policy of never telling workers the financial status of the organization. Their rationale was that they could not trust some workers, for they would tell the competi-

---

[6] Yoshida, Shuichi, "Quality Improvement and TQC Management at Calsonic in Japan and Overseas," paper prepared for the Second International Quality Symposium in Mexico, November 1989.

tion about the company's financial condition and that the competition would use this information to gain a competitive advantage.

Ironically, the leadership of the organization also wanted to build a workforce that was deeply committed to the company as a whole, one that acted with a spirit of ownership. When I pointed out the contradiction between wanting a spirit of ownership, but treating people like untrustworthy workers, some leaders of the organization simply shrugged their shoulders and said, "that's the way it has to be in this cutthroat business." When I responded by pointing out that publicly traded corporations must divulge information publicly, as a matter of course, they continued to justify their position of withholding key information from their employees.

After much debate over the course of many months, however, they have begun to share some important information throughout the company as they slowly move toward a more collaborative, more committed organizational culture. Top management finally asked themselves, "which is a greater competitive advantage, withholding financial information for fear of it leaking to competitors, or unleashing the creativity, knowledge, and commitment of our work force?" Their answer is now the latter. Sadly, however, many other organizations have not come to this same conclusion. To many organizational leaders, information is still seen as power to be guarded closely, not as power to be shared with the objective of creating an informed and committed workforce.

The critical issue here is not only how much information is shared, but also how accurate that information is. To be successful, leaders need to encourage others to provide them with as much relevant information as possible. In addition, that information needs to be accurate, reflecting a balanced and true sense of the situation at hand. Having access to full and accurate information is critical in any effort to architect an organization for the simple reason that developing one's organization requires a clear and accurate picture of where the organization is right now. The more accurate the information, the more informed the choice can be on how to proceed in the organizational development effort.

The leader who acts on the principle of full and accurate information will seek to discover the thoughts and feelings of people at all levels within the organization, and not necessarily trust that the picture painted by his immediate direct reports is the most accurate one. Their picture is indeed more likely to be biased, reflecting their wishes to paint a prettier picture than is true. The leader acting on the principle of full and accurate information will also seek to discover where problems lie in the present way of operating the firm and will want to understand how they got that way. Without such information, the leader and others will not know the best way to change for the better.

Hence, the principle of full and accurate information requires that the leader behave in a trustworthy manner, making it safe for people to share with him or her both positive and negative information about the organization. He or she must demonstrate trust in others by sharing that information, in turn both freely and fully. In addition, a leader must have a working understanding of how to collect critical information and share this information in a way that others can understand. All of this requires that the group responsible for developing the organization have the skill to facilitate open discussion of information, allowing for the fullest understanding of its significance.

Principle	*Skills Needed*
Full and accurate information	• Openness and honesty • Directness • Self-disclosure • Collect and disseminate information in a way that others can understand

FREE CHOICE

The second principle of effectively managing the process of change is that of free choice. This means that all members of the organization have both the freedom and the right to decide their fate for themselves. A choice is free to the degree that the individual can:

- define his or her own objectives
- define how to achieve these objectives
- define objectives that are within his or her capacities
- relate these objectives to his or her own personal needs[7]

When people have freedom of choice, and when their choices are both attainable and satisfying, they experience psychological success. This sense of success is the stuff of a high-spirited, high-performing organization. Of course, this does not mean that everyone can do whatever they want. It means that the person's personal wants and needs enter into the equation of what

---

[7] Argyris, Chris and Schon, Donald. *Theory in Practice: Increasing Professional Effectiveness*, Jossey-Bass, San Francisco, 1974, p. 88.

decisions get made, and that people are not forced to do anything against their will.

Lest the reader think this is heady philosophy, consider for yourself what it is like when you are strongly asked to do something that you do not want to do. What does it feel like? If you are like most people, you will either resist openly or, if coerced with few options, you will concede and go along grudgingly. Leaders who do not lead based on this principle of free choice create workers who appear to go along, but whose heart is not in their work.

In contrast, leaders who do lead based on the importance of free choice create a very different atmosphere. They create a climate that encourages the open exchange of ideas, and they create conditions where people choose their own direction, where people are therefore more committed to their actions.

> We do not always have the wisdom to make the correct choices. Woody Allen said, "more than any other time in history, mankind faces a crossroads. One path leads to despair and utter hopelessness. The other to total extinction. Let us pray we have the wisdom to choose correctly."

The skills required of the leader acting on the principle of free choice are openness with others in his or her dealings, directness in his or her expression of thoughts, and clarity in his or her own preferences and choices. This open behavior runs contrary to the "close to one's vest" type of behavior that is taught in the "protect oneself" school of management. While apparently not safe in the short run (in that you run the risk that people will not do what you want), in the long run, when the organization makes a change based on people freely choosing that change, it will be more effective and longer lasting than if it had been imposed from the top.

Principle	*Skills Needed*
Full and accurate information	• Openness and honesty • Directness • Self-disclosure • Collect and disseminate information in a way that others can understand it
Free choice	• **Ability to facilitate** • **Clarity of expression** • **Directness**

COMMITMENT

Newton's second law of physics says that for every action there is an equal and opposite reaction. Push down hard on something and it resists. So too in the world of people. When you push on them hard, they push back. Wars have been waged throughout the history of the world based on this principle. So too have gang fights, marital squabbles, and legal courtroom battles. In every case, when one person or group tries to force another person or group to do something against their will, the other person or group will push back. In brief, force breeds counterforce.

In the world of business, this counterforce sometimes occurs overtly, and sometimes covertly. Workers from the beginning of time have become masterful in developing subtle forms of pushing back. They execute work slowdowns, produce marginal efforts, come up with all forms of absenteeism, and exhibit low motivation. At the extreme, force breeds sabotage.

The word "sabotage" literally means "damage" and has its roots in the French Labor movement in the early to mid-1800s. It comes from the French word "sabot" meaning "shoe." Its origin comes from the textile industry, where workers who felt that their union was not being recognized threw wooden shoes into the looms to stop production.

After discovering some of the counterproductive consequences of exercizing force over workers, many managers over the years have discovered different ways to create change in the workplace. Some ways are manipulative, some are not. The most effective of these is to create conditions where people can buy into the change themselves. People buy into a particular change either because it is intrinsically satisfying, they value the change, or there are valuable rewards associated with that change, not because they will be penalized for not adopting it. When they buy into the change, they own it. It is theirs, and therefore they are more committed to it.

The importance of psychological and/or actual ownership of decisions has been researched considerably of late and the findings so strongly support this claim that at this point it is almost irrefutable. For example, a recent review of 25 studies found that the use of profit sharing was generally associated with 3.5 to 5 percent higher productivity in firms.[8] Another review has

---

[8] Source: *High Performance Work Practices and Firm Performance*. Background material for the Conference on the Future of the American Workplace, U.S. Department of Labor, July 1993.

shown that of the 29 studies reviewed, 14 indicated that workplace participation has a positive effect on productivity. Only two indicated negative effects. The rest were inconclusive.[9] In still a third study, among Fortune 1000 companies using at least one practice that increased the responsibility of employees in the business process, 60 percent reported that these practices increased productivity and 79 percent reported that they improved quality.[10]

The third principle of designing one's organizational architecture, then, is to create conditions where the members of the organization own the design process themselves. This means conditions where they can freely choose the changes and make a commitment to them.

The word commitment comes from the Latin word "committere," which literally means to join, connect, and entrust. The prefix "com" refers to "together," while the suffix "mittere" means "to send." The word itself has some roots in the military, in that "committere" used to mean "to send together into battle."

The creation of commitment is most effectively done by using the well-known approach of participatory management. Participatory management is nothing more than the practice of including the people affected by the decision in the creation of that decision. This

---

[9] Levin, D. and D'Andrea Tyson, L. "Participation, Productivity, and the Firm's Environment," in *Paying for Productivity*, Alan Blinder, ed. The Brookings Institute, Washington, D.C., 1990, pp. 183–235.
[10] Lawler, E. et al. *Employee Involvement and Total Quality Management*. Jossey-Bass, San Francisco, 1992.

does not necessarily mean that they actually make the decision. Nor does it mean that you, as manager or leader, abdicate your decision-making responsibility. Rather, it means that you involve others in the decision-making process in such a way that the final decision reflects their active input and takes into consideration their concerns, needs, and ideas. You not only get a decision that is potentially wiser (in that it includes their valuable input), but it also results in a far greater likelihood of their commitment. When people are involved in making the decision, they almost always feel ownership of it.

The spirit of "ownership" is not just a nice thing to have in today's organization. I believe it is essential. It results in everyone taking responsibility for mistakes or problems, rather than pointing the finger at someone else. It results in a sense of accountability, where people in the organization say in their hearts and in their actions, "you can count on me."

I am reminded of a story that for me symbolized what accountability and responsibility truly mean. The story is told about Captain Asoh, the pilot of a Japanese commercial airliner that had accidentally landed on water instead of on land. It so happened that one day, Captain Asoh misjudged the landing of his airplane. Although he landed the plane so gently that many of the 96 passengers didn't even notice where they had come down, such an act did not go unnoticed by the authorities. The National Transportation Safety Board held a preliminary hearing, with the press appearing en masse to witness the fiery testimonies. Captain Asoh was the first witness. The first question asked of him was, "Captain Asoh, in your own words, can you tell us how you managed to land a DC-8 aircraft two-and-a-half miles out in San Francisco Bay?" (read: "How Could You Possibly Make Such an Error?") Captain Asoh replied, "As you Americans say, Asoh *screwed up*" (actual expletive modified).[11]

While I'm sure there were other factors involved, what Captain Asoh said was brilliant, for in one fell swoop he totally changed the tone of the proceedings with his openness, honesty, and expression of personal ownership of the problem. This situation can only exist when people are involved in their organization and when the leaders of the organization support everyone's full participation.

One of the more graphic examples of the positive effect of participatory management is in an experiment that was done in the 1960s by the Volvo Corporation at their plant at Kalmar, Sweden.[12] Prior to this experiment, automobile engines at Volvo were built in assembly-line fashion. Due to the boredom, lack of meaning and challenge, and lack of social interaction that resulted from an assembly-line operation, the plant at Kalmar experienced high turnover of personnel, low quality output, and, at times, intentional worker sabotage.

Instead of pushing to make people work harder, Volvo tried an experiment. It built a new plant that transported the cars around on mechanical carriers to teams of workers. Each team was responsible for the production of entire units of the car such as the engine, the transmissions, etc. At first, the results were poor. It took much longer to assemble the units than in times past on the traditional assembly line. With time and practice, however, the workers got the average assembly time down such that they could put the different

---

[11] For an engaging fuller explanation of the incident, see Harvey, J. B. *The Abilene Paradox and Other Meditations on Management*, The Free Press, New York, 1988.
[12] Katz, D., and Kahn, R.L. *The Social Psychology of Organization* (2nd edition), Wiley and Sons, New York, 1978.

parts of the car together almost as fast as they would have on an assembly line. What differed, however, was not the speed, but rather the quality of the output. As a result of the change, Volvo cars had 90 percent fewer defects, there was a 25 percent reduction in production costs, morale improved significantly, and the workers took greater pride in their workmanship.[13]

Another early example of the power of worker participation occurred in a pajama factory owned by the Harwood Manufacturing Company. Up until 1962, Harwood had been managed by means of traditional hierarchical control. Through the use of a structured system of measuring organizational style, Harwood was measured at the time as being highly autocratic, controlling, and authority-obedience oriented. New owners came in and decided to move the managerial style and philosophy toward a participative, democratic, and team-oriented approach. After two years of changes in philosophy, method of operation, and managerial style, the results were extraordinary. Production efficiency improved from 85 percent of standard to 115 percent of standard. Operator turnover dropped from a monthly rate of 10 percent to a monthly rate of 4 percent, absenteeism dropped from 6 to 3 percent, and return of capital invested changed from a −15 percent in 1962 to a +17 percent in 1964. A number of worker attitudinal changes were also measured, indicating greater satisfaction with the company, the work, the compensation systems, and with fellow employees as a result of the changes in the company toward a more participative approach.

Not only were these changes remarkable, but they

---

[13] Johnson R. "Volvo's New Assembly Plant Has No Assembly Line." *Automotive News*, July 10, 1989, pp. 22, 24.

endured. In a follow-up study done in 1969, it was found that the positive gains in employee attitudes were not only maintained, but in some cases had improved far beyond the time when the formal change effort had been completed.[14]

In both cases, at Volvo and Harwood, the principle of commitment was achieved through means of participatory decision making. In both cases, the result was not only greater productivity but also greater worker satisfaction. These experiments have been reproduced time and time again throughout the United States, with consistently positive results.[15]

In a recent book entitled *Leading Self-Directed Work Teams*, Kim Fisher chronicles the productivity improvements of many experiments in high worker participation efforts. Here are a few:

- In a Proctor and Gamble manufacturing plant, worker participation produced 30–50 percent lower manufacturing costs.
- In a coal mine in Tavistock, England, output was 25 percent higher with lower costs.
- At AT&T Credit Corporation, team efforts doubled productivity.
- At a General Electric plant, productivity improved 250 percent.
- At Xerox, teams were at least 30 percent more productive than they had been with conventional approaches.[16]

---

[14] See French, W., and Bell, C., *Organization Development*, Prentice Hall, Inc., Englewood Cliffs, N.J., 1978, pp. 236–238 for a summary of this study.
[15] For more examples of the value of participatory decision making, see Zwerdling, D., *Democracy at Work*, Association for Self-Management, Washington, D.C., 1978; Fisher, K., *Leading Self-Directed Work Teams*, McGraw-Hill, New York, 1993.
[16] Fisher, K., *Leading Self-Directed Work Teams*, McGraw Hill, New York, 1993.

These are but a few of the hundreds of examples where increased worker participation produced extraordinary increases in productivity and satisfaction. In a review of organizations that shifted from traditional work approaches to more participatory approaches, John Cotter found that:

- 93 percent reported improved productivity
- 86 percent reported decreased operating costs
- 86 percent reported improved quality
- 70 percent reported better employee attitudes.[17]

Time and time again, researchers and practitioners alike have learned unequivocally that when an organization successfully involves people in decisions that affect them, the decisions tend to be more effective; people are more committed to those decisions and therefore implement them more wholeheartedly; and because their talents, skills, and knowledge are being utilized more fully, they feel a greater sense of satisfaction in their work.

This is no less true than in designing an organization's new architecture. The process of designing an organization is monumental, and calls for all of the best techniques to ensure its success. The principle of commitment calls for the leaders of the designing effort to take great pains to ensure that all key people are involved at every step along the way. While it takes longer in the front end of decision making to approach the architecting process in this way (it takes time to collaborate and come to consensus), the speed of execu-

---

[17] Cotter, J., *Designing Organizations That Work: An Open Sociotechnical Systems Perspective*, John Cotter and Associates, Inc., 1983.

tion on the back end due to greater alignment of purpose and objectives and greater commitment far out-
weighs the time lost. At the same time, the more
collaborative approach is also more satisfying for people
because it acknowledges and utilizes their ideas to a
much greater extent than the autocratic approach.

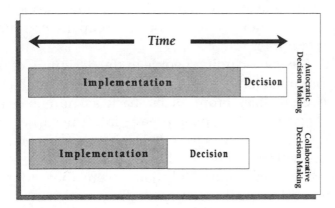

Figure 4-2. Comparative approaches to decision making.

The importance of designing the organization's architecture in a collaborative manner was reinforced for me
in a rather poignant fashion through a touching meeting that I recently had the good fortune of participating
in. This was an off-site, week-long meeting of some
of the top executives of a Fortune 100 company. This
meeting was one of a series of meetings the company
was orchestrating in order to share with people its long-
term vision for the company, and to invite further input
and ideas as the vision took shape.

At this meeting, one of the long-term employees was
moved to talk with people about the history of the company. He explained how the company was once great
and had lost much of its luster over the past 20 years

through a series of poor decisions, poor change efforts, and autocratic management. After highlighting some key areas of disappointment, he told everyone with tears in his eyes how, for the first time in years, he was hopeful about the company's future because "for the first time we are crafting this together. The CEO is asking for our input and is really listening." Upon hearing this, everyone in the room cheered and clapped, for they too felt they were part of the company crafting its vision together.

This idea of including people in the designing of their own organization is perhaps even more critical than we will ever realize. From as far back as human events have been recorded, people have introduced new and revolutionary changes into their organizations and into society, with the same results. The changes were at first rejected out of hand. Only later were they adopted. People and organizations naturally resist change. Part of why people resist is because they are uncomfortable with change. Another reason is that they feel threatened by the change in some way. Let's go back in time to a moment in our early history to understand this dynamic a bit more.

In the second century A.D., Ptolemy was the famous inventor of a highly sophisticated theory of how the planets of our solar system moved. He tracked their movement for years using the most powerful optical device of the day, his eyes. He found that they move in strange ways, sometimes quickly, sometimes slowly, sometimes in an ellipse, sometimes in a circular fashion, and every now and then they doubled back on themselves. He tracked all this movement very carefully and wrote a lengthy and popular piece of work based on his empirical observations. For centuries his theory was the basis of all studies of planetary motion.

Few disputed it. Even fewer sought to improve it, for it seemed so obvious. There was only one problem with it. It was based on the well-known and then undisputed fact that the earth is the center of the universe, and that all the planets, and even the sun, revolved around the earth. (This theory—that the earth is the center of the universe—was, of course, an advancement on an earlier theory that the earth sat on top of a giant turtle.)

Along came Copernicus in the sixteenth century, who challenged this geocentric assumption and created a highly elegant model of the movement of the planets based, instead, on the assumption that the sun is at the center of the solar system, and that all the planets, including the earth, revolved around the sun. While his theory was far more elegant (and accurate), it was dismissed by the scientific community and condemned by the church as blasphemy. At its core, it threatened the fundamental beliefs people held about how the universe works. This threat was so powerful that he was excommunicated from the church for not retracting his theory.

Time and time again, history has shown that we humans, as a species, do not take change lightly, nor do we come to it easily. It threatens the way we do things. It upsets our comfort and it challenges our fundamental assumptions and beliefs. Given this observation, the importance of including people in the process of change is more than just a welcome respite from our typical way of managing. It is essential, for without their support, people will reject change, if not in their words, certainly in their deeds. If we want people to be wholeheartedly committed to a new way of managing and to a new way of operating, we must be willing to engage them in the process.

Principle	*Skill Needed*
Full and accurate information	• Openness and honesty • Directness • Self-disclosure • Collect and disseminate information in a way that others can understand it
Free choice	• Ability to facilitate • Clarity of expression • Directness
Commitment of organization members to the decision	• **Participatory management**

THE THREE PRINCIPLES AND HOW THEY RELATE

While distinctly different in the skills they require, the three principles described above relate to one another quite strongly. Full and accurate information is needed for someone to be able to make a free choice. When someone makes a free and informed choice, they are more likely to be committed to it. Together these three principles comprise the essential ingredients to help you and your group make the changes needed to develop your organization with the least amount of resistance possible.[18]

---

[18] These three principles have also been found to be the critical features that are present in the most effective managers and in the most effective organizations. For further analysis, see Argyris, C., *Intervention Theory and Method*, Addison-Wesley, Reading, MA, 1970; Argyris, C. and Schon, D., *Theory in Practice: Increasing Professional Effectiveness*, Jossey-Bass, San Francisco, 1974.

ARCHITECTING CHECKLIST

1. There are three principles to the effective leadership of change: full and valid information, free choice, and internal commitment. Leaders who apply these principles to the process of redesigning the organization's architecture tend to be most successful.

2. Following the steps of architecting change without following the principles will likely be unsuccessful in the long run.

3. Valid information has to do with creating conditions where any and all changes are based on valid data.

4. Free choice honors the rights of all people involved in the change and treats them with dignity and respect. This in turn increases their commitment to the change.

5. Internal commitment suggests that the process of implementing change is the most critical step in the architecting process. To be most successful, the leader needs to create conditions where the people are committed to the change.

5

Communicating the Need

Managers organize, leaders disorganize.
   —Warren Bennis

In the Introduction, I described the five phases of architecting change. These phases are again demonstrated in Figure 5–1.

Each of the following chapters describes the principles underlying each phase and how to most successfully accomplish them. From here on, the book focuses on the "how to" of designing your organization's new architecture. At the same time, I will give you philosophical underpinning for each phase of the process so that you, as a leader, can not only make the right moves, but also so that you can perform them in a way that makes sense, both theoretically and practically. The first phase, the subject of this chapter, has to do with enrolling others in the need for changing your organization's architecture.

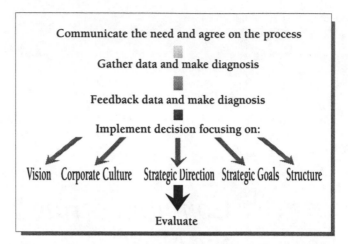

Figure 5-1. An overview of the architecture design process.

THE THREE FUNDAMENTAL STAGES OF CHANGING ARCHITECTURE

Professionals who work with organizations to help them grow often think about development as occurring in three stages:

- *the unfreezing stage,* in which the organization unfreezes its present way of operating such that change can occur more easily;
- *the change stage,* in which the actual organizational changes occur;
- *the refreezing stage,* in which the new organizational changes become solidified.[1]

---

[1] Kurt Lewin, the famous social psychologist, is noted as the creator of this simple, yet elegant, model for understanding change. I have found this way of thinking to be quite useful for it points to the importance of preparing or unfreezing an organization to make it ready to change.

The principle underlying these three stages is that you cannot effectively redesign an organization's architecture (that is, change it) without shaking up the organization first.

In the unfreezing phase, you and other leaders of the organization "loosen the bolts" in order to allow change to occur more easily. After the change has been implemented, you can "tighten the bolts" again. The things you are unfreezing are people, their attitudes, their routines, their assumptions about how work is done, and their behavior. Phase one, communicating the need, is where the unfreezing begins.

Since we know that when people are involved in the decisions that affect them they are likely to implement them more wholeheartedly, the first step in any effort to unfreeze the organization (and therefore the first step in designing your new architecture) is to let others know that you are thinking about making changes in the organization. In other words, involve people right from the beginning. Usually the best time to introduce the idea of organizational improvement is when there are some problems facing your organization. An even better time is when you have a vision for your organization that draws you toward improvement. The worst time is when there is a crisis. At times of crisis, people need to focus their energy on getting over the crisis, not on some monumental organization change. The opposite, of course, is also true: When the organization is running smoothly and no significant need exists, there is little motivation for change (see Figure 5–2).

There are three objectives to keep in mind when communicating the need:

1. Your first objective is to test the waters to see whether or not others see the need for redesigning the organization's social architecture as you do.

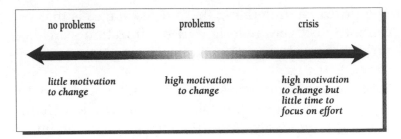

Figure 5-2. The change readiness continuum.

2. Your second objective is to discover the variety of views that people have in understanding the organization as a whole in order to use that information as you think about how to proceed.

3. Your third objective is get buy-in from the entire organization on the idea that a new architectural design is needed.

COMMUNICATING THE NEED: STEP BY STEP

In brief, the critical steps to successfully accomplish the "communicating the need" phase are as follows (Figure 5–3).

Initiate a Design Team Meeting. The first step is to identify people who you want to work with. This will be your *Design Team*, the team of people responsible for the overall designing of your organization's architecture. To have an effective design team, you will likely want to choose people:

- whose opinions you value;
- who you can trust to provide you with ideas and inputs in ways that serve to help the organization as a whole;

- who have a stake in the outcome of the design effort;
- who others in the organization can trust to take their ideas and initiatives seriously in order to design the organization's architecture.

Typically, the members of the design team will be drawn from the team of people who are considered the current leaders of the organization. This is often the top management team, but not always. Others who are not part of the current top management team may be considered potential key players in the change effort and worth including on your design team. Given the sensitive issues associated with selecting people to participate in any major change effort, it is usually best to err on the side of inclusion rather than exclusion. At the same time, a group larger than ten people can become unwieldy as a decision-making body. Do your best to keep the size of the design team at or under this number if at all possible.

Sometimes you may also want to ask others to join

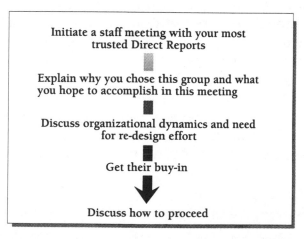

Figure 5-3. Steps to "communicating the need."

you (people lower down in the organizational hierarchy, customers, people from other parts of the company) for the initial design team meeting or the meetings soon thereafter. Such additional members may help you later at key steps along the way. For the initial design team meeting, however, simply choose those people who you believe have a significant stake in the outcome of your change effort, and whose wisdom you value. A group size of seven to ten, including yourself, is optimal for a meeting such as this.*

The selection of the design team is particularly critical, for it is through this team that you will get input, guidance, and ensure that the process is as participative as possible. Once you have decided who you want to invite to the first design meeting, it is best to contact these people personally to discuss what you have in mind. Then send a memo inviting them to the initial meeting. In the memo, be sure to explain the purpose of the meeting. Here is an example (Figure 5–4).

Explain Why You Chose the Attendees and What You Hope to Accomplish. Begin the meeting by saying that the organization has a problem to address, one that is profound enough to warrant the attention of its leadership. Be sure to point out that you have asked these particular people to attend because you trust them and you believe they each have the interests of the organization as a whole in mind. Then state that you believe that, as a group, they can have a candid discussion of the organization's effectiveness with each other. An introduction such as this indicates the importance you place

---

* *Note:* When you select the group, others will be concerned about why they were not chosen. Therefore, it is best to select a group that has some face validity for others, that is, a group about which others will agree that it makes sense for them to have been included on the design team.

Memorandum

TO: Distribution
FROM: Tom Chambers
RE: Discussion of Our Organization
DATE: April 12, 1993

....

These past few weeks have been particularly stressful for our organization as we have been trying to get our new database product developed in record time. While we have done a fine job up until recently, some of the snags we have experienced in the development cycle lead me to wonder if there are ways we can develop our products more efficiently and more effectively than we now do.

I would like you to join me in a meeting on April 23rd, from 3:30 to 5:30pm in the Main Conference Room to discuss how the development of the database product is going and whether there are ways we can improve our effectiveness as an organization.

Given the potential volatility of this subject, I'd like to ask each of you to keep this meeting confidential.

Figure 5-4. Example memorandum.

on openness with one another, and on thinking about the organization as a whole, rather than focusing on any one of its parts.

It is often useful to set some ground rules for this kind of meeting. Ground rules are guidelines for the kind of behavior that you and others want to exhibit to promote an effective meeting. They often include such things as: "no blaming," "open exploration of ideas and feelings," "honest and direct communication," "stay focused," and so on. People in a meeting such as this can be highly sensitive, where politics may play a role in what people say or do. A meeting like this can also raise people's concerns, and they can easily get defensive. At the same time, this can also be a very satisfying and revealing meeting, for if you are feeling that the organization needs to change, others are probably feeling the same way. Setting ground rules and inviting people to be open and to communicate honestly, while at the same time listening to and respecting everyone else's perspective, will go a long way towards creating the proper conditions for a successful first meeting.

In particular, it is important for you to reiterate what you hope to accomplish at this meeting and that you want a candid discussion of the organization, focusing on how well it has been meeting its goals of late. In this discussion you do not want finger pointing. Finger pointing often produces defensiveness. Instead, what you want is open exploration of potential problems and opportunities, without blame or resentment.

If your timing for holding this initial design team meeting is right, people in the meeting will feel some relief that there will be something done about the problems they have been experiencing of late. Or, if there are no significant problems now, that you have your sights set on the future and are interested in how the organization will grow. At the same time, the attendees will probably feel some anxiety that what will be uncovered is that perhaps they, personally, or their group has been a part of the ongoing problem. Whenever meetings such as this are held, you can expect this kind of ambivalence. Do not be deterred, however, for as the group becomes more effective in working together, the initial anxiety will give way to the excitement of change, and to the feeling of pride in playing a part in the organization's future success.

After covering the ground rules, you will want to give a more detailed overview of what you want to talk about in the meeting. It is best to have some structure for the meeting so that people will feel confident that you are on top of things, and that the meeting will not get out of hand. An example of a well-structured meeting agenda could be as follows (Figure 5–5).

Meeting on May 16, 1992
9:00am — 11:00am

PURPOSE OF THIS MEETING:

To discover company's present level of effectiveness and identify
ways to strengthen it for the future.

OBJECTIVES OF THIS MEETING:

- Agree on present organization and its effectiveness
- Discuss and agree on ways of clarifying future direction
- Set into motion an effort to develop the organization

MEETING PROCESS:

1. Introduction
   — explanation for why you brought the group together
   — what you hope to accomplish
   — proposed groundrules for the meeting

2. Your own observations of the organization

3. Invitation for others to express their observations of
   the organization

4. Discussion of possible future and decision on how to
   proceed

Figure 5-5. Example agenda.

Discuss Your Organization and the Need for Redesign.
Let's assume for the moment you have already done
the introduction and are now at point two of your
agenda. At this point, share with the group your own
observations on how well the organization is operating.
Try to be complete but not overly detailed. Remember,
not everyone may believe that there is a problem at all,
so they are probably not prepared to look into details as
of yet. It is probably best to focus on measurable outcomes such as quantitative output, cost controls, cycle
times, measures of quality, or customer complaints, as
these kinds of topics are tangible and verifiable. You
may also want to include human resource issues such as
turnover, absenteeism, number of grievances, etc., since
such issues may point to relevant organizational issues.
I have found that it is best to have this kind of infor-

mation presented on a flip chart or overhead projector so that everyone can clearly see and focus on the same subject as they discuss the points you are making. Here's an example of one manufacturing manager's list of concerns written out on a flip chart (Figure 5–6).

After completing your presentation (don't take too much time or it will begin to feel more like a lecture than a summary), ask for any clarifying questions, and respond to each question in as complete, open, and honest a manner as you can. Remember, the success of this meeting, as well as that of subsequent meetings, will be dependent on the degree to which people can be open and honest with each other and with you. It is up to you to set the climate for such a discussion by modeling the desired behavior in front of others.

At this point, ask everyone present for their own

Hard Data

- Backlog is 50% higher than this time last year.
- Customer complaints have reached an all time high of 35 per month.
- Maintenance costs of our printing machines have tripled over the past year.
- Absenteeism has increased by 25% over last year's numbers.
- Turnover seems to also have increased by 40% although many are appropriate transfers into the Westfield Plant.

Impressions

- There seems to be more frustration about our equipment than there used to be.
- More conflicts seem to be emerging between groups than in the past.

Figure 5-6. Example list of concerns.

views on how well the organization is doing. Invite them to say whatever is on their minds on the subject; as they are talking, you should summarize all of their main points on a flip chart. Putting everyone's main ideas on a flip chart communicates nonverbally that you care about everyone's point of view. It will also help you to focus attention on specific items later.

Here are the first six items that were put on a flip chart and discussed by the same manufacturing manager described in the meeting mentioned above (Figure 5–7).

Once you have everyone's main ideas listed on a flip

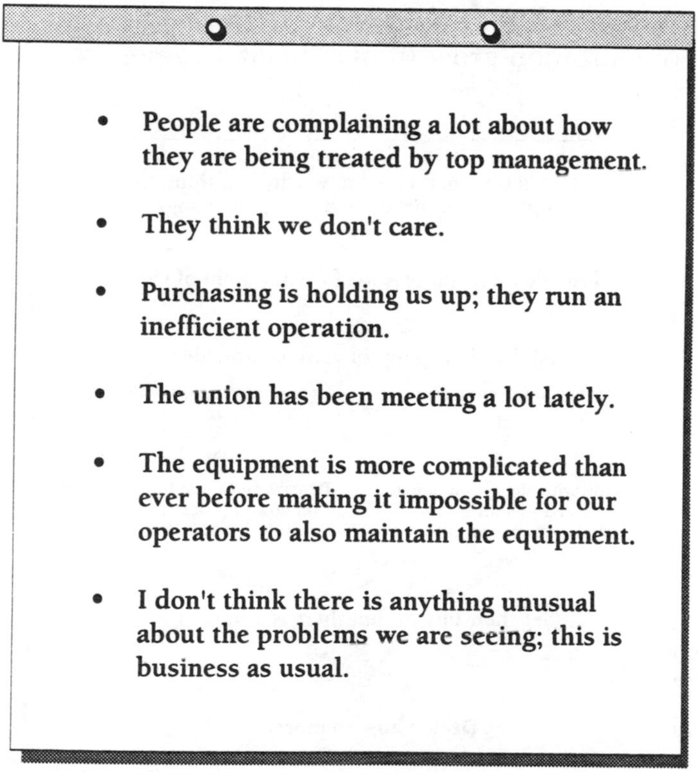

- People are complaining a lot about how they are being treated by top management.

- They think we don't care.

- Purchasing is holding us up; they run an inefficient operation.

- The union has been meeting a lot lately.

- The equipment is more complicated than ever before making it impossible for our operators to also maintain the equipment.

- I don't think there is anything unusual about the problems we are seeing; this is business as usual.

Figure 5-7. Example manufacturing items.

chart, try to summarize all their various points in a more condensed list that highlights just the key points. Then ask the group if this condensed list represents roughly the thoughts of the group as a whole. If this is, indeed, a fair representation, go on to talk about how to proceed further. If it is not, discuss the separate items until everyone is reasonably comfortable that their own personal view is represented.

Here, then, is a summary of the steps to managing the part of the meeting that allows you and others to agree on the need for a redesign effort on your organization (Figure 5–8).

Decide, As a Group, On How to Proceed. Once you have obtained agreement that there is a problem (or problems) to be addressed and that there is a need to have the organization grow from a qualitative point of view,

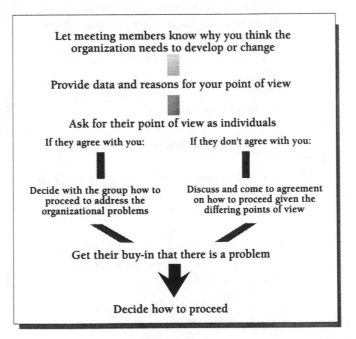

Figure 5-8. Steps for agreeing on need for architecting effort.

now is the time for you to introduce the idea of redesigning the organization's architecture. There are two basic approaches you can take at this point:

1. Share with the group your idea that you would like to begin an overall organizational change effort. Explain what would be involved (diagnosis, decision, implementation, etc.) and then ask whether or not the others see this as the proper way to proceed. *This approach works best when the group is looking to you for leadership and guidance, and where the group has a history of taking ideas such as this and running with them.*

2. Ask all the members of the group how they think they ought to proceed, given the organization's current problems; and then facilitate a discussion leading toward reaching consensus. *This approach works best when the group needs to come up with its own ideas in order to own them and buy into them.*

In either case, the key to your success is facilitating the discussion on how to proceed in a way that explores a range of alternatives, includes all the various points of view, and results in agreement about how to proceed. You want to push hard enough to get results, but you don't want people complying with the idea of architecting the organization just for the sake of going along. *YOU WANT THEIR BUY-IN.* So proceed gently yet firmly, allowing for discussion and expression of differences along the way. Here's how one successful meeting went:

This was a meeting that occurred in the R&D department of a large computer company. The department was responsible for hardware design, and had approximately 250 members. The top management had just

---

Note: This discussion about "whether or not everyone agrees at this stage" need not be long. While consensus is desirable, it is not absolutely essential. It is most essential that people have the opportunity to express their thoughts and feelings, and that they have been heard. If it is difficult to reach consensus, but most people present agree that there truly are significant problems, then go through the following steps:

1. acknowledge that one or two members disagree;

2. ask the group what would explain why these particular people have a different point of view;

3. acknowledge that their differing point of view has merit;

4. ask the group if they would feel comfortable proceeding from this point.

Nine times out of ten, the group will prefer to go on rather than trying to resolve all of their differences of opinion at this stage.

---

completed a one-hour discussion about the problems the organization had been having. In brief, they were:

- sizable employee turnover
- slow product design
- not enough compatibility between products
- low employee morale

The group is now at a point where it needs to decide on how to proceed from here. The cast of characters is:

Ellis: Director of R&D Department, who called the meeting
Bill: Manager of small systems hardware
Susan: Manager of large systems hardware
Fred: Manager of peripherals

Mary: Director of operating system software
Sam: Supervisor reporting to Bill
Jean: Human resources representative

Ellis: It is clear we have some problems we need to address. I think there are two ways we can proceed. I think we can try to tackle each of these given what we already know. Or we can try to do a more complete diagnosis of our organization as a whole, you know, list its strengths and weaknesses, and then decide what are the kinds of things that we might want to change on the basis of more full information. Are there any other ways of proceeding that come to mind?

Fred: We can leave it alone and hope it goes away (laughter).

Ellis: Actually, that may be a good idea. Sometimes you don't want to call attention to problems so that they naturally go away. Are there other ideas as well?

Susan: I think that whatever we do, we need to do it soon. The troops are getting anxious about the possibility of buying our hardware from outside vendors so that their jobs will be reduced to simply vendor baby-sitting. When the natives are restless, we have to take action.

Jean: I agree.

Ellis: How about others. Any ideas come to mind?

Fred: I think we need to resolve these issues as soon as possible. Why don't we just decide what to do on each of the items listed and then go for it. It shouldn't be all that complicated.

Bill: Damn it, Fred. You're always taking the easy way out. I don't think it is going to be so easy. Like Susan, I think these problems have existed for quite a while. If they were so easy to resolve, why haven't we done it yet?

Fred: And you're always trying to make things complicated. This situation requires action. Let's get to it.

Ellis: You know, you may be right. At this point, I'd say I'm not sure. I think sometimes I know what is needed, and therefore, I can act quickly. This time I feel unsure. Like I'm not sure how the problems have gotten to be so extreme. I'll tell you this, though, I'd like to understand the situation better.

Bill: I'm unsure as well. Ellis, you have mentioned two ways to proceed. Could you say a little more about the "diagnosis" thing.

Ellis: Well, the idea here is to gather some data about the organization, You know, do a survey or interview people, trying to uncover where people are frustrated and why. The survey would be given to all members of the organization, the results tallied, and then we would have a better idea of where the problems lie and what to do about them. We could then make some decisions about how to proceed that would more likely solve the problems in a way that keeps them solved. That's the overall idea, but to pull it off, we all need to agree that this way is the best way to go. I'm not sure we have that agreement right now.

Bill: I like the idea a lot. I would feel a lot more confident if we had more information.

Mary: I do too. Of course, it's your department, not mine. But let me say that we did the same kind of thing in Software two years ago and we learned a heck of a lot about our organization that we didn't know. That information helped us make changes that we otherwise wouldn't have thought of.

Jean: I participated in that process and my thoughts are very similar. It could work here too.

Ellis: How about the rest of you?

Sam: Makes good sense to me. I'm concerned, however, about whether this survey will be stirring up things too much. Won't it set expectations that we are out to change the world? There's only so much we can do.

Ellis: My guess is that if we set it up properly, we can manage the expectations by telling people that we are simply gathering data, and that we are not making promises until we have a better sense of how to proceed. I think that if each of us communicates that effectively, people will not expect too much. How does that sound to you?

Sam: I'm a bit skeptical about it, but I like the overall idea anyway. So count me in.

Fred: Okay, I suppose we should do it this way.

Ellis: You seem reluctant.

Fred: Well, I am. I think it is an exercise in futility. Let's just do something.

Ellis: You know, I like your drive to get things done. We sure need a lot more of that around here. My sense, however, is that maybe now is not quite the time to move fast. Maybe if we were to gather some data, not take a ridiculous amount of time, and then act fast, the results might be more complete and lasting. Are you willing to go along with this way, given the assumption we need to move fast once we get a more complete analysis on why our problems are the way they are?

Fred: When you put it that way, how can I resist? But I want us to be sure we don't stretch this out forever. Okay?

Others: Agreed!

Ellis: Okay, the way I'd like to proceed then is to have some of us put together an outline for how to conduct the diagnosis, some likely questions to ask, etc. We can all look at the outline and discuss it this Friday at the end of the day. Any volunteers?

Note how Ellis takes a more facilitative, less directive role in this meeting. He takes special care to get everyone's point of view and to acknowledge the validity of each person's idea. At the same time, he is not bashful in putting out his own point of view. When he does, knowing that it will carry a lot of weight, he is careful to ask for reactions, testing to see whether people agree or not. Since he communicates respect for others' ideas, when the group decides to go for a more full diagnosis, he is confident they are not just going along because it is his idea. They are doing it because it makes sense to them as well. That is the aim of phase one of the redesign process, to ensure that the Design Team members are committed to taking the next steps towards redesigning the organization's architecture.

ARCHITECTING CHECKLIST

1. Put together a design team made up of top management and a cross-section of "influence" leaders in the organization.

2. Explore with the design team the need for a redesign of the organization's architecture and gain buy-in. Do not force buy-in. Listen carefully to the views of others and discuss them in an open dialogue.

3. Once agreeing that change is needed, agree on how to proceed.

6

Assessing Your Organization

Discovery consists of looking at the same thing as everyone else and thinking something different.
—Albert Szent-Gyorgyi

Once you have communicated the need for redesigning your organization's architecture and established the buy-in needed from key members of the organization to move forward, it is now time to begin an assessment of your organization. The purpose of the assessment is to create a firm understanding of your current organization so that you will know how best to proceed, and where to focus your attention. How can you get to where you want to go if you don't know where you are starting from?

WHAT TO ASSESS

Organizations have many systems that need to function well in order for the business to be profitable. There are financial systems, marketing systems, production systems, manufacturing systems, etc. These systems are all at the foreground of your organization and as a whole represent what I will call the *technical* system. Each requires an appropriate set of technical skills and technical knowledge for its effective functioning.

People do not do their technical work in a void, however. They do it with each other. And they interact with their environment (customers, vendors, government agencies, etc.). Interspersed throughout the organization's technical system, then, is the *human* system. This system is composed of the organizational culture: the way the company is organized, how people interact with one another. Conceptually, the technical systems and the human systems are wholly different: the technical systems are designed to produce output most efficiently while the human systems are designed to create linkages between departments and operating units in order to manage the technical systems effectively. Both have to be running smoothly in order to have a high-performing organization.

In this book, it is assumed that you, the leader of your organization, already have the technical background needed to analyze to what extent the technical systems of your organization are running well. Given that assumption, where you need to explore to improve productivity is in the human system.* For this you need a set of processes that will result in an effective organizational diagnosis. *Diagnosis means gathering data on the current state of the organization (both formal and informal) to determine where the problems lie and the causes of these problems.* In addition, you will want to uncover potential future opportunities and new challenges that will

---

* Given the scope of this book, I am intentionally focusing more attention on diagnosing the social system, recognizing this is but part of the larger picture socio-technical relationship.

strengthen your organization as a whole. This analysis is typically done using interviews, questionnaires, observations, records, and other forms of data collection. The data need to be collected and then organized in a fashion that helps members make sense of their organization.

When done well, the assessment identifies the features of the organization's architecture that need redesigning, and does it in a way that is convincing to the organizational members. Therefore, the process of data collection needs to:

- include key individuals and groups in the data-gathering process so that the results represent their multiple point of view;
- rely on multiple methods of data collection so the results are completely representative of the organization; and
- be comprehensive in scope for people to have confidence in the findings.

Put simply, the *scope* of the assessment has to be complete and valid, and the *process* has to help generate commitment to the changes that will result from the findings.

How to Assess Your Organization

Here is an overview of the critical steps to accomplishing these objectives (Figure 6–1).

It is best if each of these steps is done along with your design team responsible for the change. Indeed, throughout the design process, you can work with the design team at each step along the way to help generate involvement and commitment from the rest of the orga-

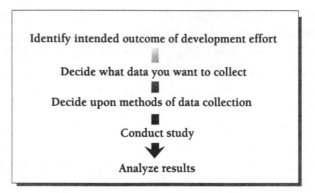

Figure 6-1. An overview of the assessment process.

nization. You may also want to include others at this phase of the process who have experience and expertise in research methodology or data collection to help ensure the process of organizational analysis is fair, and that you get high-quality information from all your efforts.

Agree on Intended Outcome of Design Effort. Conducting an organizational assessment begins with determining what things to diagnose. To help guide this selection, it is useful to begin by deciding on or reviewing what the intended outcome of your organizational architecting effort will be, and how you will measure the overall success of that effort. Most people skip this important first step, believing either that everyone knows what the objectives are, or believing that objectives are not that important. Defining the desired outcome will be a critical step, however, inasmuch as you need to find some ways of guiding your choices about where to focus your effort, and you need to know whether or not you are accomplishing what you intend to accomplish.

The desired outcome should be stated in specific terms, and should be realistic and compelling. Examples of possible outcomes are:

- increased market share
- reduced employee turnover rate
- increased customer satisfaction rating
- enhanced productivity
- increase profitability

Presumably, all the stated objectives or intended outcomes of your architecting effort should flow directly from the problems stated in your initial planning meeting.

These objectives help you focus the diagnostic process. They define the scope of the data-collection effort and provide some guidance as you make decisions later about what to do or not to do.

At this point you are faced with two key questions regarding how to approach the data-gathering process:

1. What are the data I want to collect?

2. What are the methods I want to use in collecting the data?

An Exercise:

1. Take a few minutes to think about what objectives you have for your organization architecting effort. Write these down on a piece of paper. Write down as many as you can think of. *Don't edit them.*

2. Go through your list and prioritize them. Pick the top two or three.

3. Now state these objectives in clear and specific terms, like those listed above.

4. For each of these objectives, answer the question, "How will I know when I have achieved this objective?"

Decide What Data to Collect. Before you begin to collect data, consider the following. There are three levels in which you can focus any change effort. The first level is to solve the immediate problem. Let's call this *first-order change.* This is what most people do, only to find the problem reoccurs later.

The second level is to solve the problem in such a way that it remains solved. Let's call this *second-order change.* This type of change requires some fundamental shift in the organization as a whole. You must get to the real cause of the problem and eliminate it. Few people take this larger view of a problem. Those organizations that do tend to be more successful in the long run.

The third level is to increase the capacity of the organization to solve problems in the future. Let's call this *third-order change.* This requires that you find and eliminate built-in flaws in your architecture and create conditions where you strengthen your organization as a whole. The whole purpose of consciously designing an organization's architecture is to create conditions where the organization can grow, adapt, and self-renew. Hence, third-order change is the aim of the design process.

At the same time, you don't want to ignore immediate problems, for these are the ones that people focus most of their attention on. In fact, if you ignore these immediate problems for too long, people will feel that your rearchitecting effort is too grandiose and impractical. Ideally, whenever you try to redesign an organization's architecture, you want to accomplish change at all three levels (see Figure 6–2).

The eventual goal of the assessment will have a profound effect on what questions you choose to ask. You need to ask questions (1) about the nature and scope of the "presenting problem" (first-order questions); (2)

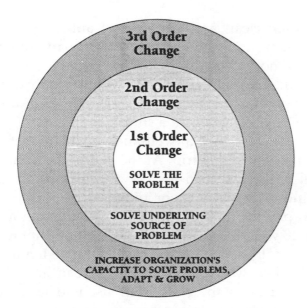

Figure 6-2. The three levels of organizational change.

that help identify the multiple causes of the "presenting problem" (second-order questions); and (3) about the nature of the organization as a whole (third-order questions). You also need to discover the organization's readiness for change so that down the road you have a sense of what buttons you can push, and how hard, in order to affect change.

An Important Concept. Typically, we think of organizations as having relatively clear boundaries, clear purposes, clear lines of authority, and as being rather simple. Therefore, we think that solving problems means you identify the cause of the problem, change the cause, and, voila! the problem is solved.

Unfortunately, organizations do not always conform to our simplistic views of them. They often have highly "squishy" boundaries, purposes are usually more vague than clear, and the lines of authority are constantly being transgressed. Moreover, parts of organizations almost always impact other parts. If this is true, finding the *cause* of the problem will be highly difficult. And changing one thing may indeed cause another problem. Let me give you a simple example.

Recently I visited a well-known chain restaurant while on a consulting trip. At the end of the meal I took my bill to the cash register. To my surprise, I found a long line of about eight or nine people waiting their turn to pay for their dinners. I was quite annoyed by having to wait, for I was tired and did not want to wait. When I finally arrived at the cashier, some ten minutes later, I asked why we all had to wait in line. Apparently, waiters in the restaurant used to take money from customers who were paying for their meals right at the table, and some had pocketed the money. To protect themselves from theft, the restaurant owners instituted a policy that customers henceforth had to pay at the cash register. Hence, in trying to solve one problem, management had unwittingly created another.

Of course, they could have easily solved the latter problem by hiring another cashier and by buying another cash register, but this would have cost money, money that they were trying to save. So they suffered the consequences of their decision, a decision that did not get at the real source of the problem at all, but completely bypassed it.

What you need, then, is a model of organizational behavior to guide your diagnosis effort, one that conforms well with the nature of organizational life. A useful model is one that views the organization as an open system. The open-system model of organizations has the following premises:

1. *The organization is more than a sum of its parts.* Each part is connected to each other part in some way. A change in one part of the system will almost inevitably produce a change in another part. Therefore, you cannot find a single cause of the problem. To effectively change a part of the system, you will, more often than not, have to change the whole.

2. *Systems have boundaries.* These boundaries separate them from their environment. Closed systems have relatively impenetrable boundaries; open systems have highly permeable boundaries. When diagnosing the organization, you need to be clear about which system you are looking at. If you want to effect change in a sub part of a larger organization, it is best to include in your analysis the larger organization and how it impacts that part.

3. *Systems interact with the environment.* The behavior of systems and people within them cannot be understood fully without understanding the environment in which they live and how this environment impacts them. Changes in the environment will surely influence the behavior of people within the system and vice versa.

4. *All systems have a natural tendency towards maintaining the status quo* (known in systems theory as Homeostasis). If you want to change a part, the organization will resist. You have to deal with this resistance if you want to see change.

5. *All behavior functions for a purpose.* What is perceived as a problem from one point of view may be quite functional from another point of view. For example, some organizations have a tendency called "not invented here." This is a condition where if an outsider comes up with an idea or recommendation, it will almost automatically be disregarded by the organization. This can easily be viewed as a problem in that it reduces learning. Seen from another perspective, however, the "not invented here" syndrome functions for a purpose. It usually develops in organizations that are highly creative and that place great emphasis on promoting ideas and innovation. Hence, the seemingly dysfunctional behavior is quite functional. If you want to change what is considered to be a problem, understand its function first.[1]

With this model in mind, what you are looking for when you make a diagnosis is a whole view of the organization, one that touches on all of the key features of the organization. You need to look beyond the initial set of organizational problems in order to help you discover and analyze the overall functioning of the organization as a system. Indeed, depending upon the magnitude of the change you seek, the diagnosis should at least touch upon, if not assess, all of the elements of an organization's architecture: vision, culture, strategic direction, strategic goals, structure. In addition, the diagnosis needs to have as a backdrop an appreciation of where your organization is in its life cycle. Let's look at an example.

Bill is the president of a 350-person biotechnology company. Of late, his organization has been experiencing high employee turnover and there seems to be a

---

[1] See Kast, F. E. and Rosenzweig, J. E. "General Systems Theory: Applications for Organization and Management," *Academy of Management Journal*. Dec. 1972, pp. 447–465, for an overview of general systems theory and its application to understanding organizations. See also Senge, P., *The Fifth Discipline: The Art and Practice of the Learning Organization*, Doubleday, New York, 1990, for an excellent treatment of the importance of understanding organizations as systems.

lot of malaise throughout the company in general. Exit interviews are conducted regularly by human resources representatives, and the data are shared with Bill. Initial reports seem to indicate that almost half of the people are leaving for higher pay, and over a third are leaving because they do not feel there are significant opportunities for growth and promotion in their jobs.

If you were in Bill's shoes, would you take action on this basis and pay people more? How would you handle the career issue? Would you immediately set up a job rotation system? While swift action might be best in this situation, Bill was not satisfied that he knew what the causes of the problem were. He conducted a deeper organizational diagnosis and found the following:

1. Most people were more dissatisfied with their lack of career opportunities than they were with the lower pay. They were particularly upset that new opportunities for higher-level positions were being filled from the outside with "MBA types" who had little understanding of their technology.

2. Most people felt that there was little communication between and within groups, and they had a strong yearning to know more about what was going on at a corporate level.

3. Promotion represents more responsibility, and it was responsibility they sought, not necessarily a higher position with more administrative hassles.

4. Many managers were too tightly controlling their groups, leaving people feeling like they were not treated as professionals.

5. Most of the younger professionals expected and needed more training for their jobs. They felt they were being thrown into the fire with little or no protection and that their peers in other companies were not experiencing it as bad as they were.

6. The mission of the company was vague to most people, as was their strategy, leading people to lose confidence in Bill's leadership.

Since all of this occurred in a company that was rapidly growing and had not come close to exploiting the market, Bill also assessed his organization as being in the growth phase of its life cycle.

On the basis of this, Bill took steps to clarify the mission and strategy, develop ways to train younger employees, and worked with his management staff to set up more self-motivating control systems. Moreover, he began to look at the balance of promotions from outside compared with those from within, and explored ways to produce a better balance. None of these steps would have been taken had Bill made decisions on the basis of the limited (and potentially inaccurate) information he had gotten in the initial exit interviews.

In summary, you want to collect data on three key areas if you are going to do a comprehensive development effort. You want data that provide you with:

1. Insight into the presenting problem, its causes and consequences.

2. Information about the overall health of your organization's architecture.

3. Insight into the organization's phase of development, giving clues to its challenges for future growth.

Decide on What Data Collection Methods to Use. To assess the relative health of your organization, and to discover the causes of enduring problems your organization faces, in effect you will be conducting research on your organization. As with any good researcher, your existing interest should not be to prove your theories about your organization, but rather to learn about how it functions or why it does not function in the way you would like it to. Hence, as you select your data collection method, and define the questions you will be asking, be sure to take an open view of the organization, one that enables you to discover its underlying dynamics, whatever they are.

There are two methods of data collection typically used by organizational researchers. Either of them can be appropriate depending on the information sought, and the aims of the inquiry.

- interviews, both structured and unstructured
- survey questionnaire

Let's take each of these two methods and explore their advantages and disadvantages.

Interviews. Most interviews are conducted in order to get an in-depth understanding of the points of view and feelings of the respondents. Interviews can be designed to get factual information (through structured, closed-ended questions) or to get information about the thoughts and feelings of the respondent (through unstructured, open-ended questions). Their strength is that they provide the researcher with an opportunity to establish rapport with the interviewee, to discover how relevant the study is to him or her, how he or she feels about being questioned, and what is on his or her mind, in addition to the answers to the questions being asked. This additional information can be particularly useful when you need to assess the relative readiness of the organization's members for change.

The weakness of the interview for data collection is that sometimes interviewers can interject their own bi-

ases in asking the questions; and interviewees sometimes are not candid, either by responding in the way
he or she thinks the interviewer wants, or by not telling
the truth for fear of reprisal.

⌐ *Surveys.* There are many kind of surveys: projective,
open-ended, scaled, forced choice, etc. Most organizational surveys that are used for organization development purposes are scaled surveys designed to elicit and
quantify how people feel about a number of aspects of
organizational life. Here is an example of a portion of
such a survey (Figure 6–3).

Questionnaires and surveys have the clear advantage
over interviews of being more concise, quantifiable, and
eliciting information from a larger population. They
generally take less time to administer and their conclusions are often easier to present. They are, however,

JOB

The following statements are about you and your job. Please circle the number that
best represents how much you agree with each statement.

Strongly Disagree	Disagree	Slightly Disagree	Neither agree Nor disagree	Slightly Agree	Agree	Strongly Agree
1	2	3	4	5	6	7

1. I have little opportunity to use my abilities in this organization.

1	2	3	4	5	6	7

2. I understand the relationship between the goals of my job and the overall mission
of the company.

1	2	3	4	5	6	7

3. I find the goals in my job to be challenging and meaningful.

1	2	3	4	5	6	7

4. Sometimes I feel that my job counts for very little in this organization.

1	2	3	4	5	6	7

5. I feel I am paid fairly for the kind of work I do.

1	2	3	4	5	6	7

Figure 6-3. Example questionnaire.

more impersonal and shallow. They do not get at the depth of feeling of the respondents, and they do not satisfy the need of respondents for more direct contact with the organizational researchers, in this case, the leaders of the organization.

Some of you may be familiar with a third method of data collection: direct observation. This is a method where the researcher observes those events that give them the most realistic and full sense of how the organization operates. It is useful for outside researchers to use this method and report back their impressions to the organizational leaders. When managers of the organization use this method, however, it usually does not work so well. People alter their style of interacting in front of important others. They may try to impress, or they may hold back. Moreover, the person making the observations, if they come from within the organization, will usually have difficulty seeing the dynamics clearly because by being a part of the organization, they are immunized from seeing some of the counterproductive features of the organization's culture. Put differently, it is hard for a fish to see that it is in water. In either case, by using insiders to observe, it is not likely that you will get a candid and accurate picture of what goes on. Therefore, I do not recommend it as a useful approach unless coupled with the use of an outside consultant.

Given that interviews and surveys have both strengths and weaknesses, I strongly recommend that you combine both of these methods to get a full and accurate picture of the organization as a whole. Appendix A is an example of a set of interview questions used for a typical organizational assessment. Appendix B is an example of some questions asked in a larger organizational questionnaire. Use these as a guide to construct your own organizational assessment.

Here, then, is an overview of how to do a diagnosis.

Step One: Get your original design team together and set objectives for the study.

Step Two: Decide what parts of the organization you need to study. Also select those people outside the organization (customers, other organizations, etc.) whose impressions you also need for the study. If there is some doubt, err on the side of being inclusive rather than exclusive. This, then, is your study population.

Step Three: Decide which key people's points of view are important to the study. These are the people you will interview. Generally, you will want to interview between 20 and 50 people. If your organization is small, this may represent your whole organization. That's okay. You will later also ask them to fill out a confidential questionnaire so that people will feel that they can be more candid in their responses.

Step Four: Choose the questions you want to ask in the interviews. Use Appendix A as a guide and add or delete as you see fit. Tailor the questions to fit your own organizational study needs.

Step Five: Prepare your organization by communicating the need for a study.

Step Six: Conduct the interviews and summarize the results.

Step Seven: Create a questionnaire using Appendix B as an example guide.

Step Eight: Determine the people you want to survey.

Step Nine: Administer the questionnaire.

Step Ten: Analyze and feed back the results, including the interview results, to the company, starting with the design team.

CONDUCTING THE STUDY

Rather than give a detailed view of each step described above, I will focus on the core of the effort, steps five through ten, and will explore each of these more in detail.

Step Five: Preparing the organization by communicating the need for a study of the organization. The first step in conducting the study is to inform the rest of your organization about your intentions to do an organizational diagnosis. Bear in mind as you proceed that the study will likely feel disruptive to some people and *will* raise all sorts of questions about why this study is being done. Are you going to fire people as a result? Are we in trouble? What do I get out of this? Is this just another half-baked effort to help the organization develop that will go nowhere? These feelings are a natural part of any change effort. This fact makes it particularly critical for you to communicate fully and freely about the process you are undertaking. If you don't, people will naturally fill in the blanks and, given people's natural fears, rumors will run rampant.

A humorous story comes to mind about how rumors occur. A colleague and I were once leading a week-long executive seminar that was part of an overall organizational redesign effort. This seminar was to be offered to managers throughout the company as a way of creating strong alignment among managers regarding the future direction of the company. Someone said at the beginning of this particular seminar that he had heard of a training program where they gave ice water enemas.

With a grin, he asked if we were going to do anything that drastic as a way of shaking people up. We all laughed. From time to time, someone referred to this in a humorous way and it became one of the playful themes of what otherwise was a serious learning process. I would have thought nothing further of it except that, to my surprise, in every seminar we did in this company thereafter, at least one person asked us about the ice water enemas that we administered at one of the seminars. Were we going to do it here too? Apparently, what was a joke to a few people was translated through the rumor mill into perceived fact.

Informing your organization in advance about the study is critical, given the fears and reservations people have about significant changes. Informing people fully and clearly up front serves many functions:

1. It gives employees a chance to plan out their work in advance during the administration of the survey.

2. It permits the administration of the study to proceed more smoothly because the details were made clear in advance.

3. It helps members understand the rationale of the survey.

4. It provides people with an opportunity to raise issues such as confidentiality, and to express their hopes and fears.

5. It reinforces the importance of the study and the importance of their involvement.

6. It is an opportunity to model the kind of openness that will be essential to get the results you seek.

7. It reduces the likelihood of rumors.

Informing the organization in advance should both generate some interest and excitement in the study, as well as allay whatever fears and concerns people have. Know however, that *no matter what you say to people, many will likely still have their fears.* Do not try to convince everyone, particularly those who are convinced that you have something up your sleeve. The more you try to convince these people the more you will fuel some of the fears ("me thinks the lady protesteth too much"). For these people, let your actions, not your words, be the proof.

You can inform people in two ways:

1. through an internal memo, or

2. at a large organizational meeting.

I find memos impersonal and sometimes frustrating in that they are often not read carefully, and they do not give people a chance to respond. They are very useful, however, as a way to inform people in a low-key way about what you are about to do and to provide a record for organizational memory. I do not recommend them as the sole means of communication when doing a redesign effort, however, in that you want people to be candid with you during and after the study. How you conduct yourself now sets the stage for the future. If you communicate impersonally and do not invite feedback now, you run the risk of getting incomplete, impersonal and safe (surface-level gratuitous feelings) data from your interviews and surveys. Meetings, while sometimes difficult to manage, provide people with opportunities to ask questions and raise concerns. This is the kind of climate you want to create if you want people to believe that this is an important study to you. By creating trust, you will get more trustworthy data. Both writing a memo (in case some people have to miss the meeting) and holding a meeting is the preferred approach that will be most effective overall.

Hold the meeting with your organization, either as one whole group, or by breaking into smaller subgroups. Choose the forum that maximizes efficiency and personal connection. In this meeting you want to communicate:

1. the purpose of the study,

2. what you hope to get out of it,

3. how the study will be conducted, and

4. what you plan to do with the results.

Here is how one senior executive handled a meeting. The meeting was held in a small auditorium with about 175 people attending. She and her design team members were seated together in front of the group in a semicircle. She opened the meeting and said the following:

> I want to thank all of you for coming today on such short notice. The group around me and I have been meeting for the past few weeks to discuss the overall state of the organization. While we are all working hard to accomplish our goals and have had significant success in the past, it is my belief that there is a lot we are not doing as well as we could. Our sales are beginning to slow (sales numbers are shown on overhead) and our products did not receive high praise from industry analysts this last year. After a few meetings we have decided that we need to know more about how we can re-create some

of the success of our recent past. Do we need to make different strategic decisions? Are there ways we can work together more effectively? Are our incentives fair to you and to us? We do not know the answers, but we'd like to learn more about our own organization, particularly from your point of view. Here's the plan.

We have selected a few of you to interview in depth to get a fuller understanding of your perspective. These interviews will be conducted by Karen, an outside consultant, who will ensure that each interviewee's responses will be kept confidential. Results of the interviews will be summarized by Karen and shared with the task force and then with all of you. In addition, the rest of you, including the interviewees, will be asked to fill out a questionnaire. This questionnaire is designed to get your impressions and feelings about a number of aspects of the organization. Like the interviews, your responses will be kept confidential. This way, everyone can feel free to answer openly so that we get valid information from all of you as a whole. Karen will also administer the questionnaire and tabulate the results. These too, like the interviews, will be shared with the task force first, and then with all of you as a whole. On the basis of this, we will all have a better sense of what we can do to strengthen and develop our organization together. Hopefully, we will make some changes from this that will help all of us. We may also find that we are doing just what we need to be doing, and that the problems lie elsewhere. Whatever the case, we will learn.

I want you to know that I'm very excited about this learning process and think we will find things that may help us reestablish our strong position in the industry. At the same time I am a bit scared as well.

I expect I'll discover things that I am not doing well as the director of this group. The good news is that I want to learn this, and grow as a director as well. At any rate, I'm sure you have some questions for us about the study. This is the time to ask them.

The audience then raised questions about who was selected for the interviews and why, whether their jobs were in jeopardy in any way, what they will do with the findings of the study, and why management has never done this before. The design team fielded these questions, as the executive played it more low key, thereby symbolically communicating that this was not just her study, but theirs as well. The meeting ended with Karen telling people about where and when the questionnaire would be administered.

Usually top management or the design team and human resources people are briefed first on the study; next the information is passed on to the management staff; and given finally to the rest of the organization as a whole. This gives top management adequate preparation to deal with questions and concerns raised by other members of the organization.

Step Six: Conducting the Interviews. Since the purpose of interviews is to obtain valid and accurate information about the thoughts, feelings, and opinions of your interviewees, it is important that the leadership of the organization does not conduct the interviews themselves. Experience shows that people rarely will give the leaders of an organization the kind of information they want directly. They will likely not be open about their negative feelings, and they will not talk directly about their concerns about the leadership team as a whole. In effect, if you or other members of the leadership team conduct the interviews, you will only get a whitewashed version of what is really going on.

Select people, either from another part of the company, or from outside the company, to conduct the interviews. These people need to be skilled in research type interviews and must be people who you can trust will effectively summarize the results for you. Let them do the leg work in interviewing for you. At the same time, work with them closely to ensure that you get the information you need upon which to make effective decisions.

Step Seven: Creating the Organizational Survey. To summarize the earlier discussion, the survey needs to be designed to give you insight into the organization's dynamics, particularly those that relate to your organization's architecture. It needs to be managed in a way that ensures you get valid and useful data. To accomplish this, your design team needs to be mindful of how they go about developing and conducting the survey. The design team will be responsible for managing the survey process at each step along the way and for ensuring that there is the required level of buy-in and commitment to the survey process to achieve the highest levels of success.

If yours is a large organization, you may want to create a separate task force whose function is to orchestrate and manage the survey process. If you do go in this direction, be sure to have a couple of members of the design team on this task force to ensure overall continuity and coordination with the overall architecting effort. Regardless of which direction you go, the process of creating and administering a survey is quite complex and extremely technical. For this reason, it is important to secure the help of a knowledgeable expert in the design, administration, and analysis of survey data.

The key task of the design team at this point is to determine the dimensions of the survey. To do this, first clarify with your design team the broad categories of things you may want to get information on. They might include such things as:

- people's satisfaction with their job
- the effectiveness of managers in managing people
- the effectiveness of your performance management system
- the quality of information flow
- the degree to which people are clear about the strategic direction of the organization
- level of morale in the organization
- the effectiveness of the decision-making process

Use the information you derived from the interviews to guide and determine what dimensions to survey.

Take each dimension and write a list of behaviors that seem to be examples of each dimension. For example, if one of your dimensions is the degree to which managers *empower employees,* ask yourself, "What does that look like in actual behavior?" Your answer might look something like the following:

Managers Empower Employees
- ensuring that people who implement decisions are involved in making the decisions
- supporting risk-taking by acknowledging and reinforcing risks even when a mistake is made as a result of the risk
- pushing decision making down to the lowest possible level

In effect, for each dimension you want to survey, you are asking questions: What does this mean to us? How would I know if I had it? What types of behaviors would I see? The answers to these questions will form the basis for constructing questions in the survey.

Take the input above and construct the questionnaire (use Appendix B as a guide for formatting the questionnaire). Be sure to use language like that in Appendix B. These questions are worded in a way that are easy to read and understand. Avoid ambiguous words or confusing sentences.

Step Eight: Determining Whom to Survey. Having the background information you need to conduct an organizational survey, you now need to determine your survey population. To do this, use the following steps as a guide:

1. Get your design team together with anyone else who will be responsible for managing the process of data collection and feedback.

2. Decide what parts of the organization you need to survey. Also determine which people outside the organization (customers, other organizations, etc.) can provide the impressions you need for the study. If there is some doubt, err on the side of being inclusive rather than exclusive. This is your study population.

3. Pick a representative sample of your larger population. These are the people you will administer the survey to. If your organization is less than 500 people, you will probably want to administer the survey to all of them. If it is more than 500, you may elect to pick a random sample of the population and administer the questionnaire to them. For a larger organization, try to get at least 300 people to take the survey. This will increase the likelihood that the results will be statistically significant.

Step Nine: Conducting the Survey. Most readers will want to skip reading about this step for it is quite detailed in nature. For interested readers, see Appendix C for a detailed explanation of what to consider in conducting an organizational survey.

Step Ten: Analysis and Feedback of the Results. Once you have conducted your survey and have collected all your data, you are ready to analyze the results. Sometimes when the results are clear, this can be relatively easy. When the problems are complicated and the causes intertwined, however, analyzing the data can be extremely complex, requiring some expertise in organizational diagnosis. I would recommend that if you anticipate the latter being true, get an expert involved early on in the organization assessment effort to help you design the study and interpret the results. The following explanation assumes that the problems and their causes are relatively clear, requiring some thought in the interpretation, thought that you and your task force are capable of handling yourselves.

Your first step is to take the raw data from the survey and tabulate the results. It is best to do this by computer, getting rich statistical information about how many people responded in what way to each item on the survey, and how the various items relate to one another. If the survey is simple, and the analysis you seek is equally simple, you can do the analysis by hand. Using a computer, however, gives you many more options, and although more costly initially, may be more efficient in the long run. Ultimately, at the very least you will want to know how many people responded to each item, the averages or means for each item, and averages for the larger dimensions as well.

Your results can be shared with the organization in raw form or they can be summarized along with the results of the interviews in a report. I find it best to provide the top level of the organization with the raw data and a summary so that they can look at whatever detail they find important. For the rest of the organization, usually a complete summary will suffice. Appendix D is an example of an excellent summary report given to a medium-sized company in the financial services industry.

The report needs not only to report the critical elements of the study, including both the strengths and the weaknesses of the organization, but also must make some tentative hypotheses about what factors have been causing the problems. For example, if one problem in the company has been high employee turnover, the report should highlight those items that seem to relate most fully to employee turnover. This relationship can be done through statistical analysis using a computer, or can be done on the basis of some information given in the interviews about how people feel and why. This is where the interviews and the survey together become most potent.

Ultimately, the report or the summary should have the following elements:

- a statement of the intended outcomes of the redesign effort
- an analysis of the organization in relation to those intended outcomes
- other problems uncovered in the study

Once the report is complete, you are now ready to feed back the survey data and begin to make organizational decisions on the basis of the results.

ARCHITECTING CHECKLIST

1. It is often best to take a whole systems approach to organizational assessment. Assessing the whole organization and all of its key elements will reveal the greatest and most useful amount of information to help you craft the architecting process.

2. Begin the assessment by reaching agreement among the design team members regarding the intended outcome of the redesign effort.

3. Look at the deeper organizational causes of problems. It is there that opportunities for significant improvement lie.

4. Take the approach that you are interested in the truth, not in verifying your hopes and beliefs about your organization. Like a good scientist, suspend judgment and seek to learn.

5. Conduct the organizational assessment using a combination of interviews and survey methodology. This provides the proper balance between rich qualitative data and measurable quantitative data.

7

Deciding Where to Focus Your Design Efforts

He that is everywhere is nowhere.
—Thomas Fuller

You now have a clear and concise assessment of your organization. If you have a relatively open organization, you are probably not surprised with the results. If you have been buffered from bad news, however, you may learn a lot from the data you have just collected. Whatever your reaction, you are now at a critical juncture in your redesign effort. From here on, you need to be deeply concerned not just with a conceptual understanding of your organization and its strengths and weaknesses, but rather with how you are going to actually make changes in a way that makes a real difference in your organization's functioning. You can sit back and make all the decisions you want to. The key difficulty now will be in getting the organization to implement these decisions.

Consider the following riddle:

*Five frogs sat on a log. Four decided to jump off. How
many are left.*

The correct answer is "five." Many people, of course,
say "one," but they fail to recognize that *deciding* to do
something and *actually doing it* are not at all the same
thing. Organizations have exactly the same difficulty.
Many decisions are made; few are implemented effectively.

Before we look at how to handle this phase effectively, let's look at how managers typically make decisions.

Here we have Joe Executive. Having just come on
board to turn the organization around, Joe has just
replaced the former executive who had grown up
with the company but had recently demonstrated
that he could no longer manage the challenges facing
the growing organization. The former executive was
encouraged to take a generous early retirement
plan.

Joe Executive was hired as a highly experienced
manager, noted for his creative ideas and brilliant
capacity to organize and plan. Just the right person,
said the president, who strongly recruited him. So
Joe Executive comes in and asks a lot of questions
about what is going on in the organization. He even
does an organizational study, with all the bells and
whistles of the most recent techniques. Sure enough,
he discovers a lot that is wrong and not much that is
right.

Joe Executive then starts making decisions. These
decisions come in the form of proclamations, written
memos, and edicts given out in management
meetings. In effect, he says, "here is the problem,
here is the answer, go off and do it." Everyone agrees

that he is on target with his analysis (or so they say). And everyone agrees, with some qualifications, with his solution. Unfortunately, that is where it ends. Most of his decisions are not implemented. Interestingly, the "yes men" of the organization are quick to implement the decisions. But the rest are not. As a result, few changes actually occur. Joe Executive blames the organization for being incompetent, unmotivated, and not committed to changing.

The above scenario is not at all atypical. It is happening in companies all over the country. Why wasn't Joe Executive able to implement his ideas? If they were good ideas, and people agreed with them, what got in the way? I believe the fundamental error in organizational management that Joe made was to separate the three functions of organizational diagnosis, decision making, and decision implementation. No different than most managers, Joe assumed that diagnosis and decision making should be done by the manager while implementation should be done by the workers. When you split up these activities, you are requiring people to carry out someone else's decision. It is not their own decision. They did not make it. They do not "own" it. They are, therefore, less committed to it. The worst possible way to get commitment when the manager makes the decision is to force people to do it because the manager said so. This tendency to separate the decision makers from the decision implementers places a lot of burden on leaders and managers to run around and make people do things. No wonder "monitoring" becomes important for managers to do. They are monitoring people who are implementing decisions they care little about. Such are the limitations of the old school of management (see Figure 7–1).

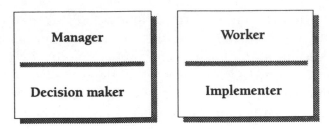

Figure 7-1. The old management model.

Managers often fall into the above trap because they believe:

- they are smarter than the workers and therefore can make better decisions;
- that is what they are supposed to do: managers manage, workers do the work; and
- they fear that if they are not making decisions, what would they be doing?

The best leaders of companies do not fall into this trap. Instead, they involve their workers in the process of decision making to the point that whatever decisions are made, they are owned by the workers, and therefore are more apt to be carried out. The significant contribution the effective leader makes to the organization architecting effort is not in the decision making (although the leader is also involved in the decisions), but rather in creating conditions where the organization can discover the best courses of action to take and the best ways to take them. This is a more facilitative function, not a decision-making one (see Figure 7–2).

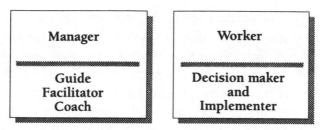

Figure 7-2. The new management model.

DECIDING HOW TO PROCEED

Given the above premise, as the leaders of the redesign effort, you and the other members of the original design team need to be particularly mindful of how you proceed at this juncture in the architecting process to ensure that the decisions are not only good ones, but implementable ones. The key is to include different groups to make different decisions, each depending on where the locus of control is or ought to be. To make things simple, let's assume two levels:

1. organization-level decisions that involve changes in the organization as a whole; and

2. department-level decisions that involve changes in each department affecting how the work gets done.

We will take each separately.

Organizational-Level Decision Making. Whether you are a leader of five people or 50,000, you will differ from those below you in the degree to which your view of your organization is strategic. You should be looking at the big picture. For some, the big picture has to do with how well your organization operates. For others it will include issues of how to compete better or how to capture a greater market share. Whatever the case, the first step in digesting the diagnosis developed earlier and in making the right decisions now is to look at the data as a whole. Again, as you did in prior phases of the design process, you will want to use your design team as your advisory group. Here's how to develop effective decisions regarding how to proceed with the process of designing the organizational architecture.

Step One: Ask each member of your design team in advance of a meeting to analyze the data and to think about what the major areas are that the organization needs to work on. These major areas should be broken into very broad categories such as: unclear mission, little strategic focus, inefficient production process, low employee morale, etc.

Step Two: Get your design team together to discuss with one another their impressions of what needs to be addressed by the organization. In this meeting, ask people to tie their ideas to the bottom-line problems or objectives stated at the beginning of the architecting effort.

Step Three: Come to agreement as a group regarding the major areas that need to change in order for the organization to function more effectively.

Step Four: Take each agreed-upon area and decide whether the implementation is: (a) within the domain and control of top management; or (b) within the domain and control of other parts of the organization.

Typically, issues such as mission, strategy, structure, and management philosophy are the appropriate domain of top management. Specific issues that are part of specific areas in the organization—such as efficiency, production processes, specific policies and procedures, and behavior between groups—need to be handled by the areas responsible for them. The rule of thumb is that if the group is responsible for its implementation, then it is responsible for its decision.

Step Five: In those areas that are appropriately within the immediate control of the top management group, decide how you will implement the changes. For example, if a clearer strategy is needed, decide how the group will develop a clear strategy. You can use the next chapters as a guide.

Step Six: For those areas that need to be implemented by the rest of your organization to be successful, decide upon a process that will include key people in the rest of your organization to help make the organizational change work.

How you decide to proceed now depends to a large extent on the particular issue that needs to be addressed. How you will know what issue to address will depend primarily on what you learned in your diagnosis phase earlier. If the primary issue is production efficiency in the manufacturing area, you may want to convene a task force made up primarily of people in the manufacturing area whose responsibility is to gather information and make recommendations on how to improve efficiency. If the issue is about low company-wide employee morale, you may want to get people together who understand the morale problem and who have a stake in the outcome, analyze the data taken from the diagnosis, collect whatever new data are needed, and make some recommendations on how to improve morale. If the issue is about redundancy between two groups, let a small subset of the two groups get together and decide how to eliminate the redundancy. Whatever the issue, typically you will want to create a task force made up of a cross-section of people who represent the groups that will be the implementers, together with one or two members of the design team. Then have the task force look further into the issue, and make recommendations as to what to do about it.

Since you have probably chosen to architect your organization in some fundamental ways, the issue are likely to be deep and complex. Therefore, you can expect that the analysis and recommendation process may take a few months, if not more. If the issue is simple and easy, the process should not take more than a couple of weeks. Whatever the case, it is important that the task force members bounce their ideas off the people they represent so that whatever recommendations the task force makes will already have been tested to some extent with the part of the organization that will be impacted.

Department-Level Decision Making. For the areas that are appropriately in the domain of the different departments, you are going to need to feed back the data about the organizational problems to each of them, and to recommend a process for how to proceed. You do not want to have them sit with the data not knowing what to do with it. Rather, you will need to have a plan in mind for how you would like to see their organization address its issues. This is not a statement of what to do. It is statement about how you would like each department to go about deciding what to do. In this way, you will be taking charge of the process, but not the outcome.

FEEDING BACK THE DATA

If you have been following the process as described in earlier chapters, you will probably have made a promise to your organization to feed back the results of the organizational assessment. Even if you haven't made that promise, most people in the organization will naturally be curious about the results. They too are interested in the company and finding ways of improving it.

Many organizational leaders I have worked with face a tough choice at this point. More often than not the survey will reveal a number of features of the organization's present architecture that are not strong. This is predictable for at least a couple of reasons. (1) Few people start a redesign effort because the company is in great shape. Hence the data will naturally lean in the direction of demonstrating organizational weaknesses. (2) This may have been one of the few times that people in the organization have had an opportunity to express some of their frustrations and feelings. This often results in the organizational survey uncovering strong negative feelings.

As a result, when leaders see the data, they are often surprised that the data are so negatively weighted. This is particularly the case if the leadership team has been previously buffered from hearing about problems. Given the surprising negative flavor of the data, some leaders of organizations resist feeding back the data to the rest of the organization for fear of sending a message that the organization is in trouble, or for fear that the data show the organization they are not good leaders. In their fear, they consider not sharing the data at all. Some consider sharing only part of the data. I have even been in meetings where the leaders consider changing the data so that the picture does not look so bad.

While you and other members of the design team may be compelled to withhold data, such an act, I believe, would always be a mistake. If you had promised to feed back the data, you would be violating a promise, thereby engendering mistrust. If, on the other hand, you had not made this promise, think about the kind of organization you want to create. If you are like many leaders, you want an organization where everyone feels responsible for the organization and its results, and were everyone feels ownership for its solutions. They best way I know how to create such an organization is to have open and honest communication. Sharing the data, openly and honestly, no matter what it says, sends a powerful message throughout the organization that you want to create an organization characterized by open communication, valid data, free choice, and personal commitment. The first step in sharing the data is to discuss it with key leaders of the organization in a feedback meeting.

This feedback meeting, as well as others you will probably hold later throughout the organization, is more than just a presentation of the results of the data collection and diagnosis. It is an opportunity to elicit reactions from your organization and take its pulse in terms of its readiness for change. Primarily, you want people to be willing to take action on the basis of the data. Therefore, you want to manage the feedback meeting in such a way that it engenders an open discussion of the diagnosis and helps motivate the organization toward action. For purposes of this discussion, we will assume you are holding a feedback meeting with 75 people or less. (If it is a larger group, you may want to break the meeting down into smaller groups.)

Here, then, is a breakdown of how to effectively orchestrate feedback sessions of this kind:

1. Restate the original agreement made prior to the start of the data collection process.

2. Explain how this meeting will proceed.

3. Describe the data collection process.

4. Present the data.

5. Ask for reactions.

6. Communicate your plan for how to proceed.

1. Restate the original agreement. This step is intended to communicate to your organization that you are fulfilling your agreement with them. This not only communicates that you care about keeping your agreements, but also communicates that they can trust that in the future, when you ask for data, you will always share with them what you have learned. You should also take this opportunity to remind people about the original impetus for the study. This helps people become focused again on the bottom-line results that you are seeking. Without this reassurance, people will often feel that this is just another study (yawn).

2. Explain how the meeting will proceed. You are in charge of this meeting. Without stating that explicitly, you need to act like you are in charge. If you are looking for people's reactions, state that. If you want to answer people's questions, let them know you want them to ask questions. In effect, say, "Here's how I have planned this meeting, and here's what I would like everyone to get out of it."

Also, be sure to propose some ground rules for the

meeting in order to establish a climate for open discussion. You will be well served to strongly assert your desire for an open exchange of ideas and a focus on shared responsibility for the survey results. Let people know how difficult this is for you and/or your concerns about how people may respond. In effect, by establishing the climate for the meeting, you are settling the tone for the nature of the discussion that you want to take place.

3. *Restate the data-collection process.* This is intended to remind people of what has happened thus far, and to ensure that everyone knows how the results were obtained.

4. *Present data.* Here you and other members of your design team should share with the group the results of the data collection efforts. For this meeting, you will want to present two levels of information:

(a) the raw numbers developed by the interviews and survey, and

(b) the summary of the data.

In this part of the meeting, state that you will focus the discussion on a summary of the data since the raw numbers are too lengthy and detailed to discuss here. At the same time, let the participants of the meeting know that the raw numbers are available to anyone who is interested. Then share with the group the diagnosis. This should be done using flip charts, an overhead projector, or slides. However it is presented, the diagnosis should be concise and to the point.

5. *Ask for reactions.* At this point you want people to share with you their reactions. How people react will tell you a lot about whether and to what extent the organization is ready for change. So tell people that you

wonder whether or not the diagnosis is on target. If you have done a good job of creating an open forum for discussion, they will then tell you, with varying degrees of truth, their reactions.

If you expect or are finding that people are reticent to react to the data, it would be helpful to let them know how you feel about the data and then ask for their thoughts. By sharing your own, you are paving the way for an atmosphere of open communication of thoughts and feelings.

Here, more than at any other time in the feedback meeting, you will want to take a facilitating role. When they respond, thank them for their reaction. If you want further clarification, say things like, "That sounds important, could you say more?" When you hear ideas about which you are curious what others think, ask: "How about others, what do you think?" Whatever you say, be sure to signal that you appreciate hearing their thoughts. And by all means listen!

If people do not respond, ask the group what is making it difficult to respond. Then respond to their concerns or their thoughts. Whatever the case, this is not a time to tell then what's wrong with them, but instead to encourage open and honest communication. Your positive and appreciative reactions to them will go far in facilitating full discussion about the data.

You may also want to get some impressions from people about their ideas for how to affect change. Every now and then, when someone gives you a useful reaction, you may want to ask them if they have any ideas about what needs to be done. This will give you an additional sense of people's readiness to change. At the same time, this meeting could easily drift into problem solving. While that may be useful at some point, it is best not to try to solve the problems too quickly or in a reactive mode. At this phase in the process, the most important thing is to have a good sense of the problems and how people feel about them. Problem solving will come later. Premature problem solving can cut off the exploration of thoughts and feelings. (I say this in particular to those of you who, like me, as soon as you sniff a problem, you want it solved. My wife thankfully reminds me of this. Often, when she tells me something that is bothering her about work, or family, or me, my first reaction is to want to solve it. She often points out that what she really wants is to be heard.)

6. *Recommendations on how to proceed.* At this point, you should state how you would like the organization to address its key issues. These ideas, presumably, have been developed by you and the other members of the design team in advance. The plan could have to do with things your top management team is going to do, or it could be a recommendation for what you want from the organization. If it is the latter, spell out as clearly as you can what you want to accomplish, and ask for feedback as to whether or not that makes sense to the group.

THE NEXT STEPS

At this point in the redesign process, the possibilities for what each individual reader will want to do to help achieve higher and more enduring performance in his or her organization will diverge significantly. What you will do depends largely on what the issues are that your organization needs to address. The following five chapters provide guidance on how to handle each of five different features of an organization's architecture: vision, culture, strategic direction, strategic goals, and structure. Separately, they represent tried and true methods for improving each of them. Together, they represent a holistic and comprehensive development effort; one that, if managed effectively, will enhance your organization's productivity in significant ways.

ARCHITECTING CHECKLIST

1. In thinking about the process of redesigning your organization's architecture, place particular emphasis on the implementation phase. Decisions are often the easy part. The challenge is in carrying those decisions out.

2. Take a risk and share openly and fully the data about your organization. This typically engenders a stronger spirit of ownership throughout the whole organization.

3. Use the feedback process as an opportunity to get further input and guidance, and to sense the feelings of the organization. This information will be critical in the decision-making process.

4. Give the data away and let appropriate people make decisions that are in their area of responsibility.

8

Clarifying Your Vision

Some men see things as they are and ask "Why?" I dream of things that never were, and ask "Why not?"
—George Bernard Shaw

A colleague of mine is the director of human resources development in a large industrial company. Until recently, his organization has focused on providing a comprehensive set of management and organization development services to the whole company. Hard times, however, have rocked the company, such that cutbacks have forced him to lose 50 percent of his staff. Dejected, he and his group mourned their loss and feared that they would no longer have the impact on the organization they so strongly wanted to have. After a week of soul searching and discussion with others, the director decided that his staff was now too small to provide all the various services that it could in the past. The only logical thing to do was to offer training programs, and to do some consulting on the side. This idea, he believed, would be deflating to the rest of the organization, and would run the risk of losing the rest of his people. Undaunted, he worked on his plan with the president of the company, and then prepared to give the news to his troops. After a few introductory remarks, he shared with the group the new vision. This is roughly what he said:

> After a lot of thought, and discussion with the president of the company, we have decided to focus our efforts on management training and development. While this will not allow us to do some of the things we have enjoyed in the past, let me tell you what I have in mind. Our industry lacks effective management training programs. The general consensus in the industry is that we don't have good management people, and those we do have, we don't train well. Our programs, too, have suffered, from lack of creativity and impact. This is from no fault of ours; we have been too busy doing other things for the company. I'd like to turn our situation from one of disappointment to one of opportunity. For the next 18 months, I want us to develop and deliver the finest management training programs ever developed in our industry. And if we can't develop them here, we will buy them, sparing no cost. In two years time, I would like to hear everyone in our company say they have not only benefitted from taking our courses, but are proud of the standard we set for our industry.

This is not just any old vision. This is a vision of which anyone involved can be proud. This is not just a goal, or an objective; this is a cause to rally for. That is the essence of an effective vision. It is a cause. It provides people with a sense of purpose. It gives meaning to their work. It is, in the words of Peter Block, a vision of greatness.[1]

WHY IS VISION SO CRITICAL?

When I ask people what the vision of their department or organization is, I get all sorts of answers, few of which constitute what I would consider to be an effective vision. I get answers like:

> "Our mission is to provide quality assurance for our bleep line."

> "Our goal is to raise our customer satisfaction index from 8.3 to 9.1."

> "Our function is to configure the systems and then send the material lists to the production unit for completion."

> "Our vision is to develop the widget line according to blankety blank specifications and in such a way that it keeps abreast of our competition."

These are not powerful visions. They are goals or brief statements of an organization's charter. They represent an effort to explain what the group is supposed to accomplish. But they lack excitement. They lack vigor. They lack meaning. They are dry, uninviting statements that specify, but do not inspire.

A great vision inspires. A vision is not a goal, not an objective, not a statement of function. It is a reason for being. A great vision is not just a reason for coming to

---

[1] Block, P., *The Empowered Manager: Positive Political Skills at Work*, Jossey-Bass, San Francisco, 1991.

work each day, but a reason to want to come to work. A great vision takes work out of the realm of toil and makes it fulfilling.

> Said one bricklayer when asked what he was doing, "I am just doing my job." Said a second, "I'm just laying these bricks here." Said a third, "I am building a cathedral."

A great vision also differentiates the organization from others like it. A key factor in any successful organization is its identity. It is an organization's purpose, mission, and values that give it uniqueness and identity.

A great vision also provides the grounds for key strategic decisions. Vision is at the core of an organization's architecture, for it provides meaning and direction for all that an organization does. Without a vision, the organization is too subject to the twists and turns of its environment, always other-directed, never focused. A great vision is, in effect, the heart and soul of an organization as it breathes life into it and drives it toward greatness.

Finally, a great vision stretches an organization beyond its perceived capabilities. The most powerful value of a vision is not the getting there, for few organizations truely achieve their vision. It is in the striving toward the vision that propels an organization toward greatness. Peter Senge, in his book, *The Fifth Discipline*, offers an excellent example of the power of a great vision. He talks about Bill Russell, perhaps the finest professional basketball player of his era. Bill Russell, at the end of each game, graded his performance on a scale of one to one hundred using a standard or vision of excellence he had developed for himself early on in his career. Each game he fell well short of his vision, some games more so than others. In fact, he never achieved more than a 65. Yet he never despaired, for by comparing his accomplishment with his vision, he learned and continued to push himself to accomplish even more.[2]

For the past ten years, numerous best-selling books on management excellence, such as *In Search of Excellence,*[3] *Managing for Excellence,*[4] *Creating Excellence,*[5] *Corporate Cultures,*[6] and *Leaders,*[7] have been saying the same thing. The best managers and leaders inspire their organizations through their passion for achieving a powerful and compelling vision of their organization's future.

Most organizations are not vision driven. They are problem driven. Their *modus operandi* is to seek problems, and solve them. While that works to some extent, it does not drive an organization to achieve greatness, for the absence of problems does not result in excellence. Achieving one's vision, in contrast, brings the organization far beyond the absence of problems: it draws toward achieving something of distinction. It pulls the organization to stretch its boundaries and create something that has not existed before (see Figure 8–1).

When an organization has a vision, you can feel it when you enter its doors. It permeates the organization, providing unity and meaning in everyone's efforts. You could feel it at Polaroid when the first instant

---

[2] Senge, P., *The Fifth Discipline*, Doubleday Currency: New York, 1990, pp. 153–154.

[3] Peters, T. and Waterman, R. *In Search of Excellence*, Warner Books, New York, 1982.

[4] Bradford, C. and Cohen, A. *Managing for Excellence*, John Wiley & Sons, New York, 1984.

[5] Hickman, C. and Silva, M. *Creating Excellence: Managing Corporate Culture, Strategy, and Change in the New Age*, New American Library, New York, 1984.

[6] Deal, T. and Kennedy, A. *Corporate Cultures: The Rites and Rituals of Corporate Life*, Addison Wesley Publishing Company, Reading, Mass., 1982.

[7] Bennis, W. and Nanus B. *Leaders*, Harper & Row, New York, 1985.

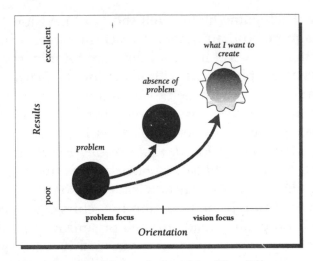

Figure 8-1. Vision/problem relationship. The difference between vision focus and problem focus.

camera was being produced. You could feel it at Data General in the group that was creating what was then called the Eagle Computer.[8] You could feel it during the early days of People Express. You could feel it at Chrysler Corporation after Lee Iacocca took over the reins of the sagging automobile company. And you could feel it throughout most of the history of Apple Computer. These were organizations that were not just following a mission, they were on a mission. The feeling in the workplace was one of excitement. People were working hard. There was enthusiasm in its leadership, an enthusiasm that permeated the entire organization.

That is the essence of a vision. Vision is not just a check-off item on your management "to do" list. It is that force which keeps people focused on a larger issue;

---

[8] See Kidder, T., *Soul of a New Machine*, Avon Books, New York, 1981, for a wonderful look at the inner workings of a group developing a computer.

it provides guidance for decisions; it motivates; and it helps to sustain attention to excellence.

Thomas Alva Edison's well-known dictum says it well: "Invention is 1 percent inspiration and 99 percent perspiration." It is vision that holds a person or group's attention and commitment through the tough times.

It was vision, for example, that helped Spence Silver and Arthur Fry persevere for years at 3M in trying to convince people that their new semiadhesive substance was worthwhile. At first people at 3M said it was worthless. So did the people who were asked to do test marketing of the idea in four cities. What use is adhesive if it only does half the job? But in spite of some people's resistance, Silver and Fry persisted.

Eventually, after much trial and error, Silver and Fry produced a product that made ideal use of their semiadhesive surface. You and I know it as those little yellow sticky Post-It™ note pads that we use to leave notes.

It was vision that helped Taiichi Ohno persevere with his "just-in-time" approach to inventory in the face of a whole industry, nay, a whole planet's conviction that one needs large inventories to ensure manufacturing efficiency. Ohno felt otherwise. His notion was that inventories take up time to maintain and space to hold them, both of which cost money. If you could create a system that gets the inventory to you right at the time you need it, not before, and not after, you will create a far more efficient, far more cost-effective system. In spite of experts saying it couldn't be done, Ohno persisted. It took him 30 years of trial and error at Toyota to perfect the system. It is now widely accepted throughout the business world as the best way to manage inventories, and it has saved Toyota and countless other businesses millions and millions of dollars.

It was vision that helped Arthur Jones perservere in

his attempts to create an efficient machine for helping people build muscle strength. Up until 20 years ago, it was widely known and accepted that to build strong muscles, one needed many repetitions of an exercise or movement, many times a week. But Arthur Jones challenged this notion. Through careful research, he found that 8–12 repetitions of a single movement at maximum weight was optimal. He also corroborated some earlier research that demonstrates that one should rest at least 48 hours between exercise sessions. He also found that rather than working many muscles at a time, isolating muscles and identifying the optimal flexible movement of those muscles, facilitates the muscle-building process.

On the basis of his research, he developed a set of machines that isolated different muscles and controlled their movement. He took these machines to the leaders of the muscle-building community, who scoffed at the idea. No one would finance his efforts. So he decided to build and market his machines himself. He built them in his garage (why is it that so many inventions start in a garage?) and little by little sold them to exercise businesses throughout the United States. You and I know these as Nautilus machines, one of the most popular forms of muscle-building exercise in the Western world. As a result of his vision, in a thirty-minute period of focused exercise, three times a week, one can build strong muscles and/or attractive muscle tone.[9]

Almost every innovation known to human kind was at one point or another developed in the face of enormous doubt or resistance. Such is the nature of vision.

---

[9] The three examples above were drawn from Nayak, P. and Ketteringham, J., *Breakthroughs: How the Vision and Drive of Innovators in Sixteen Companies Created Commercial Breakthroughs that Swept the World*, Rawson Associates, New York, 1986.

It perseveres in spite of resistance, and from vision comes great accomplishments.

WHY IS VISION SO RARE?

While vision in effective leadership is critical, it is also rare. This is in part due to the fact that as a society, we are extremely short-term oriented so that we tend to focus on what is immediately around us rather than on the big picture. This scarcity is also due to the fact that few people naturally take a visionary approach to their leadership or their life. Recent groundbreaking research on the process of adult development sheds significant light on this dynamic.

For years, psychologists have known that different people see the world very differently, and that how they see the world— their attitudes, assumptions, values, and beliefs—directly impact the choices they see and the decisions they make. What is less widely known, however, is that these different ways of seeing or different worldviews develop through late adolescence and into adulthood in a clearly definable progression of steps or stages (see Figure 8–2).

As each progressive step is taken in one's development, a new way of seeing and a new way of under-

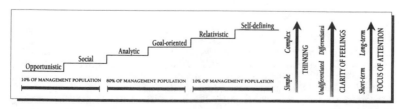

Figure 8-2. Stages of adult development.

standing or interpreting the world emerges.[10] These stages of development can be summarized as follows:

Stage One: *Opportunistic.* Self, others, and events are treated as external things to be manipulated according to one's own desires.

Stage Two: *Social.* Person tends to focus on others' needs and desires and aims to please them. Events feel like they occur without person's ability to significantly influence them; a person needs to adapt to these events to feel successful.

Stage Three: *Analytic.* People and events tend to be treated as technical systems to be influenced by finding the right "key" to their inner workings.

Stage Four: *Goal-oriented.* Self, others, and events are treated as rational systems that can be influenced by substantive argument and calculated action.

Stage Five: *Relativistic.* Self, others, and events are treated as an interaction of differing perspectives. No perspective is inherently right. Conflicts are managed and resolved through tolerance and discussion.

Stage Six: *Self-defining.* Self, others, and events are treated as developing systems, to be influenced by frameworks that permit freedom to hold different values and views. A person's aim is often to engage with others to mesh these differences into a mutually satisfying whole.[11]

---

[10] For some of the more central theories of adult development, see Loevinger, J., *Ego Development: Conception and Theories,* Jossey-Bass, San Francisco, 1979; Kegan, R., *The Evolving Self,* Harvard University Press, Cambridge, Mass., 1982; and Kohlberg, L., *Collected Papers on Moral Development and Moral Education,* Center for Moral Education, Cambridge, Mass., 1976.

[11] Adapted from Merron, K., Fisher, D., and Torbert, W., "Meaning Making and Management Action," *Group and Organizational Studies,* Sage Publications, Newbury Park, Ca, Vol. 12, No. 3, September 1987, pp. 274–286.

These stages of adult development are ordered in a precise manner, for research has found that adults at successive stages of development see the world in more complex ways, and experience greater degrees of self-understanding and emotional maturity. In addition, research has found that one cannot move on to "later" stages of development without progressing through the earlier stages. That is to say, a person cannot skip a stage.

It is also now known that at some point adults slow down in their developmental process and "land" on a relatively stable worldview. While some may progress in adulthood to another stage, few do. Most adults arrive at a world view and remain there for long periods of time, until either they move on through a focused effort at self-development that pushes them toward more complex ways of being and knowing, or a major event occurs that shakes up their world and causes them to question the way they view it.

What is particularly relevant to our discussion is that one's stage of development seems to impact one's effectiveness as a leader. Research has shown, for example, that leaders at earlier stages of development exercise power in a more coercive manner, whereas managers at later stages tend to build power in a more collaborative manner, and tend to be driven by their needs for achievement rather than by their needs for personal power or personal gain.[12] It has also been shown that leaders at later stages of development are more likely than those at earlier stages to seek feedback from others

---

[12] Smith, S., *Ego Development and the Problems of Power and Agreement in Organizations,* Unpublished doctoral dissertation, George Washington University, 1980. Lasker H., *Ego Development and Motivation: A Cross-Cultural Cognitive-Development Analysis of an Achievement,* Unpublished doctoral dissertation, University of Chicago, 1978.

about their performance, and to explore new ways in which they can increase their effectiveness.[13] Finally, it has been found that leaders at later stages of development are able to see multiple ways of understanding problems and their causes, are more able to understand and manage complex problems, and take a more collaborative approach to solving them.[14]

In brief, adult developmental theory strongly suggests that effective leadership is not a haphazard event, but to a large extent a function of the leaders' world view or stage of development. The implications of this are far reaching and revolutionary. For example, if it is true that one's developmental stage affects one's leadership capability, then leaders are indeed made and not born, for anyone and everyone has the capability of growing and maturing from a developmental point of view. Inaddition, if one's world view directly impacts one's leadership capability, then businesses that desire to cultivate effective leadership should be spending as much effort on encouraging the human development of its people as they spend on developing their technical skills.

Adult developmental research also helps us understand why few managers exhibit true vision in leading their organizations. The ability to take a long-term approach to management, and to see and integrate complex processes and events, seems to be most strong in people at later stages of development. Managers at later stages seem far more able than those at prior stages to see integrated patterns, to perceive and accept ambigu-

---

[13] Merron, K. and Torbert, W., "Offering managers feedback on Loevinger's ego development measure," Unpublished manuscript, School of Management, Boston College.

[14] Merron, K., Fisher, D., and Torbert, W., "Meaning Making and Management Action," *Group and Organizational Studies*, Sage Publications, Newbury Park, Ca., Vol. 12, No. 3, September 1987, pp. 274–286.

ity and paradox, to see multiple ways of looking at events, and to reframe problems in ways that increase their ability to solve them effectively. In effect, their "world view" corresponds more closely with the world that most businesses occupy.[15] Since fewer than 10 percent of the management population have patterns of behavior associated with later stages of development,[16] few managers seem to be naturally visionary. In addition, regardless of one's stage of development, the physiology and function of some features of the human brain seems to inhibit visionary thinking.

How the Brain Functions. It has long been known that the primary driver of our thinking is that part of the brain known as the reptilian brain. The reptilian brain focuses on threat or survival, and calls us to behave in ways to protect ourselves. This reptilian brain, a throwback from our animal ancestry, governs much of what we focus our attention on. When a threat occurs, we are poised for response (see Figure 8–3).

What we focus on in the short run is also governed by the part of the brain known as the limbic system. This part is controlled by the hormonal secretion of chemicals. These chemicals, to a large extent, influence our emotions. Given that we are emotional beings, our emotions often drive our behavior and determine our focus of attention. Witness the mood swings adolescents often feel, much of which is governed by rapid changes in their hormonal system.

These two parts of the brain then, the reptilian brain and the limbic system, often override the third and

---

[15] Fisher, D. and Torbert, W., "Transforming Managerial Practice: Beyond the Achiever Stage," in *Research in Organizational Change and Development*, JAI Press, Inc., Vol. 5, 1991, pp. 143–173.
[16] Torbert, W., *Managing the Corporate Dream: Restructuring for Long Term Success*, Dow Jones-Irwin, Homewood, Il., 1987.

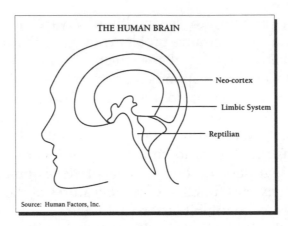

Figure 8-3. The human brain.

largest part of the brain, the neo-cortex, and keep us focused on fear, threat, and survival. The neo-cortex is the part of our brain where data are processed, where thinking occurs, and where decisions are made. It is the neo-cortex that distinguishes our brain anatomy from that of other animals, for human beings have by far a much larger neo-cortex as a proportion of their total brain than does any other animal.

Yet we rarely use our neo-cortex to the fullest. To a large extent, we are still instinctual, reaction-oriented, fear driven, and emotionally wired. Given this, we often do not act differently than other animals. We react first and think later. "Ready, fire, aim" characterizes many of our decisions. It is no wonder that most organizations are fraught with fire-fighting, and that people in them feel that they do not have the luxury of long-term planning and continuous improvement. They created this by the very way they organize, and by where they focus their attention.

This tendency, however, not to look into the future is often the undoing of our businesses, and has the potential for leading to the destruction of our planet. As a consequence of our short-term, self-protection focus, we create products that pollute the environment, and we continue to create a growing human population that will, within a not-too-distant future, exceed the planet's ability to sustain it. If we were to look into the future, we would notice the trends that we are in the process of creating. If we were willing to live for the future rather than to indulge ourselves in the present, we would perhaps choose alternative paths for governing our society, ones that build up the environment rather than destroy it.[17]

But we have yet to come to this conclusion as a society. Why? Because we do not look and act for the long term. We act for the short term. We are a society that reinforces the benefits of immediate gratification. Not surprisingly, according to Scott Peck in *The Road Less Traveled*, the sign of individual maturity (and I believe societal maturity) is in delaying gratification to experience long-term satisfaction. Few people seem to do this. Our society certainly does not reinforce this. The same is unfortunately true in business.

An example of the consequences of short-term thinking was a trade that recently occurred in professional football. In 1989, the Minnesota Vikings were on the verge of becoming a powerhouse in the National Football League. They decided that what they needed to get over the top was a world-class running back. So they sought out and traded players to the Dallas Cowboys for Hershel Walker, one of the premier running backs in the league. What they gave up for Hershel Walker was five established players on their roster, their 1992

---

[17] See Ornstein, R. and Ehrlich, P. *New World, New Mind*, Simon and Schuster, Inc., New York, 1989, for a revealing book on this subject.

future first round draft pick, plus six other draft picks in 1990.

At the time, the Cowboys were one of the more mediocre teams in the league and were interested in building a foundation for the future. The Vikings, on the other hand, wanted an immediate opportunity for the Super Bowl championship. They mortgaged part of their future to get it. The rest is history. In three years time, the Cowboys went from a record of 1–13 to the championship of the National Football League in 1993. The Vikings are still not serious contenders.

The kind of decision made by the Vikings is being made every day by hundreds of companies throughout the United States, where immediate return on shareholder investment drives the thinking of our business leaders, and sows the seeds of eventual mediocrity. One major retail company recently announced an aggressive shipping date to their customers. They overextended themselves and had to put delivery off many times over. As a result, they finally shipped significantly later than initially promised, and their customers are no longer confident in the company's ability to deliver. A large software company shipped everything they had on hand at the end of the month to make quarterly earnings look good. Unfortunately, what they shipped was of poor quality. They sold and shipped products that were either incomplete or fraught with bugs. Moreover, they booked future income from service contracts as current income. While their quarterly income looked good, their credibility was seriously compromised. As a result, their stock and income dropped severely to the point that they almost lost the company. Still another company has a habit of making their quarterly income look good by fancy accounting. This works in the short run. In the long run, you can't hide the truth.

Companies in the United States do these kinds of things all the time, all in the service of short-term profit. They fear that if they do not demonstrate a robust return on shareholder investment, the investors will take their money and invest it elsewhere. And why not? That is exactly what investors do. So we are caught up in a never-ending short-term-focused spiral, and experience the consequences of this every day.

It is no surprise that the Japanese have been so successful. They are far more interested in building companies that leave a legacy behind for their children and grandchildren, and are far less interested in immediate success. So they focus their efforts on continuous small improvements, while we focus on immediate results. They drive their companies based on a long-term vision of success, while we focus on immediate short-term goals.

THE ELEMENTS OF A VISION

According to a recent study on visionary organizations, the best organizations that are driven by a vision have two critical components in their vision: a guiding philosophy and a tangible image of the future.[18] A guiding philosophy includes a clear sense of purpose as well as a core set of beliefs and values. An organization's purpose answers the question: Why do we exist? Its values are the deeply held beliefs and principles that guide behavior. A tangible image of the future includes a strong sense of mission (the overarching goal of the organization at a given point in time) and a vivid description of how that mission translates into specific

---

[18] Porras, J. and Collins, S. "Organizational Vision and Visionary Organizations," *California Management Review*, Volume 34, Number 1, Fall 1991, pp. 30–52.

behaviors and organizational outcomes. In contrast to the assumptions of most organizations, a clear vision is not a statement on the wall (although many great companies have these). It is a living, breathing sense of the future that drives the organization's behavior and gives meaning to people's work.

While not all great companies have all of these features articulated in a formal way, they all seem to have them as guiding features in their drive toward excellence in the future (see Figure 8–4).

One good example of a vision is an organization that I have worked with over the past couple of years called The Skills Center. The Skills Center is one of the leading organizations in the country providing training and employment to people with developmental disabilities. I share this example, not because this company exemplifies corporate America, but because it is like the many smaller companies throughout the United States seeking to find meaning and value in their work. In this case, the organization is taking a revolutionary stand in its field, and they are enormously successful by almost any standards one can imagine.

I have had the privilege of working with The Skills Center for the last three years. As part of that work, I

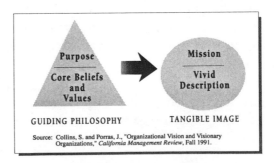

Figure 8-4. Key features of successful visions.

have been helping them to clarify and craft their vision for their organization. This particular part of my consulting work with them involved a series of meetings that took place over roughly a year's time. After much discussion and reflection on the part of the leaders of the organization, the Board of Directors, and the employees of the company, The Skills Center arrived at the following statement of their vision (Figure 8–5).

What makes this vision particularly exciting and revolutionary in its field is that much of the client population of The Skills Center has difficulty expressing verbally their wants, needs, and desires. Too often in our society, we assume that we know what is best for the disabled population. We tend to view them as perennial children, and therefore think that we are responsible for directing their lives in "their own best interests." This assumption permeates our society and the service providers we entrust to support them.

The Skills Center, in contrast, views their clients as adults, not significantly different from you or me. While they may have special needs, they are still adults, and as such are deserving of the dignity, understanding, and respect that are the rights of all people. The Skills Center takes this notion seriously, and bends over backwards to ensure that they follow the lead of their clients, just like any company might care about listening to and understanding its customers. In this case, listening to the needs and desires of their clients is not easy inasmuch as many of their clients cannot articulate their needs verbally. So The Skills Center derives creative ways of understanding their clients' needs. One example of this process is to ask the client a question about what he or she prefers in terms of transportation to and from The Skills Center. Do they prefer being driven by the center's van, being driven by their

VISION STATEMENT

The Skills Center will become a leader by following the ambitions and aspirations of the people it serves.

Values of Skills Center, Inc.

Sense of Community

- The Skills Center will be more than just a place to work. It will be an experience of belonging, teamwork and involvement.

Culture of Creativity

- We are committed to building an environment of creativity:
  - where everyone is challenged to explore, learn, and grow;
  - where pride in efforts and achievements embraced;
  - where everyone is a better person for having been here.

Driven To Succeed

- We believe that our success is directly linked to the accomplishment of those we serve and we take great pride in their successes.

Community Involvement

- We are committed to provide every opportunity for the people we serve to fully participate in their community.

The Inherent Value of People

- We believe that people are inherently good and therefore entitled to dignity and respect.
- We will listen to and learn from all involved with the organization.

Safety and Stability

- We pledge to create an environment that is stable and safe, supportive and comfortable.

Learn From Those We Serve

- We believe people with developmental disabilities are our primary customers. Their honesty, courage, compassion, and perseverance will be a model for our decisions and behavior.

Figure 8-5. The Skills Center vision.

family, or taking public transportation? When dealing with a client who has difficulty verbalizing his or her feelings, a member of The Skills Center puts these options on a piece of paper and asks the client to point to his or her preference. Another example of this process is that the employees are trained to watch for nonverbal clues that indicate what the client is feeling. Just like everyone else, their clients' eyes light up when they like something. The eyes signal their preferences and feelings, and The Skills Center's service providers are trained to watch for these clues and to respond appropriately.

The Skills Center also seeks to learn from their customers, driven by a firm belief that their clients have much to teach us about love, courage, determination, and dignity. I have this experience myself almost every time I visit The Skills Center, for I am consistently overwhelmed by how friendly and caring their clients are. I am always greeted with a smile and a handshake by one of the clients, and frequently observe them hard at work in one of their many work efforts. When I observe, I am inspired by their focus and dedication to doing a good job. Would that I were so dedicated, and could express my caring for others so freely and so fully.

These are but a few of the many ways that The Skills Center is creative in living its vision. And it works. They are one of the most respected service providers in the country, and one of the most financially sound. The people there enjoy their work, and know they are on the leading edge of something great.

HAVING A VISION
MAKES GOOD BUSINESS SENSE

It is no surprise that the concept of a vision is becoming such a critical element in the business community. In this day and age of continuous change, the victors are those who are able to envision the future of the environment around them, and then craft a mission, strategy, and approach to succeed in that future. The need to anticipate the future was not necessarily true in times past. Let's look back to roughly 100 years ago, before the industrial revolution had taken hold in western society.

Around the turn of the century, our economy and our society, indeed our world, was primarily agriculturally based. There were more people involved in agricultural activities than in any other major work arena. This had been true for hundreds of years before, and was still true up until that time. Up until the industrial revolution, the world was relatively stable. One had a sense of what one needed to do to succeed, and could expect that what was needed would not change significantly over time. You learned how to farm from your parents, who had learned it from their parents, and so on. What you learned were the tried and true methods that had withstood the test of time in previous generations. While innovations occurred to help you to succeed, such as better hand tools, these innovations did not significantly change the nature of your work, they only aided it.

Around the turn of the century, however, a shift in the larger forces that shaped our society began to occur. Industry began to displace agriculture as the primary force in our economy. Thus began the industrial revolution, where machines became the critical drivers of our economic output. This revolution has forever changed the face of our society, for in today's industrial world, success is defined more by the speed and economy of production and by the intelligent distribution of work than it is by the sweat of one's brow.

In the period of industrial preeminence, developing new and innovative products and machines to support the work became critical to one's success. This is still true to a large extent today. In the early 1900s and ever since, scientific research and development began to play a significant role in shaping society. As a result of increasing technological advances, changes in business began to occur more rapidly. Whereas before, in the agricultural age, you could look out a few decades and expect that the world would be the same, in the early and middle periods of the industrial age (roughly 1935–1965), you could only look out a few years. The ability to anticipate these upcoming changes therefore became more and more important.

Somewhere around mid-century, a new development began to occur, one that completely and forever has changed the nature of our economy and our society. This was the creation of the first commercially viable computer, the UNIVAC. The introduction of the UNIVAC in the mid-1950s, and all computers since, has brought forth a new age, one where information is the primary source of innovation, technological advancement, and power. In this new age, change is not only occurring, but is increasing geometrically with time. This is true, in part, because the nature of change in a technology-driven economy tends to follow a "J" curve where technological advances occur at an ever-increasing rate. Here are two examples (Figures 8–6a and 8–6b).

In such a world, information is king and technology is queen. Given such a rapidly changing world, the

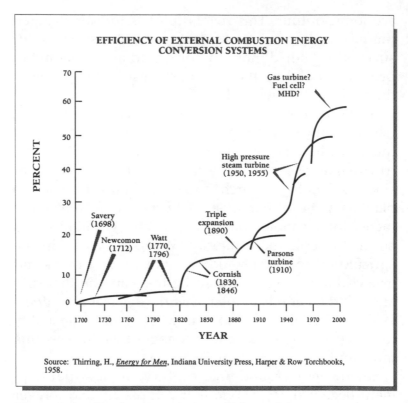

Figure 8-6a. Combustion engine efficiency J curve.

future is almost upon us at any given moment. By the time we realize that a significant change has occurred, it is often too late to adapt, react, or respond. More true today that ever in the past, success comes to those who can anticipate changes before they have come. To do this requires the ability to look well into the future, and see patterns, trends, and processes unfolding.

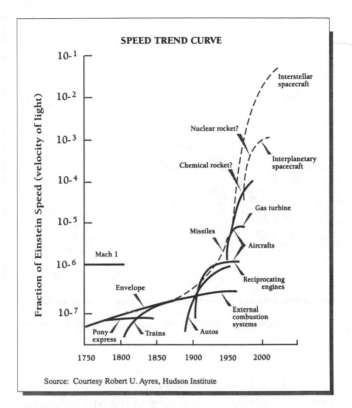

Figure 8-6b. Speed-of-travel J curve.

HAVING A VISION
HELPS PROMOTE CHANGE

It is now widely accepted among researchers and practitioners of organizational change that in order for a leader to create a fundamental change in an organization, three things need to be present: a vision for the future, a clear sense of present reality, and a path to get from the present reality to the future (see Figure 8–7).[19]

---

[19] See Beckhard, R. and Harris R. *Organization Transitions: Managing Complex Change.* (2nd ed.) Addison-Wesley, Reading, Mass., 1987, for an excellent book on the subject.

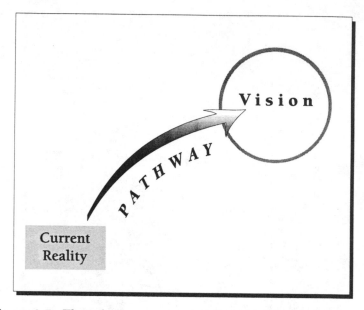

Figure 8-7. Three key components of organizational change.

Each are critical to the process. Leaders with vision, but without an understanding of reality are often referred to as dreamers, and have difficulty producing concrete results. Leaders with a strong sense of reality without vision tend to reinforce the status quo. And leaders with vision and understanding, but without a clear pathway to achieve their vision often tend to produce poor implementation strategies and their change efforts go awry.

These three elements are critical for another reason. Look at the dynamics of personal change. Whenever we have a vision for change that is powerful and compelling, there exists a tension between our present reality and that vision. Normally what we do when we experience the tension is to let go of the vision and revert to our old ways. Like a rubber band that is stretched, when our vision is far from our reality, we have a tendency to snap back to our previous state.[20] Witness, for example, Scott, a manager who has a true desire to become more participatory in his approach yet has a strong need for control. No matter how hard he tries to be open with others and include them in the process of decision making, in many situations he reverts back to his old controlling ways.

In order to produce an enduring change in his style, Scott needs to do two things: hold on to this vision of a different approach to management so powerfully and in so committed a fashion that he is inexorably drawn toward achieving that vision. In addition, he needs to explore his need to control others, understand its causes, and through insight and self-awareness, begin to change the pattern of thinking that underlies that need. Both are critical.

Interestingly, without the vision, there will be nothing drawing Scott toward self-awareness. Therefore, in either case, a powerful and committed vision of a new approach to management pulls Scott in the direction he seeks and compels him to find new, and more effective, ways of being.

Such a dynamic works the same way in organizations. The more compelling the vision, and the more committed people are to it, the more likely the organization will move toward realizing their vision. This is not to say that implementing a vision is easy. It often is not. It is, however, in the purest sense, rather simple.

---

[20] See Fritz, R. *The Path of Least Resistance*, Stillpoint Publishing, Walpole, NH, 1984, for an in-depth and revealing analysis of the dynamics of change.

HOW TO CREATE A VISION

Creating a vision in an organization that already has a partial one and is unsure about it's future is very challenging. When an organization is new, what drives the direction is the vision of the original founder or founders of the company. Over time, however, the world changes, and often some features of the vision either lose their impact, or the organizations lose touch with the original vision. This is not unusual. The greatest challenge is in taking a company that has been in existence for a while and mold or create a new vision. This is particularly difficult when people in key positions of leadership do not see eye to eye about the future of the company. Indeed, it is often considered so difficult that most organizations shy away from creating a vision, partly in fear that some members of the company will not support it and have to leave. Rather than face the challenge, and confront the differences, leaders within organizations will either consciously or unconsciously choose to avoid the potential conflict.

This is one of the reasons why there is such confusion in organizations about what they are trying to do. When the organization doesn't have a clear and compelling purpose and vision, it ends up in disorganization, and people wind up working at odds with each another. Most people, when you ask them about their organization's vision, will shake their heads and sigh. They realize that they don't have one. Or if they do, they don't know what it is. I just recently met with a senior executive of one of the largest retail organizations in the country and talked with her about the vision for her company. She revealed they had none. I then asked her about her own vision for the future of the company and for herself. After some soul searching she discovered that she had none in both cases and that her career, while successful by many standards, had no focus nor direction. She then went on to talk about how unsure she was about her work, and that she was drifting, often reacting to events around her, with little drive or passion. She also revealed that she felt she was not having the impact she sought on the organization. She is not alone. Many people and many organizations feel the same.

In brief, a vision is a clear, articulate, and compelling view of the core purpose, values, and direction of the organization. It is more that just what you are trying to accomplish in the world. It provides larger significance for the organization. It provides meaning.

In effect, creating a vision requires the leader to project his or her mind into the future and to mold a picture or image of how the organization will then be. When effective, the vision compels an organization to become that image. Hence vision draws an organization toward greatness. To be effective, your vision needs to be so far-reaching that it stretches your organization to achieve the highest level of productivity it possibly can. Yet at the same time, it needs to be realistic enough that people believe in its feasibility (see Figure 8–8). Most importantly it has to be your own. (A West Coach motel chain has the following vision: "Service that brings guests back." I doubt that would work at a hospital!)

Figure 8-8. Effective point of vision.

I want to caution the reader at this point that for a vision to work it not only must be one's own, but it must be authentic. Too often I see leaders of companies look at the research on vision, or they read an article or book about vision, and think that because most successful companies have articulated and are driven by a vision, they too will be effective if they have a vision. So they take steps to find one. This rarely works, however, for it is not the vision that produces the success. It is the passion for the vision and the commitment that underlies the vision that produces enduring performance. One cannot manufacture passion or commitment, nor can one legislate it. It must be *real*. This chapter will help the leader of an organization discover, articulate, and develop their vision. It will not, however, help create a vision or have passion for that vision. This must come from the heart.

Having said that, I think that if indeed you and others in the organization want to achieve significant and enduring performance, clarifying your vision will be key. This chapter will serve as a guide for you in developing that vision. It will focus on two features of a powerful vision: *purpose* and *mission*. In the next chapter about culture, you will be asked to articulate a set of *values* to guide the functioning of your company's internal organization. This, too, is part of the vision for your company, but pertains particularly to its culture and so it will be addressed later.

To successfully discover your purpose and mission, I recommend that you use the following steps as a guide (Figure 8–9).

Clarifying Your Purpose. In contrast to most other things that you do to design your organization's architecture when developing your sense of purpose, you should not necessarily include everyone throughout the

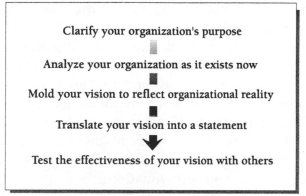

Figure 8-9. Steps to identifying your vision.

organization. A purpose statement should not be set by consensus. Studies have found that groups tend to be risk-averse. They shy away from setting lofty goals. In order to reach agreement, they tend come up with a solution or a goal that represents the common denominator. If you invited the full participation of everyone in your organization, you would not likely end up with a vision that is compelling. It would more likely be mediocre. An effective vision should be created by you and your leadership team; if truly compelling, the rest of your group will adopt it as their own.

This is not to say that you should be unresponsive to the group's sense of purpose. Indeed, the best visions tap into the spirit that is already driving an organization. They release the pent-up energy of people who are already seeking greatness for themselves. They give voice to some goal or desire that everyone shares. So your purpose should express things that most people aspire toward. Nevertheless, more than anything else, the purpose needs to be yours, and that of your leadership team. You need to characterize a purpose that, above all, is compelling to you and the rest of the leadership team. Here's how you will do it.

Step One. Bring your design team together and ask each person to identify four to eight key events or decisions that have previously occurred in your company that have helped to bring it to where it is today. Use the time line in Figure 8–10 as a guide. Then have each person think about why each of these events was so critical. What was the meaning of the key event in the development of your organization?

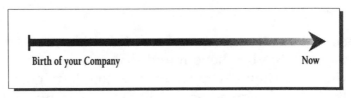

Birth of your Company   Now

Figure 8-10. Organizational timeline.

Event/Decision   **Importance to Your Company**

_____   _____

_____

_____

_____   _____

_____

_____

_____   _____

Event/Decision

Importance to Your Company

_____

_____   _____

_____

_____

_____   _____

_____

_____

Share with each other your views on each key event and write them down on a large flip chart.

Ask the group to step back and discuss what made these events so critical. What is their impact on the organization today? What did the organization gain from these events? How did they shape its identity? Leave this topic alone for now. You will come back to the discussion of these key events later.

Step Two. Ask each member to write down their purpose in working in the organization. What draws each of them to your organization and their work there? These are necessarily lofty statements, ones that give meaning to their work. One well-known example of a meaningful purpose is that of Hewlett-Packard. After a considerable amount of soul searching, they came to the following statement of purpose: *"To create information products that accelerate the advancement of knowledge and fundamentally improve the effectiveness of people and organizations."*

Another example of a well-articulated purpose is that of the Federal Home Loan Mortgage Corporation. Known by many as "Freddie Mac," the Federal Home

Loan Mortgage Corporation is in the business of buying mortgages from mortgage lenders, bundling them in the form of securities, and selling them to investors. One could easily say that Freddie Mac is in the business of buying and selling, and this would be true. But for Freddie Mac, they are playing a much larger game. As explained more fully in Chapter 13, they see their purpose as contributing to the well-being of society by helping people who otherwise might not be able to get a loan. In their eyes, they are increasing people's ability to realize their dreams of building a nest egg and owning their own homes. Such a sense of purpose gives meaning to their work, and drives them to greater and greater success. Freddie Mac came to this sense of purpose by asking themselves "Why do we bundle mortgage packages? What value does this offer? How does what we do make a difference?"

You can use these questions to help guide your design team members as they explore their purpose. Have each members of the team articulate their purpose to the others, and record their responses on a flip chart. As each one responds, you may want to ask the question "Why do that?" until the person can no longer give an answer; in other words, until the person reaches a rock-bottom sense of purpose.

For example, let's say you write software programs for the shipping industry. One person might say, "My purpose is to write the best software programs available." Write this down on the flip chart, and then ask "why build the best software? Of what value is this to people?" The person might say, "So they can do their jobs better." Then ask, "Why improve their jobs?" They might say, "So that shipping runs smoothly and efficiently." Ask why again. They might say, "To keep commerce active and alive." Ask why again. They might say, "So our economy is strong." In other words, they write software programs to support the shipping industry and thereby help make our economy strong. This regressive questioning process enables people to get to the deeper purpose behind their work.

This last statement, by the way, may or may not be most meaningful of all the statements offered. What has real meaning in all of this for the answering person may be "active commerce," or it may be "smooth shipping," or it may be something else. To determine which answer has the most meaning, ask each person which answers feels closest to what has real meaning to them. What gives purpose to their work? What enables them to get up in the morning and feel good about what they do?

Be careful not to steer the group in any particular way. If the group is stuck, one way of getting to purpose is to ask: "What is the value of our work to others?" Another way of proceeding is to ask: "What positive difference do we make to society, to our community, or to our people?" These sorts of questions will help you get at the deeper meaning of your work and help you to discover your purpose.

Post all the ideas expressed above on the flip chart in order to use them in the process described below.

Step Three. As a group, imagine yourselves in the following scenario. It is the year 2040 and the board of directors at your organization has decided to dissolve the organization as it is, perhaps to form a whole new structure. It is a time of sadness and celebration because your organization has achieved extraordinary things in the past 46 years. What is the legacy that it has left behind? What was it known for? What needs has the organization met? What has been this organization's calling?

As a group, answer these questions using the ideas from the previous flip charts as a guide. At this point, keep the ideas flowing. Do not wordsmith. Simply put down all the ideas on a flip chart.

After putting down people's ideas, see if a strong unifying theme emerges. Try to express this theme succinctly and clearly. Take these ideas and articulate your organization's higher purpose or reason for being. Do not be shy to make it a bold statement. In many ways, the bolder it is, the better.

Step Four. If the group seems to be developing only dry ideas, or the ideas seem too pedestrian, consider a more artistic approach to the question of purpose. Ask each member to draw on a large sheet of paper a picture that best describes or depicts his or her vision for your organization. How will it be, what will it be, when it achieves its greatness? Be creative! Ask them not to use words, but to use pictures only.

Have each member of the design team share with others his or her picture and what it means to them. Utilizing the impressions from all the pictures, ask the group to describe the characteristics of your organization that best represent their vision by answering the following question: "If our organization were to become all that we envision it to be, what characteristics would it have?"

Now list the characteristics on a flip chart. Then go back and ask the group what the implications of these visions are for the organization's purpose.

Step Five. Take all of the above ideas and craft them as a group into a single statement of purpose. Do not worry about wordsmithing, for you will likely want to change some of the words later. Do, however, clarify your basic ideas.

Step Six. Once you have established your statement of purpose, think about how you will track your progress. Purposes, like anything, can be measured. In

fact, given that your purpose is the single most important factor in your organization, it is that much more
important to find ways of measuring progress. By measuring your purpose, you have a mechanism by
which you can determine whether and to what extent
you are moving toward it. By agreeing on measures,
you are also putting teeth into the purpose and symbolically reinforcing its importance to the organization.

With your design team, take each feature of your
organization's proposed purpose and think of ways the
organization can measure progress on each.

Purpose   **Potential Measures**

_____   _____

                                     _____

_____   _____

                                     _____

_____   _____

                                     _____

Now pick the measures you think will be most appropriate to leverage your ability to move toward your vision.

Clarifying Your Mission. You now have a part of your
vision: a purpose. The next step in creating a vision is
to mold that part of the vision that has to do with mission. To do this, think about what unique contribution
you would like your organization to make to the world.
What differentiates your mission from other organiza-

tions with the same purpose? Write down your unique contribution below:

_____

_____

_____

_____

_____

_____

_____

_____

Ask others on the design team to do the same. Your unique contribution could be about how you work with customers. For example:

- We are considered the most friendly and cheerful firm in our business. Customers know that when they call on us, we will respond in a way that makes them feel warm and welcome.
- We are noted for our fast responses to customer problems.
- We are proactive in assessing customer needs. We never wait to hear that the problems occurred. We are on top of them at all times.
- We always take responsibility for problems we have created in our product line without being defensive.
- We work closely with our customers to ensure that we address their business needs as they define them.

Or your mission can be about what you produce:

- We provide the top-of-the-line products in our industry. We make the Rolls-Royce of kitchen utensils.
- Our dry-cleaning services come with the guarantee that if you are not satisfied, you are welcome to come back and your garment will be cleaned again, free of charge.
- We deliver our products on time, and fully documented. We meet all our customer commitments without fail.
- We provide the best price/performance ratio in the business. You can't get a better value from any product in our industry.

As you craft your mission, you will need to have your unique contributions in mind. Ultimately, what a clarification of mission does is to tell your organization, "this is where we will focus our attention in the next few years in order to achieve success." As in a battle, the mission of the organization tells the people within it, "This is the hill we are going to climb. This is the battle we aim to win." The mission does not, contrary to popular belief, tell the organization what business it is in. That is the function of a business charter, which is often confused with mission. Charters tend to only be definitions, and as such are quite bland. Missions, on the other hand, tend to attract and invite, excite and compel.

To get a better feeling for an effective mission, let's look at the results of one organization's process for developing a mission. In this organization (its name cannot be revealed in order to protect its anonymity), the leaders originally developed the following mission (Figure 8–11).

MISSION

Our Mission is to be acknowledged as the leading provider of services for our target customer population. We will achieve a status as the market leader among our most critical customers and increase our market share by 3% per year over the next 7 years.

Our business will be national in scope, with a growing intensity in international markets. Our success will be measured in terms of:

- Overall satisfaction of our customers;

- Satisfaction of our employees;

- Growth in market share

- Profitability;

- Respect in the community.

Figure 8-11. Original mission statement.

At first glance, this mission may seem quite good. Initially, it looks comprehensive, far reaching, and well-worded. Upon closer scrutiny, however, I believe it is problematic. When people in the company were asked for their responses to this vision, they said things like the following:

"The mission needs clarity."

"The mission is not inspirational."

"The numbers are picked out of the hat. Are they relevant?"

In my mind, all of these criticisms are on target. In addition, my sense is that the mission is too comprehensive. It is saying, "we are going to climb six mountains all at the same time—market leader, customer satisfaction, employee satisfaction, market share, profitability, and respect in the community. Mission, like purpose, is intended to provide focus for people in the organization. This mission does the opposite. It tries to be all things to all people.

To help the organization clarify a more effective mission, the top management team decided to develop a set of criteria upon which they might measure the effectiveness of a mission statement. They felt the mission needed to:

- be organized around a customer focus;
- help them clarify what challenge they intended to meet;
- be based in reality;
- be simple and focused (not necessarily complete); and
- help them make tough choices.

In my estimation, these are excellent criteria.

They then brainstormed various possible missions. They put words on the board in short bursts, bearing in mind that it was important not to wordsmith, but rather to capture the spirit of their aims and aspirations.

They then selected from the list those few that seemed most compelling and relevant, and from these began creating a mission statement. After exploring a number of alternatives and applying the above criteria to help reduce the possibilities, here is what the organization arrived at (Figure 8–12).

While this is a not perfect example (no mission is), the organization that created it now has a much clearer

---

MISSION

We will be the top supplier of services in our target market areas in terms of overall customer satisfaction.

- We will measure our leadership in terms of our customers'

    Δ satisfaction of our services
    Δ loyalty
    Δ growth in use of services

- We will be seen as the supplier of choice among high-quality service providers and achieve a triple star rating among industry analysts by the year 1995.

Figure 8-12. Evolved mission statement.

sense of focus, and not surprisingly, people's response to this new mission is far more positive than it was to the initial one.

To create your own mission statement, consider the following guidelines.

Step One. Agree as a design team on what the criteria are for an excellent mission statement for your organization. Use examples given above as a guide.

Step Two. Using the criteria developed above, brainstorm some features of your mission. At this point, don't edit. Simply let the ideas flow.

Step Three. Winnow your list down to the few concepts that seem most compelling, attractive, and on target. Consider merging a couple of ideas if they seem strongly related.

Step Four. Take what's left and apply the criteria you developed in step one above. Drop out those features that do not seem to meet the criteria. Add others that help to meet the criteria.

Step Five. Weave what you have left into a statement that reflects your mission as you presently see it. Do not wordsmith.

Here are some abbreviated versions of mission statements that I think are excellent.

A utilities company: "to supply electricity and gas at the lowest long-term price to our customers."

A facilities department of a major university: "to supply the most timely, cost-effective services to the University community better than what is available through commercial vendors in the surrounding area."

A retail company: "we are committed to serving the business, social, and cultural needs of our communities, and to achieving levels of profitability equivalent to the leading firms in our industry."

A computer company: "our objective is to be, and be recognized as, the best, the leaders, in both technology and business."

A consulting firm: "to always be highly respected and regarded as the finest implementors of long-term, results-oriented management."

Analyze Your Organization. Any vision, in order for it to be realistic, needs to be tempered by the reality in which your organization exists. It needs to stretch the organization, but it also needs to build upon the foundation that is already there. Your vision will fall upon deaf ears unless it is tempered by an objective analysis of your reality.

For the next few days or weeks think about your organization's strengths and weaknesses. Use your organization's earlier assessment as a guide. In particular, pay attention to the following questions as they pertain to your organization. You might want to jot down some notes for yourself as you answer the following questions:

Observations About Your Organization:

1. What historically has been the thing that distinguishes our organization from our competitors? From others with a similar function?

2. Who are we as an organization? How would others characterize our organization? How would they describe our purpose?

3. What are our organization's most important strengths? When we have succeeded in the past, to what would I attribute that success?

4. What are our most glaring weaknesses? When we have failed in the past, to what organizational weaknesses would I attribute that failure? What reoccurring mistakes do we tend to make?

5. What do our customers want? What do they want more of? What do they want less of?

Observations about your environment:

1. What trends are most significant in shaping our industry?

2. What are our competitors doing? How should we respond to them? How are they gaining an advantage? What are the best companies in our industry doing that make a difference to our customers?

3. What do I predict will be our winning products and services five years from now? Ten years from now?

Mold Your Vision to Reflect Organizational Realities. Now go back and look at your vision thus far—your purpose and your mission. Make changes in these statements where the organizational realities make the vision impossible to achieve. Modify the vision without losing its essence.

Look at your purpose and mission once more and test their effectiveness by answering the following questions:

1. Would our vision make sense to someone familiar with your company, or in our industry?

2. Have we identified all the potential benefits and liabilities of our vision?

3. Is it clear what impact achieving our vision will have on our company? On our customers? On our people? On me?

4. Do I believe we can accomplish this vision? Will others believe in it?

Translate Vision into a Vision Statement. Vision statements can be written in many different ways. They can be written in prose form, they can be a laundry list of concepts, they can focus on vision, or they can focus on results. However the statement is molded, it is best to have at least three features: what you want to accomplish (mission), why you want to accomplish it (purpose), and what you expect the results to be. Take your purpose and mission and, as a design team, answer the following questions as you begin to mold your vision into a statement or set of statements that you want to make to your entire organization in order to clarify your future direction.

1. Why are we developing a vision at this time in our organization's life? What is calling for us to clarify our direction and shape our future?

2. What is our reason for being as an organization? What contributions are we making or intending to make? Why do you want to work towards this purpose? What makes this purpose compelling?

3. What specifically will we set our sights on accomplishing as an organization in the next few years? What is or what will be our mission?

4. How will we accomplish or move towards this mission? What ways will we work together? What processes need to be in place in order for our vision to work?

5. What results do we expect as a result of accomplishing our mission? How will we know when we are successful?

Now you want to work these answers into a powerful and compelling overall vision statement, one that is:

- colorful
- compelling
- concise

To do this, you may want to start off with a statement that talks about an opportunity. Why is this timely? What is moving you to want to clarify your vision now?

Then say *WHAT* your vision is. To make it colorful and compelling, you may want to use metaphors and analogies to make the vision graphic for people. Then say *HOW* you will move toward this vision and finally what *RESULTS* you intend to create. This order, of course, is not inviolable.

Make the statement flow in whatever way comes from the heart. Above all else, this is your vision. If you are excited about it, others will naturally follow it.

Test Your Vision Statement With Others. At this point, you will want to test to see whether others will find the vision as compelling as you and your design team do. Probably the best way to do this is to show it to a small handful of people whom you trust. Ask them what their reaction is. Does it seem compelling to them? Does it reflect their own vision of your organization? In particular, you will want to be sure to check it with the person you report to. After all, your mission must be an integral part of theirs. You will also want to check it with at least one peer, a couple of customers, and then finally some people in your organization. Use all their inputs to help you further your vision.

So What Do You Do With a Vision Statement?

A vision statement is not something to be put away in a drawer. To be of any value, it needs to be a living, breathing statement that is actively referred to and reinforced. The more it is communicated, the more it is reinforced by your actions, the more others will understand it and live it for themselves, and the more likely you will all accomplish that vision. Here are some ideas about what to do once you have developed your vision.

1. Put it on the walls of your organization so all may see it. Put it in all your public relations documents, and in collateral material as well. Shout it out proudly so that all may hear it. (If you are not proud of it, go back to the beginning and create one you are proud of.)

2. Remind people what your vision is every chance you get. Reinforce it through verbal and written communications.

3. Whenever there is a conflict, help people to resolve it by finding ways to work together that are consistent with the vision.

4. Whenever you develop a policy, relate that policy to the vision.

5. In a meeting where a difficult decision is being made, remind people of the overall purpose of your organization.

6. Never do anything unless it is clearly related to the organization's mission and purpose.

7. Prioritize your work in order of the degree that it helps you accomplish your organization's vision.

8. From time to time, step back and ask yourself and others, to what extent are we moving toward our vision?

9. Measure your progress in concrete ways. When movement occurs that is desirable, reinforce that movement. When it looks like the organization or its members are moving away from the vision, correct it quickly.

I have found that the creation of a vision is an excellent opportunity to look at areas in an organization where misalignment occurs. The optimal aim of a great vision is to align the organization around a shared direction. The single greatest obstacle to achieving your vision will likely be those areas where significant communication disconnections occur. One company I have worked with, for example, found that its greatest gaps were between the 600 top managers of the company and the rest of the 15,000 employees (see Figure 8–13). Another company found its greatest gaps were between union and nonunion members (Figure 8–14). Still a third found that it had severe splits between divisions (Figure 8–15).

In summary, *having a vision statement* does not differentiate excellent companies from pedestrian ones. It is

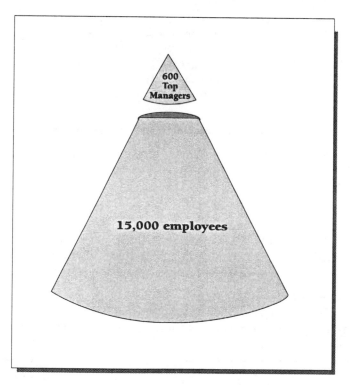

Figure 8-13. Gap between top management and rest of company.

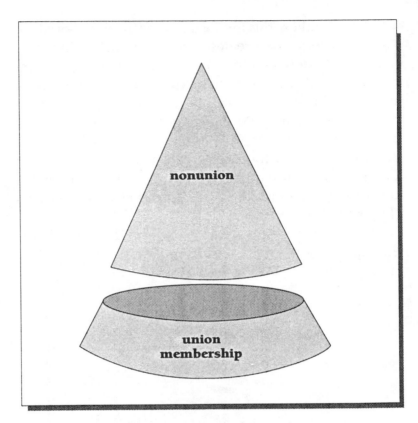

Figure 8-14. Gap between union and nonunion.

Exercise: Draw a picture of your organization. Identify the major communication disconnections. Who is the "in" group? Who is the "out" group? Where do communication gaps occur? Where does miscommunication occur?

Answers to these questions will yield a good understanding of where your vision will break down and where team building is needed to create a strong sense of alignment around your new vision.

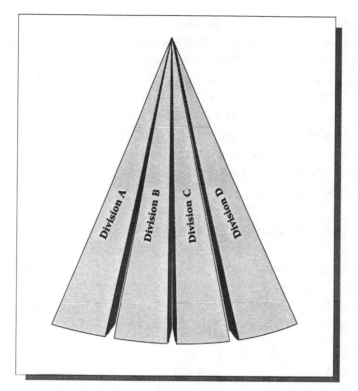

Figure 8-15. Gap between divisions.

those organizations that *live their vision on a daily basis* that are the true leaders in business.

THE MIND-SET OF A VISIONARY LEADER[21]

While the above gives a clear approach on how to go about creating and reinforcing a vision, it can also be misleading, for leadership is not just a set of actions, it is a way of being. It is not so much what leaders do that

---

[21] I am indebted to Tina Benson, whose thinking on leadership and an unpublished paper she wrote on the subject greatly influenced the ideas expressed below.

makes them great leaders. It is their attitude, values, and views that makes them great. Given this, it is not enough to explain how to generate and communicate a vision. As a leader, you must also think differently, like that of a visionary leader. By examining your values, and being willing to have the courage to stand up for your convictions, and then by following the guidelines above, you have a much greater chance for success. Here, then, are some thoughts about the mind-set of a visionary leader.

1. *Visionary Leaders Do Not Have Visions. They Are Their Vision.* Great leaders do not hold their vision as an idea outside of themselves. They live and breathe their vision. It permeates all they do. It is not something they need to be reminded of, nor is it something that needs to be expressed in words, for it envelopes them.

2. *Every Single Action of a Visionary Leader Is Driven by Their Vision.* They do not take action that is inconsistent with their vision. They feel the tug of their vision every day, in every moment. They have no time or energy to waste on activities that don't forward their vision.

3. *Visionary Leaders Declare Their Vision as a Fact and Then Collect Evidence.* When President Kennedy declared that we would have a man on the moon and returned by the end of the 1960s, he had no rational basis for making that claim. In fact, experts around him said that it was impossible. The technology did not exist for achieving that aim. He persevered nonetheless and, like a magnet, drew around him people who were willing to create the needed technology where none existed. Leaders believe "it's a done deal" and then make it so.

4. *Visionary Leaders Declare Their Vision Publicly, and are Willing to Accept Failure.* By declaring their vision publicly they put a stake in the ground and accept responsibility for their vision.

5. *Visionary Leaders Do Not Let Their Fear Get in the Way.* Most people think that leaders are those who are fearless. They are blinded by the "John Wayne" myth that leaders have no fears and are superhuman. This is absolutely not true. If you talk to almost any great leader, you will find they have fears just like the rest of us. Fears come with the game of high risks, a game all great leaders play. The difference between great leaders and the rest of us is not the absence of fear, but the unwillingness to allow their fears to stand in their way.

6. *Visionary Leaders Persevere.* Whenever one articulates a vision and commits him- or herself to that vision, barriers or obstacles to achieving that vision will naturally arise. Who ever said that great accomplishments are easy? If they were easy they would not be great. A truely great leader sees these obstacles as natural challenges along the path of achieving their vision. Their job is not to be sidetracked by the obstacles, but to overcome them.

7. *Visionary Leaders Do Not Have the Word "Problem" as Part of Their Vocabulary.* Problems or obstacles are merely challenges or opportunities to learn. Great leaders know that to view events as problems is to adopt a mindset that may create resistance. Instead, they view problems as opportunities and are motivated to take advantage of these opportunities.

8. *Visionary Leaders Have a Strong Belief in Themselves.* They are absolutely confident in their ability to find solutions to challenging situations. When they see situations that require action, they step forward. Their attitude is "if it is to be, it is up to me."

9. *Visionary Leaders Take Risks.* Great leaders take chances, they take unpopular stances, and are more committed to achieving their vision than being liked. When Christopher Columbus said the world was round, they almost locked him up. When Martin Luther King stood for equality, he faced enormous hatred and eventually death. A great leader's vision is far more important than their popularity or their desire to look good. They will do just about anything to achieve their vision.

10. *Visionary Leaders Don't Believe in Failure.* In the thinking of great leaders, there is no such thing as a failure. Failures are but temporary steps on the pathway to achieving their vision. To visionary leaders, there is also no such thing as a mistake, only opportunities to learn. Rather than fearing or avoiding mistakes, great leaders embrace them and look forward to the lessons that can be learned from them.

11. *Visionary Leaders Are Not Confined in Their Thinking by What Is Already Known.* They create new realities if the one presently existing does not work. That is not to say they make up information. They do not lie about facts or data, for these are critical. It is extremely difficult to achieve a future vision without have a strong awareness of current reality. They do, however, create new languages and new technologies to express new ways of thinking. Sigmund Freud created an entire language (unconscious, ego, self, etc.) to communicate his ideas. Our entire concept of the human being was revolutionized by his thinking (in spite of the whole medical community laughing at his ideas). Visionary leaders are not limited by what they find in front of them or what is told to them by others. They have the ability to see what others may pass by.

ARCHITECTING CHECKLIST

1. Vision draws the organization toward greatness. A powerful vision is one that is not crafted from the head, but from the heart.

2. The process of creating a vision can pull a company together.

3. Purpose, mission, and values are the key elements of many corporate vision statements.

4. There is no one perfect vision. The best vision is the one you are committed to.

5. It is not in the vision statement that makes a company great. It is in the enduring commitment and passionate desire to achieve the vision that distinguishes great companies from mediocre ones.

6. Never compromise your vision.

9

Building a High-Performance Culture

It is only with the heart that one can see rightly; what is essential is invisible to the eye.

—The Fox in *The Little Prince*

Every so often a concept comes along that is so powerful and so elegant that it wins the hearts and minds of American managers, and revolutionizes the way they think about their roles and their companies. In the early 1900s it was scientific management; in the 1960s it was human relations; in the 1970s, strategic management. In the 1980s it was the concept of corporate culture. Introduced in 1982 by Terrence Deal and Allan Kennedy in their seminal book *Corporate Cultures*,[1] and reinforced in *In Search of Excellence*,[2] the concept of corporate culture spread like wildfire. Soon the pages of every magazine and journal from *Newsweek* to the

---

[1] Deal, T. and Kennedy D., *Corporate Cultures: The Rites and Rituals of Corporate Life*. Addison Wesley, Reading, Mass., 1982.
[2] Peters, T. and Waterman, R., *In Search of Excellence: Lessons From America's Best-Run Companies*. Harper and Row, New York, 1982.

Harvard Business Review were crammed with articles describing the values, myths, and beliefs that distinguish one company from another. Today, while the concept has lost some of its luster, it remains an enduring way to both think about organizations and to discover new ways of making them even more effective.

While much has been written about the concept of corporate culture, there is still much confusion about it. Some authors suggest that a culture is a set of norms, values, and beliefs that vary from company to company. Others seem to suggest that a corporate culture is merely a reflection of many individual personalities. Still others define a corporate culture in terms of the rites, rituals, and myths of the corporation. Interestingly, the term "culture" is derived from social anthropology. Studies of different societies suggest that each society has a unique set of traditional qualities and characteristics that define both acceptable and unacceptable behavior. A society's "culture," to anthropologists, is that set of behavior patterns, accepted values, beliefs, myths, rituals, and artifacts that define the society and make it distinct from all others. In this chapter, we will define an organization's culture as the set of characteristics, behavior patterns, norms, and shared values of that company.

In their book on corporate culture, Deal and Kennedy assert that the culture of an organization has far more to do with the organization's performance than we ever considered before. They point out early in their book that "a major reason the Japanese have been so successful is their continuing ability to maintain a very strong and cohesive culture throughout the country."[3] Later

---

[3] Deal, T. and Kennedy D., *Corporate Cultures: The Rites and Rituals of Corporate Life*. Addison Wesley, Reading, Mass., 1982, page 5.

they demonstrate how "the people who built the companies for which America is famous all worked obsessively to create strong cultures within their organizations."[4] In short, they argue that the strength of the culture is a critical, or at least an essential, factor in determining an organization's success.

No statement could be more true. An organization's culture is its primary determinant of success. The culture defines the organization. It provides boundaries for knowing what is acceptable or unacceptable. In short, the culture of an organization subtly, yet powerfully, shapes people's behavior, their attitudes, and their beliefs. Too often, organizational leaders look to other features of the organization in order to affect change. If the organization is not producing results, they look to change the systems, the structure, the strategy, or the people, totally disregarding the powerful and all-encompassing nature of the culture and its impact on people's behavior. Changing the structure of an organization in a culture that is dysfunctional, for example, is like rearranging the deck chairs on the Titanic.

The view that an organization's culture directly impacts its results has been widely accepted among managers and organizational researchers for the past ten years, and little has emerged to refute this assumption. Since the early 1980s, numerous articles and books have appeared, each one giving anecdotal evidence to support the claim that an organization's culture determines its effectiveness.

Exciting new research has emerged recently that demonstrates the direct relationship between the

---

[4] Deal, T. and Kennedy, D., *Corporate Cultures: The Rites and Rituals of Corporate Life*. Addison Wesley, Reading, Mass., 1982, page 8.

strength of an organization's culture and its performance. In their book, *Corporate Culture and Performance,*
Kotter and Heskett studied 207 firms from 22 different
U.S. industries.[5] In their study, they measured the
strength of each company's culture and found that it related directly to corporate performance (see Figure 9–1).

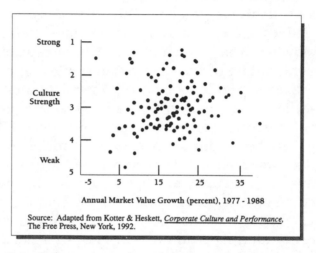

Figure 9-1. Culture strength and market value.

The relationship they found, however, was relatively
weak, suggesting that other factors also impacted corporate performance. Kotter and Heskett, in conducting
further research, found that strong cultures can sometimes become rigid and too slow to adapt to a rapidly
changing environment. They looked at firms with relatively strong cultures yet weak performance and found
that, almost without exception, these companies were
slow to change. One example is that of Tandem computers. Identified in Deal and Kennedy's book as a posi-

---

[5] Kotter, J. and Heskett, J. *Corporate Culture and Performance.* The Free Press,
New York, 1992.

tive example of a strong company culture, it has been struggling significantly in the past few years because it lacks the flexibility to respond to growing competition in the area of parallel computer processing. Another example is that of Wang Labs, described earlier. Wang Labs built its success on the basis of technological capability but was too slow to respond to changing market demands.

How a company becomes unadaptable is not easy to see at any given point in time. It can be seen, however, by looking at the process by which some companies evolve. As a given company becomes successful, its strategic direction, structure, and systems converge and coalesce over time and can become firmly fixed in place. Furthermore, over time, members of the organization develop patterns of behavior and habits that begin to take the form of rigid habits and beliefs. These self-reinforcing patterns of behavior contribute to a sense of complacency on one extreme, or rigidity and control on the other. Together, these forces conspire to make an organization incapable of adapting in a changing environment. Thus, an organization's success can easily sow the seeds for future failure.[6] Those companies that break the binds of early success are those that tend to achieve success in the future (see Figure 9–2).

Adaptability in a culture is not something that just evolves. It is something that is intentionally created by a leader willing to challenge the status quo. Companies, like societies, build in norms of behavior, norms which, when challenged, often get reinforced rather than changed. In the airline industry, for example,

---

[6] For an excellent discussion of this phenomenon, see Tushman, M., Newman, W., and Romanelli, E., "Convergence and Upheaval: Managing the Unsteady Pace of Organizational Evolution," in *California Management Review*, Vol. 29, Number 1, 1986, pp. 29–43.

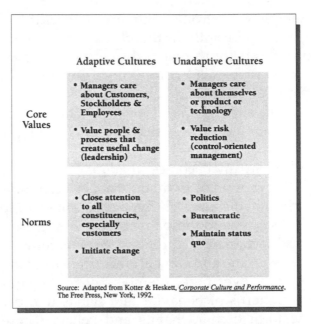

	Adaptive Cultures	Unadaptive Cultures
Core Values	• Managers care about Customers, Stockholders & Employees • Value people & processes that create useful change (leadership)	• Managers care about themselves or product or technology • Value risk reduction (control-oriented management)
Norms	• Close attention to all constituencies, especially customers • Initiate change	• Politics • Bureaucratic • Maintain status quo

Source: Adapted from Kotter & Heskett, *Corporate Culture and Performance*, The Free Press, New York, 1992.

Figure 9-2. Adaptable cultures yield highest performance.

when studies showed that customer satisfaction was important, many airlines sought to change the habits of pilots and asked them to greet the customers. For years, pilots refused, saying, in effect, "we're not going to meet customers, we're professionals." The norm of pilot separated from the milieu was viewed as inviolable. Eventually, declining profits, combined with persistent leadership, forced the hands of pilots, who, in spite of their constant resistance, have learned how to greet passengers with a warm smile and a friendly handshake. Many even show people the cockpit. (My son was shown the cockpit recently, and although he was not interested, I was fascinated. Truth be known, he is three years old and could care less. It was just an excuse for me to ask questions that I always wanted to have answered.) As a result, the experience of flying is, to many, a more enjoyable one.

The adaptability of a company's culture is one factor that impacts the effectiveness of the culture. Another factor is the fit between the culture and the company's environment. Kotter and Heskett called this "strategic appropriateness." To test this hypothesis, they measured the fit between the culture and its environment, and found that the twelve highest performers had the highest culture/environment fit. The ten lowest performers had the lowest culture/environment fit (Figure 9–3).

How does this misfit between culture and environment develop? Kotter and Heskett suggest that a fairly universal pattern exists. The company begins with some level of success. This is due early on to a good fit between the strategy of the company and the environment's demands. Over time, however, the culture becomes relatively rigid, while the environment changes. Competitors emerge, the expectations of customers change, or the economy changes, all of which suggest the need for a corresponding change in strategies. In unadaptive organizations, new strategies are not developed or are not successfully implemented in time, and

Industry	The Twelve Higher Performers	Culture/ Environmental Fit (7 = high, 1 = low)	The Ten Lower Performers	Culture/ Environmental Fit (7 = high, 1 = low)
Airlines	American	6.2	Northwest	3.7
Banking	Bankers Trust	6.5	Citicorp	3.0
Beverages	Anheuser-Busch	6.4	Coors	2.2
	PepsiCo	5.5		
Office Equipment & Computers	Hewlett-Packard	5.7	Xerox	3.8
Food	Con-Agra	6.4	Archer Daniels Midland	6.2
Oil	Shell	6.5	Texaco	2.6
Food & Drug Retailing	Albertsons	6.2	Winn-Dixie	3.0
Other Retailing	Dayton Hudson	4.4	J.C. Penney	4.1
	Wal-Mart	6.8		
Savings & Loan	Golden West	7.0	H.F. Ahmanson	5.0
Textiles	Springs Industries	5.3	Fieldcrest Cannon	3.6
	Mean	6.1	Mean	3.7

Source: Adapted from Kotter, J. & Heskett, J. *Corporate Culture and Performance*, The Free Press, New York, 1992.

Figure 9-3.   Culture/environment fit.

the culture becomes strategically inappropriate. As a result, overall performance deteriorates significantly. Again, the experience of Wang Labs is instructive. They held on to their proprietary software while the market was demanding industry-standard, open systems. In addition, they held on to their focus on the minicomputer, while the whole field of computers was moving more and more toward smaller personal computer-based systems. The inevitable consequence was that Wang Labs' performance rapidly deteriorated.

In short, effective corporate cultures have three distinct features:

- They are strong—the guidelines for behavior are clear and are regularly reinforced.
- They are strategically appropriate—there is a strong match between the culture and the environment.
- They are adaptable—they are flexible in a changing environment.

Part of the challenge in creating an effective culture is in finding the right mix between creativity, associated with independent thinking and action, and the efficiency and ability to change associated with collective effort. Too much independence yields chaos and internal conflict. Too much collective effort stifles creativity. In a high-performance culture, you want both. Too often, however, organizations and societies are too heavily weighted toward one extreme or the other. In companies in the United States, we tend to extol the virtues of individual freedom, yet have difficult mobilizing groups of people toward a shared cause. In companies in Japan, where collective action is paramount, they tend to suffer from lack of innovation. Interestingly, many organizations, in the face of this realization, seek a compromise between the two extremes. I think this limits the possibilities. Great organizations focus on a synergy between both values: creativity and individual freedom on the one hand and collective effort on the other. The great French Revolution of 1787 had as its motto: *Liberty, Equality, Fraternity*. Such a vision, I believe, reflects the aim of a high-performing organizational culture: the expression of individual freedom, the importance of honoring and valuing all people, and the spirit of teamwork and collective effort (see Figure 9–4).

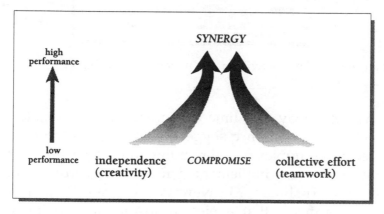

Figure 9-4. The synergy of creativity and teamwork.

How do you create an effective culture? The evidence suggests that it is not at all easy. In fact, there is much to suggest that of all the five key dimensions of an organization's architecture, culture is by far the most difficult to change. This makes very good sense, given that strong cultures take time to emerge. Therefore, the stronger the culture, the more difficult it is to change. Kotter and Heskett, for example, demonstrate that, for large companies, it takes as much as ten years, sometimes even more, to significantly change its culture (see Figure 9–5).

Firm	Size When Change Initiated	Length of Major Cultural Change Effort
General Electric	Very large	10 years and continuing
ICI		6 years
Nissan		6 years and continuing
Xerox		7 years
Bankers Trust	Large	8 years
First Chicago		10 years
American Express TRS		6 years
British Airways		4 years
SAS	Medium	4 years
ConAgra		4 years

Source: Adapted from Kotter, J. & Heskett, J., *Corporate Culture and Performance*, The Free Press, New York, 1992.

Figure 9-5. Time taken to affect major cultural change.

While it may take time for an organization's culture to change, experience suggests that some of the more effective examples of redesigning an organization's architecture were implemented rapidly. According to a study by Tushman, M., Newman, W., and Romanelli, E., "it appears that a piecemeal approach to frame-breaking changes gets bogged down in politics, individual resistance to change, and organizational inertia."[7] Because of its inherently risky and uncertain nature, and because of the intensity of global competition in most industries, a total redesign effort executed swiftly and aggressively will have far greater chance for success than a piecemeal effort.

Now we can see why one must have a clear plan of attack in order to change a culture. My own experience with companies leads me to conclude that it takes three

---

[7] Tushman, M., Newman, W., and Romanelli, E., "Convergence and Upheaval: Managing the Unsteady Pace of Organizational Evolution," in *California Management Review*, Vol. 29, Number 1, 1986, p. 10 of reprint series.

key elements to intentionally change a culture in a positive direction:

- A clear *vision* of the kind of culture you want to create.
- A clear *plan* for creating the necessary changes, based on a strong understanding of the dynamics of systems change.
- *Courage* to carry out the changes in the face of potentially strong resistance.

Few leaders have all of these capabilities, yet I agree with Kotter and Heskett, who state that "the single most visible factor that distinguishes major cultural changes that succeed from those that fail is competent leadership at the top."[8] Given that few leaders have the kind of leadership capabilities to impact large cultural change, few organizations successfully change their cultures to meet rapidly changing environmental demands.

There are examples, however, of organizational cultures that have successfully changed. General Electric, under the leadership of Jack Welch, has been enormously successful in shifting its culture. Nissan has been in the process of changing its culture, with seemingly significant success. AT&T has had some striking success of late. All of these efforts suggest that cultural change is not only possible, but no company is immune from the need to change its culture at some point in time.

Transforming, renewing, or changing an organization's culture requires no less than total attention to the following features of the organization:

---

[8] Adapted from Kotter, J. and Heskett, J. *Corporate Culture and Peformance*, The Free Press, New York, 1992, p. 105.

- The organization's *purpose*
- The organization's *values*
- The organization's *norms* of behavior
- The organization's *systems and policies* that reinforce the culture

Together these factors comprise the most critical features of the organization that impact on its culture. The organization's *purpose,* as described in the prior chapter, is its "reason for being." Distinct from its objectives, the purpose of the organization is why it is in existence. The organization's *values* are the stated principles that guide people's behavior and define the ideals the company aspires to. The organization's *norms* are the codes of acceptable behavior that have emerged over time to tell people how to handle different situations appropriately and how to interact effectively. And the *systems and policies*—such as the performance management system, the salary policies, and information systems—dictate what people pay attention to. To change your culture, you must be willing to examine and impact each of these separate factors.

Because changing a culture is not easy, and because of the unique aspects of every different culture, I strongly recommend that if you intend to change your culture, you hire an experienced consultant to help you. This step is often necessary for at least two reasons: it is hard to see one's own culture from within, and changing a culture often requires a willingness to confront the present culture. An outside consultant can be extremely helpful in both of these areas. Let's explore these dynamics in more detail.

The nature of a culture is that it is very difficult to see one's own culture in action. We rarely question, for example, the appropriateness of being direct and upfront in giving someone corrective feedback, yet in

Japan this process can often be seen as insensitive, indelicate, and arrogant. We don't even see that being direct and up-front is part of our cultural assumptions or norms. It is simply a part of how we in North America operate. Culture, like water to a fish, is essentially invisible. Because it is so familiar to us, it recedes into the background of our awareness.

How the familiar recedes into the background came home clearly to me a few months ago. My wife and I recently moved into a new house. I was in charge of setting up the waterbed in our master bedroom. I was so exhausted from the overall move, that I did a fairly sloppy job of putting the bed in the right place. Without being careful, I put the bed on a visible angle to the wall and proceeded to fill it up with water. My wife came into the room and was aghast at the poor job that I had done. We debated whether to let all the water out and start all over again, but since we were in the middle of a drought in the San Francisco Bay area, we elected to leave it as I had set it up.

After a couple of days of feeling disappointed, we both accepted the fact that our bed would be on an angle. Months later, I remembered that I had originally put the bed on an angle, and was struck by the fact that I never once noticed it since then. I mentioned this fact to my wife, and she too said that she never saw it on an angle anymore. Either the bedroom had shifted significantly (in earthquake-ridden San Francisco, I don't rule out this possibility) or else we had grown so accustomed to the bed's placement that it receded into the background of our awareness.

The same is true of culture. Our cultural norms are so familiar and so assumed that we no longer see them. An outside consultant, however, is far better able to see the existing culture and some of its counterproductive features than can any of the insiders.

In addition, because our cultures are such a part of us, and so familiar to us, they are often hard to change. We believe (and it is often true) that they are a big reason for our success. "This is the way we do things here," is often the justification for holding on to our approach to the way we operate. It is difficult to let go of whatever we believe in. To change a culture often requires confronting the culture (and therefore the people within the culture) and saying, in effect, "What you are doing is not working." An outside consultant, without any axes to grind, can be a useful aid in challenging the counterproductive features of the existing culture.

Ultimately, of course, it is still up to the leadership of the organization, and the people within it, to change their culture. The steps to successfully transforming a culture are shown in Figure 9–6. Let's take each of these steps one at a time.

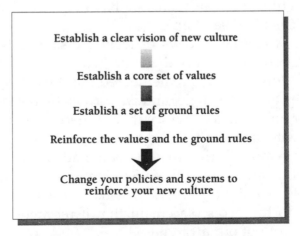

Figure 9-6. Steps toward transforming your culture.

ESTABLISH A CLEAR VISION OF YOUR NEW CULTURE

Creating a vision of your culture is, in effect, the act of looking into the future and articulating what you want your culture to look like. As described in Chapter 8, a good vision is clear, concrete, and compelling. To help you create your new vision, pull together your design team and ask them individually to answer the following questions:

1. Imagine that your organization's culture is now exactly the way you would want it to be. What would it feel like? How would people behave in your company? Would people be adaptive? Would everyone behave in a uniform fashion? Would people be open and honest? Would people be polite? Write your thoughts here.

_____

_____

_____

_____

_____

_____

_____

_____

_____

2. When you as a company have done your best work in the past, what qualities characterized your personal interactions? (An example of what some people report

here is that people are both direct and honest with one another and at the same time sensitive to each others' needs.)

_____

_____

_____

_____

_____

_____

_____

_____

3. Think about your organization's external environment. What kind of organizational qualities are critical for being effective as an organization in your current environment?

_____

_____

_____

_____

_____

_____

_____

_____

4. Some organizations and the people within them tend to communicate more effectively through visual means than they do with words. If you are more comfortable in this mode of communication, draw a picture, without words, that depicts the kind of organization that you want to see in terms of how people relate to one another.

5. Now take each of the above four inputs and write below some words or phrases that capture your personal view of the kind of culture you want your organization to have.

_____

_____

_____

_____

_____

_____

_____

_____

_____

Now gather up all these inputs from each individual on your design team, and on a flip chart transcribe what was described by each individual in Step Five. Then step back as a group and look for areas of commonality. Are there similarities? Are there differences? Are these differences insurmountable? If so, what would explain so many differences? Compare your overall list with the list of characteristics below that research has shown are common to most effective organizational cultures.

- An attitude of openness to others' ideas
- A respect for differences
- A strong ability to adapt and change
- Personal honesty and integrity
- A strong emphasis on teamwork
- A strong sense of community

If your list does not have at least some of these features, consider the possibility that you are envisioning an organization that may not be optimal as a culture. On the other hand, if you come up with significant differences, and the environment or market in which your company lives warrants these differences, you may be on the right track.

Regardless of whether or not you have included some of the above features on your list, come to an agreement as a group on your overall vision of the ideal organization for your company. If you have difficulty achieving consensus, discuss as a group how best to proceed in light of the lack of agreement. Talking about the differences and finding ways to bridge those differences will be important for they likely represent differences that exist throughout the company. Remember that in the case of developing your culture, while uniformity of agreement is not critical, having a strong shared commitment to creating a culture certainly is. So continue to work together until you have reached consensus.

ESTABLISH A CORE SET OF VALUES

Once you have a vision of your culture, it is time to flesh it out and be specific in articulating your values. Almost all strong and effective cultures are actively driven by a commitment to a core set of values. Values are the principles that guide behavior. These become the foundation and conscience of the organization. Values like "honesty," "respecting one another," "the customer comes first," and "openness to learning" are more than mere platitudes. They distinguish the pretty good companies from the ones we respect the most. If you are interested in creating a strong, viable organizational culture, go through a process of value clarification. To do this, I have found the following procedure works well:

1. First, as individuals, imagine you are on your death bed and thinking about the things you want to be best remembered for. What are some of those things?

_____

_____

_____

_____

_____

_____

_____

2. As you look at these qualities or characteristics or actions, think about the values that these qualities reflect. Write below the values that underlie them. (For example, one of the things I want to best be remembered for is how much I cared for others. When all is said and done, I want to be known as a loving husband and father, and someone who was always sensitive to the needs of others. I think the value that underlies this is love and care for others.) State them in value-laden terms like honesty, care for others, commitment.

_____

_____

_____

_____

_____

_____

3. Based on the above, what are the top five values that you hold as a person and as a leader in your company? A value is a principle to guide behavior. Remember, you do not have to live these values at all times to aspire to them. At this point you are articulating what you aspire towards, as opposed to how you live on a daily, moment-by-moment basis. Next to each value write what that value means to you.

Value: What that value means to me:

I. _____   _____

                          _____

II. _____   _____

                          _____

III. _____   _____

_____

IV. _____   _____

_____

V. _____   _____

_____

4. Take each individual's input and put them on flip charts. Post them around the room. Then have the group look around and get a sense of where there is a merging of shared values. When you think they are ready, ask the group to articulate what they think are the values that are shared by the members of the design team. Using whatever technique makes most sense, winnow the overall list to select the four to six values that seem to be the most critical and are shared by all.

5. Take this list of critically shared values and construct a page for each one that specifies the value and what it means to you as a group. Do not try to wordsmith this statement perfectly. Rather, capture the essence of what people are feeling. Figures 9–7 and 9–8 demonstrate examples of values statements that two companies noted for their enduring success have written.

6. Now have each member of the design team share this set of values statements with their direct reports. Ask each design team member to explain the purpose of the values and to ask their direct reports and/or their peers for feedback regarding whether or not these values are shared by the next layer of the organization, and what changes, if any, would they recommend. Continue this process on down to the next level in your organization, if appropriate. (Note: As your design

HEWLETT PACKARD'S VALUES

HP's values are a set of deeply held beliefs that govern and guide our behavior in meeting our objectives and in dealing with each other, our customers, shareholders, and others.

- *We have trust and respect for individuals.*

- *We focus on a high level of achievement and contribution.*

- *We conduct our business with uncompromising integrity.*

- *We achieve our common objectives through teamwork.*

- *We encourage flexibility and innovation.*

Source: *The H-P way*, official company document.

Figure 9-7. Hewlett-Packard's values.

team members discuss these values with others, they need to be prepared for skepticism. Often, when others see a list of values that the company violates from time to time, they will see them as unrealistic. Often I hear people say something like: "How can you say these are our values. We don't behave this way." It is important to listen openly and without defensiveness to this feedback and also to remind people that the purpose of the values statement is not to reflect our present behavior, but to draw us toward desired behaviors. This will often shift the reaction from one of skepticism to one of hope.)

LEVI STRAUSS & CO.
ASPIRATIONS STATEMENT

What type of leadership is necessary to make our Aspirations a Reality?

New Behaviors:
> Leadership that exemplifies directness, openness to influence, commitment to the success of others, willingness to acknowledge our own contributions to problems, personal accountability, teamwork, and trust.

Diversity:
> Leadership that values a diverse work force (age, sex, ethnic group, etc.) at all levels of the organization, diversity in experience, and diversity in perspectives.

Recognition:
> Leadership that provides greater recognition — both financial and psychic — for individuals and teams that contribute to our success.

Ethical Management Practices:
> Leadership that epitomizes the stated standards of ethical behavior.

Communications:
> Leadership that is clear about company, unit, and individual goals and performance.

Empowerment:
> Leadership that increases the authority and responsibility of those closest to our products and customers.

Source: Levi Strauss & Co

Figure 9-8. Levi's values.

7. Take all the inputs from the next layer(s) of the organization on down and revise the values statement as appropriate.

8. Take this semifinal version, invite further feedback, and construct the final statement.

9. Make a public commitment as a group to these chosen values.

> Commitment means jumping off a cliff and building your wings along the way.
>
> —Anonymous

ESTABLISH A SET OF GROUND RULES

Once you have articulated and agreed upon on a set of values, it is time to put them into operation by being explicit about the kind of behavior you want to reinforce in your new corporate culture. For this purpose, a set of ground rules or behavioral guidelines is particularly useful. They may flow directly from the above values, or they may stand alone as a set of guidelines for the organization. These ground rules will create or reinforce the kinds of norms you want all the members of the organization to adopt and to abide by in their daily working lives. Ground rules are desired guidelines like:

We will:
- only make commitments to our customers that we will keep
- communicate honestly, openly, and directly
- focus on the bigger picture
- play team at the highest level
- have fun

Notice that while these ground rules are not specific enough to tell you exactly what to do in every situation, they are more specific than values, and they provide guidelines for making choices. For example, if given the choice, the above ground rules say to be open and honest in raising issues, rather than to hold back and protect oneself or another person. While we may individually disagree about what "open and honest" might look like, we aspire to be that way. To create effective ground rules or behavioral guidelines, I have found the following process to be particularly effective:

1. As a design team, brainstorm a list of ground rules you would like to see everyone use to guide their daily behavior in the organization. When you do brainstorming, do not evaluate or disagree. Allow the creative juices to flow freely.

2. Take the overall list and eliminate any redundant or similar items. If two items look about the same, eliminate one of them, or integrate both of them into a single new phrase.

3. Ask the group to vote on which of these proposed ground rules they like the most and are most directly related to the organization's values. A simple method to use for this process is to give each person a total of six votes with the instruction that they are to distribute one vote to each of the six ground rules they like the best. Tally up the total of all of the votes and determine which ground rules have received the most votes.

4. Discuss the ground rules that got the most votes, and as a group, agree on a final list of six to nine ground rules. I have found that more than nine makes them difficult to remember, while less than six may not be encompassing enough for your organization.

5. As you did above with values, have each member of the design team share this proposed set of ground rules with their direct reports and/or peers and invite feedback regarding whether or not these ground rules are shared by them, and what changes, if any, they would recommend. Continue this process down to the next level if appropriate.

6. Take the inputs from the next layer(s) of the organization and revise the ground rules as appropriate. It is now appropriate to wordsmith the statement, for you are close to a final version.

7. Take this semifinal version, invite further feedback, and construct the final statement.

8. Make a public commitment as a group to these ground rules.

REINFORCE THE VALUES AND THE GROUND RULES

Too often I have seen elegant and carefully crafted values statements on the walls of corporations throughout the United States and heard that people within the company complain bitterly that these statements are empty, because people, particularly the leaders, do not behave in accordance with them. Indeed, according to Robert Levering, co-author of the book, *The 100 Best Companies to Work For*, over half of all U.S. companies have a values statement, more than double the number he saw years ago.[9] Yet many if not most of these companies do

---

[9] Farnham, A., "State Your Values, Hold the Hot Air," in *Fortune*, April 19, 1993, pp. 117–124

not approach living consistent with them. Says Andrall Pearson, former president of a large U.S. industrial company now teaching at the Harvard Business School, the gap between a company's espoused values and actually living them is "the largest single source of cynicism and skepticism in the workplace today."[10]

While there will always be a few disgruntled employees in large corporations, the frequency of such complaints is sobering. I believe there are two dynamics involved in making this situation happen:

1. By publicly declaring these values and ground rules, the company is inviting closer scrutiny. Had management said nothing, there would be no perceived gap between the commitment and the actual behavior.

2. There is always a significant gap between our stated values and ground rules and our actual behavior.

The purpose of declaring values and ground rules is neither to pretend to perfection, nor is it to invite criticism. Rather, the purpose of the declaration is to challenge the organization to aspire toward and behave consistently in a way that will help transform the culture over time. Naturally, there will be many instances where people do not behave consistently with these published values and ground rules. After all, if there were no gap, the culture of the organization would already be transformed. Therefore, the close scrutiny will be valuable, productive, and often quite sobering.

Cultures have a natural tendency to persist, in spite

---

[10] Farnham, A., "State Your Values, Hold the Hot Air."

of our well-meaning efforts to change them. Like the movement of rivers, they are powerful drifts. If you do not focus on and support the desired new behaviors, the organization will likely revert to its old behavior patterns. To support people in shifting their behavior and the culture, the leaders of the organization need to model the values and behaviors they seek to engender in others, and to find ways of reinforcing new and desired behaviors. By modeling, I mean that the leaders need to exhibit behaviors consistent with the behaviors they seek in others. This does not have to be demonstrative acts. On the contrary, demonstrative acts and inflated platitudes often are not seen as real. Rather, it is in the relatively unobtrusive acts and mundane daily behaviors that people see the new, desired behaviors as real. Some examples of mundane behavior that, when taken together, can have a great impact are:

- asking questions
- in meetings
- in how one manages one's calendar
- through stories and humor
- in day-to-day interactions
- in luncheon gatherings
- surprise get-togethers designed to appreciate a small success

In addition, it helps to highlight positive examples of the desired behaviors in others and to acknowledge them accordingly. In this way, positive role models and examples serve to reinforce and support the desired change. For this, both feedback and informal reward mechanisms will be valuable in helping you to reinforce what you want to see in the future.

Feedback. Early on in the process of reinforcing a new culture, feedback is critical. The purpose of feedback is both to remind people in the organization of the importance of the new behaviors, and to help them get a sense of how well they are doing in relationship to the desired new behaviors. I have found that if you do not structure feedback sessions for this purpose, people will slowly drift back to their old ways of behaving.

One way of structuring feedback is to, on a regular basis, have each work unit or department (groups of five to nine work well) meet with another, and give and receive feedback from one another as a group. Here's an effective way to set this feedback process up:

1. Agree on the ground rules for the feedback process. In particular, emphasize the importance of open, honest feedback, and a supportive attitude.

2. Have each person in each work unit or department fill out a sheet giving each other person in that group feedback on a scale of 1–10, where 1 is low and 10 is the highest possible. Be sure to have people fill out each other's sheets without looking at what others have already written so that the feedback is truly from one person to another.

3. After each person has filled out all the sheets, ask for a volunteer to go first in receiving feedback. This person then shares with the group his or her total scores and asks the group to elaborate on whatever areas the person receiving the feedback wants to understand better. One at a time, each person in the group gives the selected person feedback and communicates both their sense of where the person is strong and where they can improve. The form of communication that seems to work best is something like the following:

"I see you as particularly strong in the
following _____ ground rule" (be specific and
give examples)

"I think you can be more effective in _____
by _____" (be specific and give examples)

4. It is important that the person receiving the feedback
does not respond in any way, either to agree or to disagree. Each person may want to explain, defend, or
deny what they hear, but this will only inhibit their
ability to receive and integrate the group's feedback.
They should only listen carefully, and if something is
not clear, ask for a clarification. Other than that, the
norm should be "no response," except for a "thank
you" at the end. It is helpful to have someone else in
the group take notes for the person receiving the feedback so that his or her attention can be purely on listening. (An alternative to this process is to do a
feedback mingle, where people pair up and exchange
feedback. Continue the pairing process until each person has met with every other person in the group and
given and received everyone's feedback.)

5. Have each person in the group take a turn much like
the first person who volunteered until everyone in the
group has received all the feedback.

6. After each has received feedback, ask the person to
write down some of the most salient comments they
heard, and identify one or two areas in particular to
work on and improve. After all the feedback has been
given and received, take a few minutes and ask each
person to craft a development plan for his or her own
improvement. This plan should be specific for each person as to what the behavior is that they want to change,
what their desired behavior is to be, and how they will

change their behavior. The more specific each person can be, the better.

7. Have each person in the group share with the other members the key points he or she heard and what his or her development plan looks like. At this time, it is helpful to invite response and/or support from others. This way, everyone in the group will be reinforcing everyone else's new behavior.

A second, and extremely valuable, way of structuring feedback is to introduce into your performance review process a section on values and ground rules, and, if you use performance evaluations to determine salaries, to assign a percentage of each person's performance evaluation to their effectiveness in living according to the values and ground rules of the company. In New York City, where many of my friends grew up, this process is known as "putting your money where your mouth is." I have seen companies assign as much as 25 percent of their performance evaluation to the degree to which a person exemplifies (or does not exemplify) the values and ground rules of the organization. While you may choose to put less emphasis on this aspect of performance evaluations, the mere step of assigning a value and evaluating people on it sends a strong positive message that you and others are serious about creating a new and more healthy and productive culture.

While I believe very strongly that living the values should be a part of performance reviews as a way to highlight their importance and give feedback, at the risk of contradicting myself, let me point out that I am growing increasingly ambivalent about using performance evaluations as a basis for determining salaries. Connecting these two tends to create or reinforce internal competition, and it does not recognize the fact that variation between employees often has more to do with forces outside employees' control than their own skill level or capability. There are alternatives, ones that a growing number of companies are exploring. These include paying everyone within the same job level or category the same, increasing their pay based on group performance, while at the same time continuing to give people feedback and guidance to support their growth, development, and increased effectiveness.[11]

CHANGE YOUR POLICIES AND SYSTEMS TO REINFORCE YOUR NEW CULTURE

This last feature of changing your organization's culture is perhaps the single most critical of all. Too often organizations have great plans and intentions for having an effective, high-performing culture, but their internal policies and systems work against them. A simple and all-too-common example of this situation is a company that stresses the importance of teamwork, yet has a performance evaluation system that focuses on individual contributions. Even worse, they may have a performance evaluation system that evaluates and pays people based on a predetermined distribution, or using what is known as "forced ranking." It used to be that people believed this form of personnel evaluation motivated people and promoted excellence. While that may be true for some, for most people it reinforces an over-

---

[11] See Scholtes, P. "An Elaboration on Deming's Teachings on Performance Appraisal," in *Performance Appraisal: Perspectives on a Quality Management Approach.* Ed. by McLean, G., et al., University of Minnesota Training and Development Research Center and American Society for Training and Development, Alexandria, Va., 1990.

emphasis on individual contribution and promotes competition within a company. Moreover, this form of evaluation tends to put too much focus on the achievement of goals and not enough on the process one uses to achieve them. There are alternative ways to determine salaries, such as pay based on knowledge, pay based on responsibilities, or pay based on team or organizational results. These alternatives are growing in their popularity and seem to go hand in hand with greater teamwork and a greater focus on company needs as a whole.[12]

Without change in the systems and policies to support and reinforce your new organizational culture, your new culture will not last. This is because systems and policies are in part designed to impact decisions, influence choices, and affect behavior. Consider, for example, the way you use your information systems. If you are inundating your executives with information at a highly detailed level about operational issues that are most germane to the workers and their supervisors, you will draw your executives towards micromanagement. Overviews and executive summaries, combined with details when relevant, tend to help executives focus on the broader, long-range issues.

There are at least four major systems that have significant impact on the quality and the nature of an organization's culture: human performance systems, information systems, financial systems, and physical plant and office layout.

---

[12] See O'Dell, C. and McAdams, J. "The Revolution in Employee Rewards," *Management Review*, March 1987 (pp. 30–34) for an excellent report on the growing interest in alternative pay systems based on a study jointly conducted by the American Productivity and Quality Center and the American Compensation Association.

The human performance systems have to do with performance management and reward systems. If, for example, you seek to develop greater teamwork within your new culture, it would be best to reinforce teamwork in performance feedback sessions, and in what you reward.

Information systems have to do with how, when, and with whom information is shared throughout your organization. If, for example, you want to promote a strong sense of ownership and commitment throughout your organization, it is best to share openly all critical information with all your employees.

Financial systems have to do with how you keep track of money, how you budget, where it is coming from, where it is going, and how decisions will be made from that information. If, for example, you want to empower employees to make decisions that are in the best interests of the organization as a whole, sharing financial results on a regular basis will promote a larger focus on the part of your people.

Physical layout has to do with how your physical space is organized and the condition it is in. If, for example, you want to promote open communication and teamwork, do not put up walls to divide people up into groups. Create more open physical spaces instead.

While developing effective management systems and policies are not within the scope of this book, it would be well worth the reader's while to look at the systems and policies of his or her organization and, for each of them, examine the degree to which they either reinforce or inhibit the desired new culture. If they tend to inhibit, change them. If there are only a few that reinforce your new culture, consider creating a few new ones to help support your new organizational aims.

Here are some questions for you to consider:

1. Look at your financial reporting systems. Do they provide information fully and completely to all people in the company, or do you withhold key financial information out of mistrust?

2. Look at your reward systems. What kinds of behaviors do you reward? Do you reward individual accomplishment or team accomplishment?

3. Look at who you promote and who you don't promote. What message are you sending in your promotion policies? Are you reinforcing the kinds of behaviors your new culture needs to have?

4. Look at your management information systems. What information is collected and provided? How does that influence your culture?

5. What is your policy about dealing with customer complaints? Does it take forever for a customer to experience satisfaction in response to a problem? What message do you send to your customers by the way you as a company relate to them?

6. How does your salary system impact your culture? What messages do you send your people from the way your salary system is designed and implemented? Do people get raises automatically or due to their improved performance? What does that say to your employees about your culture?

To change the policies and systems of an organization requires painstaking examination of everything you do, and a willingness to alter your approach to create your new culture. The above questions highlight only a few of the many areas you will want to look at and perhaps change as you create your new organizational culture. To do a more complete job of changing your systems and policies, I recommend that you assign a committee of people to oversee the process. This committee should be made up of people who have both the responsibility for the policies and systems and also have the ability to authorize changes. Have the committee organize an effort where a team from each part of your company that is involved in creating or upholding policies and systems goes through all of their official policy statements as well as their supporting systems, and analyze each in terms of the degree to which they reinforce or conflict with your organization's purpose, values, and ground rules.

Have them come to the committee with their analyses and recommendations for appropriate changes to reinforce the new culture. Then, as a committee, authorize the changes you deem to be most effective and thank the teams for their efforts.

Know that the above process of changing the culture, including all of the systems and policies within it, is not easy. Nor will it happen overnight. The commitment and courage it will take you to alter or transform your organization's culture is huge, and not for the faint at heart. If you do choose to embark on this task, however, the rewards are often far greater than the time spent and well worth it.

ARCHITECTING CHECKLIST

1. Anecdotal evidence of the relationship between corporate culture and performance has new been substantiated with some valuable research.

2. The culture of an organization has a powerful impact on the actions and behaviors of people in that organiza-

tion. It impacts, to a large extent, how people think and how people approach decisions and problem solving.

3. There are three criteria for an effective organizational culture: strength, adaptability, and appropriate match with the environment.

4. The key to a strong and adaptable culture is one that is driven by values and reinforced by the leadership of the organization.

5. To create a strong and viable culture, create a set of values and ground rules, and reinforce these consistently and without reservation.

10

Clarifying Your
Strategic Direction

*Business more than any other occupation is a continual dealing
with the future; it is a continual calculation, an instinctive
exercise in foresight.*

—Henry R. Luce

In spite of a proliferation of research, books, training programs, and materials on strategic thinking and planning, there is an enormous amount of confusion in some organizations about what a strategy is, and how it ought to be used. Said one CEO of a large industrial firm, "Our strategy is to be the number one provider of products in our industry." Said another CEO in a Fortune 500 company, "Our strategy is to be the top price/performance leader in our industry. We aim to provide the best performance at the lowest cost, bar none." *In most cases, these are not strategies!* They are extremely broad goal statements. A goal is *what* you want to attain, a strategy is *how* you will attain it. Even though corporate executives are knowledgeable and experienced people, they often confuse the two concepts, thereby adding confusion for the rest of the company as to what the company's strategy is.

At the same time, there is confusion among people about what a strategy is and an enormous difference among experts about how to devise a strategy. Options abound, ranging from time-intensive, quantitatively derived long-term strategic plans, such as the portfolio approach conducted by the Boston Consulting Group, to the competitive analysis methodology advocated by Michael Porter, down to relatively short-term analyses of industry trends and organizational strengths and weaknesses. To add to the confusion, each expert claims that theirs is the best way to devise a winning strategy. Whichever particular method is recommended, however, depends heavily on the biases and assumptions of the practitioner. Faced with this morass of confusion, you, the leader of an organization, still have to figure out how much effort to spend in determining strategy, and which method to use.

In spite of the confusion surrounding what the most effective strategic planning process is, or ought to be, companies are still in love with the idea. Most Fortune 500 companies have a strategic planning department that develops reams of paper on product strategy and product positioning. Indeed, many live (or die) by their strategic plans. What we have here is a problem of overuse.

The problem began in the late sixties and early seventies when numerous companies, each one following the guidance of consulting firms such as the Boston Consulting Group, invested huge sums of money in strategic planning with the belief that this would give them an edge over their competitors. Many of the analyses were based on a "portfolio" approach to business strategy, where the consulting firm conducts a market share/market growth matrix to determine how the client-company can gain the largest market share with respect to its competition.

There are at least six difficulties with most traditional strategic planning processes, rendering them relatively ineffectual in today's business climate.

1. First of all, a "growth for growth's sake" strategy is no longer a guarantee of success. Witness the number of monolithic companies like IBM or Digital Equipment Corporation, whose sheer size is rendering them unadaptable to the rapidly changing conditions of the marketplace.

2. Companies following the advice of the growth-strategy model tend to make acquisitions solely for financial reasons, and end up spreading themselves too thin. No longer is diversification a guarantee of financial stability. In some cases, it guarantees ruin.

3. Much of strategic analysis being done is based on present market conditions, so it provides little help in determing how to shape the business for the future.

4. Much of the advice of strategic consultants falls on deaf ears as it is either overly ambitious in nature or too rational for the tastes of quick decision makers. To follow the recommendations of the strategic planners often requires making enormous organizational changes, committing a company to a strategy that will likely need to be changed in only one to two years time. The more entrenched the solution, the less realistic it is in a changing environment.

5. Even if the leadership of the organization was prepared in principle to implement the strategic plan, a strategy is no good if the rest of the organization does not fundamentally believe in it. I have seen many strategic plans collect dust on the bookshelf from lack of commitment to its implementation. Said Robert Haas, CEO of Levi Strauss, reflecting on a past failed strategic effort, "We had a strategy in the late 1970s and early 1980s that emphasized diversification. We acquired companies, created new brands, and applied our traditional brand to different kinds of apparel. Our people did what they were asked to do, but the problem was, they didn't believe in it."[1] Part of the reason why people in organizations do not believe in the strategy is that they did not participate in its creation and therefore feel little ownership for its implementation. A decision without implementation is worse that no decision at all for it ties up a great deal of the organization's time.

6. Finally, while the advice of the consultants may be sound from a rational point of view, few organizations are in a position to change their organization to fit the strategy. To change an organization, one needs to do more than just develop an appropriate strategy. One needs to develop a way to change the organization structure, its policies, and sometimes its whole philosophy of management. This is an enormous task, one that many organizational leaders shy away from.

Given these problems with traditional forms of strategic planning, it is no wonder that so many companies develop formal planning strategies that never see the light of day.

The key to a good strategy is that it is developed not by a group of planners whose sole job it is to analyze competitors, industry trends, and customer needs, but

---

[1] Quoted in an interview by Robert Howard, *Harvard Business Review*, Vol. 68, No. 5, September–October 1990, p. 134.

by a group of key decision makers throughout the organization to enable them to become more strategic in their thinking, and to create conditions in the organization where people can and do own the strategic direction. Through ownership comes commitment and implementation. One example of this kind of strategy was, up until recently, formulated regularly by the leadership at IBM.

At least once a year for over 30 years, IBM held a strategic planning conference. The purpose of the meetings has been to give the company's leadership an opportunity to analyze the direction the company has been going in, and to adjust that direction in view of changes in the marketplace. The participants over the years have been the heads of each of the operating divisions in the company. So successful have these meetings been in the past that a few years ago IBM started inviting key customers to come and help shape the company's direction for the future.

Each meeting started with an analysis of significant trends in society, in the industry, and in customers' needs. Problems that need to be addressed are raised, and significant changes have occurred in the company as a result. For example, as a result of the original conference in 1956, Tom Watson, then head of IBM, reorganized the company into product groups for the first time, and established the Corporate Management Committee. As a result of the 1977 conference, IBM decided to sell rather than lease its products, to invest heavily in upgrading its production facilities, and to position itself for the coming revolution in small computers.

While at first glance it appears that the company makes decisions on the spot, nothing could be further from the truth. In fact, IBM does not make final decisions in any of these meetings. Rather, they are an opportunity to discuss and debate in an open forum, thereby adding to IBM's ability to think strategically in an on-going manner.[2]

These strategic planning conferences have, up until recently, helped IBM achieve a level of success unprecedented in the history of American business. They have helped IBM to clarify its business approach and to achieve alignment of purpose and focus among its leaders.

Of course, no approach is without its flaws. While to a large extent effective in the past, their approach has also had a couple of major drawbacks. By placing so much emphasis on seeking input from present customers, they have missed some new customer and new market opportunities. Similarly, they have subordinated their efforts in the new PC market to the old cash cow, the mainframe business. As a result, they have mortgaged the future by holding on to the past. Secondly, as a corporate culture, IBM's emphasis on mutual reinforcement has dissuaded many within the company to challenge the decisions from people at the top.[3]

Many of IBM's severe difficulties of late come not as a result of their process of strategic planning, but as a result of the consequences of their size on their ability to change. Their enormous size, coupled with a strong tendency toward bureaucratic decision making, has rendered them slow to respond to changing market conditions in each of their major product areas. Long gone are the days when "bigger is necessarily better" and where economies of scale justify larger size. Large size now is often equated with slowness of foot. In

---

[2] The above illustrations and quotes were drawn from an IBM publication entitled *Directions, '87: A Think Special Report*.
[3] For a more detailed explanation, see Carrol, P. *Big Blues: The Unmaking of IBM*, Crown Publishers, Inc., New York, 1993.

a rapidly changing environment, slowness can be fatal.

Hewlett-Packard has been engaged in highly successful strategic direction-setting processes for many years, with a particular emphasis on tying their strategic direction to specific, short-term business goals. It is different than IBM's approach in the past, however, in that Hewlett-Packard is highly decentralized, made up of relatively autonomous business divisions. Each division is responsible for the success of its business effort. On a regular basis, each division or product line identifies and examines the critical issues it faces as a business. With Hewlett-Packard's vision, mission, and values as a guide, they craft a set of strategies for how that business line will compete in the coming years. From this, they create a set of three-to-five-year business objectives that, if reached, will leverage its ability to move in the proper direction. They also ask each division to look at how their objectives will impact other divisions, thereby ensuring there is product and service coordination throughout the company. While not fancy or terribly elaborate, this approach, combined with talented research and development and effective execution, has helped Hewlett-Packard become one of the most consistently successful companies in the high-tech arena.

Why does this kind of strategic planning work? The answer lies in its simplicity, and in its ability to mobilize the organization to act on the basis of its strategy. It ingrains in people the value of planning, not as an isolated process, but as an integral process of doing business. Let's look into this more deeply.

Warren Bennis, one of the founding fathers of the field of organizational change and development, argues that an organizational leader attempting to create a high-performing organization cannot succeed without two key conditions being present:

- The leaders' vision for the organization must be clear, attractive, and attainable.
- The leader's position must be clear. We tend to trustleaders when we know where they stand in relation to the organization and how they position the overall organization relative to the environment.[4]

How an organization positions itself is the essence of strategy at its most fundamental level. Like product positioning done by marketing experts, organizational positioning is the focus an organization must have to make the company more profitable. This requires that the organization know what trends and factors will impact its business, what the company is capable of doing, and how to blend these into a relatively clear stance regarding its strategic direction for the future.

The following is a step-by-step approach for doing just that (Figure 10–1).

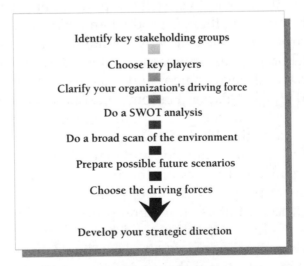

Figure 10-1. Steps to developing your strategic direction.

---

[4] Bennis, W. and Nanus, B. *Leaders*, Harper and Row, New York, 1985.

DETERMINING YOUR STRATEGIC DIRECTION, STEP BY STEP

Step One: Identify Key Stakeholding Groups. Identify the different groups that have a stake in defining your organization's strategy. Your options might include:

- trusted members of your organization
- people in peer organizations with which your organization is interdependent
- key customers
- key investors

Your key stakeholding groups:

_____

_____

_____

Step Two: Choose Individual Players to Represent the Stakeholding Groups. On the basis of the above identification process, think about people from each stakeholding group that you would like to include as part of the strategic planning process. Aim to be inclusive rather than exclusive. Include at least one or two members from each stakeholding group, ones who will both be representative and will have a strong influence on the stakeholding group once a strategic decision is made.

However you structure the group, remember that a key reason for getting such a diverse group of people together is to generate support for whatever strategic decisions eventually do get made. Commitment and ownership are what you are after, not a perfect decision. No strategic decisions are perfect. At best, they are decisions that are the organization's current best guess as to how to steer the ship in choppy waters. Too often, organizations and their leaders see the process of strategic planning as an analytic process and therefore separate others from the process. The result may be a brilliant analysis, but little buy-in and follow through.

The group should be composed of, at the very least, the leader of the organization and the top leadership team. Contrary to some people's assumptions, strategic decisions should not be delegated. They are the appropriate responsibility of top management and whomever else they choose to include to create ownership and commitment. The size of this team will best be somewhere between five and fifteen, depending on the size of the organization and its make-up. If it looks like the size of the group is going to exceed 15 people, you may want to have some of these people act more in an advisory capacity, as a larger group can easily become unwieldy for purposes of strategic decision making.

Think carefully about whether to invite any customers to the meeting. In the long run, this can be very valuable, particularly if you have a small group of long-term, high-impact customers. If you choose to invite customers, be sure to invite a good representative group, ones you trust will be open and honest with you.

Write down whom you would like to invite to the strategic planning meeting below:

_____   _____

_____   _____

_____   _____

Step Three: Clarify Your Organization's Driving Force. The idea of a driving force in an organization has been around for a number of years. It was originally popularized by Kepner-Tregoe in the late 1970s and early 1980s and has since been a key ingredient in their work with companies.[5] It is based on the idea that the best companies are the ones that are clear about what provides their competitive advantage.

Apple Computer is one example of this kind of company. While the nature of their products has changed somewhat, they are clear about one thing: their success, past, present, and future, has been and will continue to be dependent on their ability to produce exciting, innovative, and user-friendly products. This focus is distinct, for example, from IBM's core focus, which has been market savvy and product-integration capability.

There are a number of strategic areas that can provide strategic direction for a company. According to Michel Robert, one of the leading proponents of the driving force concept, there are ten key areas to consider:

- Product/Service Concept
- User/Customer Class
- Market Type/Category
- Production Capacity/Capability
- Technology
- Sales/Marketing Method
- Distribution Method
- Natural Resources
- Size/Growth
- Return/Profit

---

[5] Tregoe, B., et al. *Vision in Action: Putting a Winning Strategy to Work,* Simon and Schuster, New York, 1989.

Product/Service-Driven Strategy. A product-driven company is one that has "tied" its business to a certain "product concept." As a result, this company's future products will greatly resemble its current and past products. Future products will be modifications, adaptations, or extensions of current products. Future products will be derivatives of existing products.

The automobile industry is a good example. The "look" and "function" of cars has not changed for 100 years and probably will not change for the next 100. Thus, Daimler-Benz and Volvo's business concepts represent product-driven strategies. Boeing also follows this type of strategy. Its business is built around the concept of the airplane and the next product from that company will probably be another flying machine.

User/Customer Class-Driven Strategy. The company pursuing this strategy has decided to "anchor" its business to a class of *users*. It then communicates continuously with that customer to identify a variety of needs. Products are then made to satisfy those needs. A user-driven company places its destiny in the hands of that customer or user.

Johnson & Johnson, whose strategy of making products for "doctors, nurses, patients, and mothers" is an example of a company pursuing a strategy anchored to four specific types of users. It follows that J & J will not make products for mechanics, electricians, brick layers, and so forth.

Market Type-Driven Strategy. This company is one that has "anchored" its business to a describable or circumscribable market type or category as opposed to a class of users.

An example of the *market-driven* concept is offered by American Hospital Supply, which caters to the needs of *hospitals* and thus offers a wide range of products that all end up inside of a hospital, the market it has tied itself to.

Production Capacity/Capability-Driven Strategy. This company usually has a substantial investment in its production facility and the strategy is to "keep it running" or "keep it full." Therefore, such a company will pursue any product, customer, or market than can optimize whatever the "production facility can handle. Paper mills, hotels, and airlines are good examples of capacity-driven organizations. Keeping the facility at full capacity is the key to profits. Print shops are another class of business pursuing this strategy. A printer will tend to accept any job that the presses can handle, and optimizing the use of those presses leads to profit.

Technology-Driven Strategy. This organization uses technology to gain competitive advantage. It fosters the ability to develop or acquire hard technology (e.g., chemistry) or soft technology (know-how), and then looks for applications for that technology. When an application is found, the organization develops products and infuses into these products a portion of its technology, which brings differentiation to the product. While exploiting this edge in a particular market segment, it looks for other applications in other segments. Technology-driven companies often have "solutions looking for problems" and usually create brand new markets for their products. "The funny thing about this business," says CEO Edson de Castro of Data General, "is that things are designed and brought out when no market exists—a syndrome that a technology-driven company frequently encounters. "It's always been technology that has driven this company," de Castro adds. Sony, DuPont, and Polaroid are other examples of technology-driven companies. DuPont's invention of nylon led it to market segments as diverse as nylon stocking, shoes, thread, sweaters, fishing line, tires, and nylon-laminated packaging materials. The only thread between all these diverse businesses is that they all stem from one technology—nylon.

Sales/Marketing Method-Driven Strategy. This company has a *unique* way of getting an order from its customer. All products or services offered *must* make use of this selling technique. The company does not entertain products that cannot be sold through its sales method, nor will it solicit customers who cannot be reached through this selling or marketing method. Door-to-door direct-selling companies, such as Avon, Mary Kay, Amway, and Tupperware, are good examples.

The direction of these companies and the products and markets they pursue is determined by their selling method. Amway or Tupperware would never operate in an area where door-to-door selling was prohibited. Their decisions regarding future products are also determined by their selling method. Whatever their salespeople can place in their carrying bags will determine the nature of the product these companies promote.

Distribution Method-Driven Strategy. Companies that have a *unique* way of getting their product or service from their place to the customer's place are pursuing a distribution method-driven strategy. Telephone operating companies, with their network of wires from their switches to the outlets in the walls of your home of office, are an example. A telephone company will only entertain products or services that use or optimize its unique distribution system. Food wholesalers are another example. Department stores such as Sears are a third. Sears' jump into real estate and financial service [was] an attempt to optimize the use of the company's distribution system. Karl Eller, chairman of Circle K convenience stores—the nations's fastest-growing chain—has a very clear understanding of his companies driving force: "We're a massive *distribution system*. Whatever we can push through the store, we will."

Natural Resource-Driven Strategy. When access to or pursuit of natural resources is the key to a company's survival, then that company is natural resource-driven. Oil and mining companies are classic examples.

Size/Growth-Driven Strategy. Companies that are interested in growth for growth's sake or for economies of scale are usually pursuing a strategy of size/growth. All decisions are made to increase size or growth. LTV and Gulf & Western in the 1960s and 1970s were examples of companies following this strategy. Peter Grace's "philosophy of size and diversification, often at the expense of earning" for W. R. Grace & Company is another example. Currently, Wickes & Company seems to be in this mode. Sanford Sigoloff, its CEO, has had a voracious appetite for acquisitions in his quest "to be a $10 billion company by 1990."

Profit/Return-Driven Strategy. Whenever a company's only criterion for entering a marketplace or offering a product is profit, then that company is profit/return-driven. Conglomerates are usually good examples. They are usually organized along the lines of a corporate control body with fully autonomous subsidiaries. There are usually few or no links between these subsidiaries except a certain level of profit. Subsidiaries are bought or sold on this criterion alone. ITT, under Harold Geneen, had such a strategy. His dictum of "an increase in quarterly earnings, regardless what" and the subsequent acquisition of some 275 unrelated businesses, showed strategic disregard for all other criteria.[6]

---

[6] Robert, M., *The Strategist CEO: How Visionary Executives Build Organizations*, Quorum Books, Westport, Conn., pp. 39–42.

While conceptually distinct, none of these areas are independent of the others. One can have two or three key driving forces. Nevertheless, only one driving force is strategically most important to a company's success at any given point in time. The process of clarifying in an organization exactly what the current strategic driving forces are provides a shared focus of direction and alignment.

One excellent example of the value of clarifying one's driving force is that of AT&T. Long viewed as one of the titans of U.S. industry, Ma Bell has buckled under fierce competition in the past few years. Recently, however, CEO Robert Allen has worked hard to stem the tide of declining market share. One of the many things he and other key leaders at AT&T have done is to clarify one of its most critical driving forces—the distribution channel. Allen considers its intricate web of wires, computers, optical fibers, and software as AT&T's "crown jewel." To protect this major source of revenue and strategic advantage, AT&T has asked all its business units to not only grow and be profitable in their own right, but make sure they contribute to the success of the core telecommunications network. In addition, it has taken aggressive legal action against competitors who, they believed, were trampling on their turf. These and other actions have stabilized market share and placed AT&T back in the driver seat in the telecommunications industry.

AT&T has also done a lot more to build itself back up as a company. It has spent huge amounts of money promulgating a set of company values, ended a tradition of promoting only from within, and installed a new corporate structure that encourages cooperation among otherwise independent businesses. These and other efforts have resulted in strong profits of late, and a robust rise in stock price.[7]

To identify the best driving forces to guide your organization, it is important to take the next steps in understanding your internal and external environments, and then come back to select the best driving force or forces.

Step Four: Do a SWOT Analysis. Any strategic direction, in order to be effective, has to take into account two critical factors: (1) your present strengths and weaknesses as an organization, and (2) the environment in which your organization exists. In the parlance of strategic planning, this involves a SWOT analysis. *SWOT* stands for *S*trengths, *W*eaknesses, *O*pportunities, and *T*hreats. A SWOT analysis helps you and other members of your organization understand your organization and its environment at this point in time, including such questions as:

- What are the key products or services you provide?
- How are they currently perceived in the marketplace?
- How do you stack up against the competitors in your industry?
- How satisfied are your customers?
- What factors inside your organization have caused your present level of success?
- What factors have inhibited further success?
- Where are you most strong in your current product line?
- Where are you most vulnerable?

---

[7] Kirkpatrick, D., "Could AT&T Rule the World?," *Fortune*, May 17, 1993, pp. 55–66.

To do a SWOT analysis, begin with strengths and weaknesses. Take your strategic planning team and break it in half. Ask one half of the team to identify the strengths of the organization. Ask the other half to identify weaknesses. Invite both groups to use some of the above questions as a guide and any others that are germane to your effectiveness. Be sure they look at operational factors, ability to meet customers' needs, as well as other factors that make up your capability. The answers to these questions will provide you and others with a snapshot of the current state of your organization.

Have each group post their thoughts on a flip chart and share with the other group. Then discuss and come to a shared understanding of your strengths and weaknesses. It is not important here to come to consensus. This is not a point of decision making. Much of what you are doing here and elsewhere is generating a shared view of your organization. For this, dialogue and open exploration is more critical than agreement. The dialogue that ensues needs to be brutally honest. If done well, it will reveal much about your organization, and provide an important understanding upon which to craft your strategic direction. The above understanding will be both a conceptual and practical backdrop for the remaining conversations.

Now look at opportunities and threats. Divide the group in half. Have one group focus on opportunities in the environment, both present and near term, that your organization can exploit to its advantage. These can be new customers, new technologies, changes in government regulations, etc. Have the other group focus on threats to your success. These can be threats from competitors, from regulatory changes, or any others to which you must respond to remain viable. Follow the strengths and weaknesses process.

Step Five: Scan the Environment for Broad Trends That May Affect You in the Long Run. The next stop is to look at the external environment and generate a strong understanding of the forces that will shape its future. In contrast to the earlier look at opportunities and threats, which was a look at more recent and immediate factors that affect your success, this is a long-term broad view of the environment. The external environment is made up of at least each of the following key factors:

- Your customers' growing and changing expectations
- Key technological innovations
- Government regulations, legislation, etc.
- Your competition, their strategies, and their products
- Economic trends
- Societal trends
- The availability of materials

For each industry, there may be other factors as well that will affect the business.

As a group, consider each of these factors. Based on whatever information you have or can acquire, develop your best guesses as to what each of these factors will look like in the future. For most industries, a five-to-twenty-year view is best. How far you look into the future will depend on how quickly your industry changes, and how long of a strategic direction you want to define. Generally, the farther the reach, the better.

To develop an understanding of the above trends, send to each member of the strategic planning team as much information as possible on each of the above topics in advance of your meeting in step six. Give them ample time before the meeting to study these trends and form their own understanding of them. When you do convene as a group, consider having industry experts and outside strategic planners provide presentations on the above topics to stimulate participants' thinking and provide critical appreciation for what's involved. The aim here is to have the presenters provide useful information and thought-provoking questions. It is the planning team's responsibility to come up with some tentative answers. From the above input, as a group create a list of key trends that will affect your organization.

Step Six: Prepare Possible Future Scenarios. From the information you generate in the preceding step, develop a set of possible future scenarios. These scenarios represent your current best guesses as to what the future will look like. Different scenarios may be appropriate depending on differing assumptions. For example, one scenario might unfold assuming slow economic growth and little change in political forces. Another scenario might unfold if rapid economic growth occurs. Still a third might focus on a breakthrough in technology or in the regulatory environment in which your organization operates. Look at such factors as changing technology, energy availability, shifts in global politics, changes in attitudes about the environment, economic forces, and so on.

As you develop these scenarios, bear in mind that past trends do not necessarily determine future ones. Let me give you a simple example to illustrate what I mean.

In California, up until around 1989, housing prices had been going up steadily for over 20 years. Indeed, in the mid-to-late-1980s, the value of housing had been growing at almost 15 percent a year with no foreseeable end in sight. Around that time, many people entered the market and sought to generate considerable wealth based on this assumption. What many of these investors did not notice was that mortgage payments as a percentage of income were already higher in California than in almost any other state in the country, and that unless incomes rose, housing values could not possibly continue to rise. Eventually it would become too expensive for most people to live in California, and many would start to leave. In other words, people's ability to buy could not go up unless their incomes went up correspondingly.

In 1990, the domestic economy went into a recession. By 1992, the California economy was in a tailspin, and it experienced one of the highest jobless rates in the country. The California housing market had by then reached the point where the supply of houses was beginning to exceed the demand. Indeed, if you looked at the values of houses in other regions in comparison to California, housing values were overinflated and demand had to naturally go down.

In 1989, the 20-year trend of increasing housing values began to slow significantly, and in 1990–1993, they stayed the same or went down. Many people who had expected continued growth and invested on that premise were forced to sell some of their real estate at a loss. Some even lost the fortunes that they had gained earlier. In short, trends do not always continue unabated. Other factors affect them. It is these trends and other factors that must be understood before developing appropriate future scenarios.

On the basis of your understanding of the trends and factors that are shaping your environment, generate three to four likely scenarios along with your best guesses as a group as to the likelihood of each scenario. If you have the resources, you may want to have a strategic planning group develop these for you in advance for your consideration and discussion as a group. It is best to keep it to three or four as any larger number will be difficult to discuss and anticipate its implications.

Here is an example of what this process looks like. One large company (to protect its anonymity, we'll say it was an insurance company), in preparation for a strategic planning meeting for one of its major divisions, asked its strategic planning department to put together a presentation that described key trends in the environment, their implications for the insurance company, and then a set of possible future scenarios upon which the leadership of the division can explore its strategic direction (see Figure 10–2).

The planning group identified and analyzed such trends as changes in consumer behavior, demographic changes, changes in product needs from consumers, and federal regulations and their impact on the industry (see Figure 10–3).

They then looked at changes in the industry infrastructure, including increased competition from other insurance companies as well as other companies in the broader financial services industry, technology and its impact, and unusual tragedies that had occurred that had affected its main markets (see Figure 10–4).

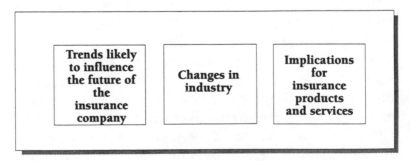

Figure 10-2. Model for analyzing trends and their implications.

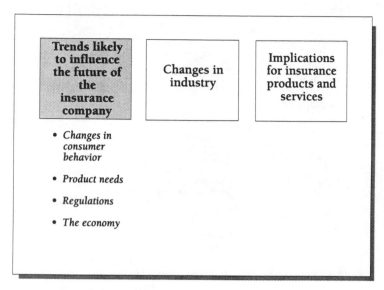

Figure 10-3. Analysis of key trends.

On the basis of all of these factors, they identified the implications for the company. These factors affected their product mix, whether and how to exploit new market opportunities, and their investment portfolio (see Figure 10–5).

The strategic planning department explored all of the above in detail with the top 25 executives in the company and then described three possible future scenarios to consider in creating its strategic plans. One scenario saw the economy growing at a solid pace. The second scenario assumed slow to stagnant growth in the economy. A third scenario looked at the possibility of significant shifts in the political climate affecting the insurance industry—in particular the high likelihood of significant changes in the health care industry if Bill Clinton got elected. For each, the planning department described the scenario in detail, explained the assumptions under which the scenario was created, offered its

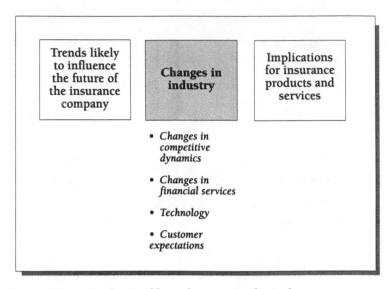

Figure 10-4. Analysis of key changes in the industry.

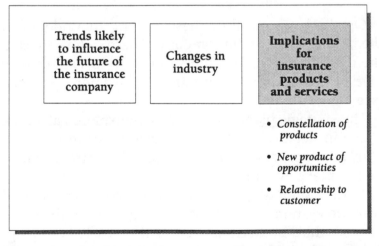

Figure 10-5. Implications for company's products and services.

best guess as to the likelihood of the scenario coming true, and explored some of the implications of the scenario on the company key businesses. The aim of the discussion with the executive team was to ascertain the likelihood of these scenarios as a group and to explore their implications on the strategy of the company.

The above presentation and discussion took three days, the outcome of which was a predicted likely scenario that the group agreed to and a clear strategy to respond based on this scenario. Of course, if they are off target, the future success of the company is at stake. If they are on target, however, they will have prepared their organization for significant success in the future. Any critical strategic direction setting has this effect. It creates the possibility of significant positive change in the direction of the company, and by virtue of the fact that the organization is putting a stake in the ground, it has its risks as well.

Step Seven: Choose the Driving Force(s). The analysis of your internal and external environments will provide you with clues as to the strategic driving forces that are most critical for your company's future. On the basis of the above scenarios, choose the driving force(s) that will best leverage your present abilities. It may be the one that will reinforce your present strength. Or it may be one that requires you to shift your focus. Your choice needs to be both strategically appropriate given the likely scenarios identified above, and culturally appropriate given your present and potential strengths and weaknesses.

One way of selecting the most significant driving force for your current position is to create a matrix that positions each scenario on one axis and the possible driving forces for that scenario on another axis. By identifying the best driving force for each scenario, you can get a good sense of the impact of the various driving forces on your future direction.

Step Eight: Develop a Strategic Direction. On the basis of the above selection, generate a list of strategic challenges that you face. These may include how to further develop your major driving force, how best to exploit new markets, how best to respond to changing customers' needs, and how to respond to particular competitive threats. Put the list on a flip chart for all to see and identify the ones that are most likely to enhance your success given the scenarios you have chosen. You are now ready to provide focus and translate all of the above effort into a clear and guiding set of strategic goals for your company.

ARCHITECTING CHECKLIST

1. The company's strategic direction provides the focus, aim, and direction of business activities.

2. The success of an organization is as much if not more dependent on commitment and coordinated execution than on having the right strategy.

3. Commitment and coordinated execution are produced by creating a shared process of strategic direction setting where key stakeholders together craft the future direction of the organization.

4. An effective strategic direction is organized around a clear driving force that defines the organization's greatest strength.

5. An effective strategic direction is also dependent on an understanding of the forces that shape its changing environment. Effective strategies are a match between the organization's present or emerging strengths, and the unfolding future business and market conditions.

11

Setting Your
Strategic Goals

Over the years I have seen an enormous amount of confusion on the part of organizations over how to create effective strategic goals. Many organizations create an overwhelming number of goals that, rather than providing focus, contribute only to organizational confusion. Many organizations create strategies, yet provide few measures or concrete milestones upon which to determine how well those strategies are being implemented. Still others get so overwhelmed with measurement that they lose sight of the larger picture.

Not only are there problems within organizations regarding the nature and value of strategic goal setting, organizational consultants and researchers do not agree on what the best approach to goal setting is. On the one hand, there is over 25 years of experience saying that management by objectives (MBO) is a powerful method for motivating employees, and an effective means of ensuring that people are focused in the same direction. On the other hand, Dr. W. Edwards Deming, one of the leading gurus in the total quality movement, had for years insisted that MBO, with its associated overemphasis on numeric goals, is part of the reason that our country is rapidly losing our ability to compete globally. He called managing by objectives one of his seven deadly sins. It is little wonder that organizations are confused about the nature and value of strategic goal setting.

Strategic goal setting is neither a panacea nor a curse. When done properly, it is an effective method for ensuring that everyone in the organization has a shared focus, is moving in the proper direction, and is achieving directly observable results in its efforts to grow. When it is used to motivate employees, however, it produces mixed results. Some employees are extremely goal-driven. For them, goals and measures provide valuable stimulation and feedback. For others, goals can sometimes be limiting, and provide an annoying structure that inhibits creativity. Still others, who are not committed to achieving results and focus on their own personal success, can manipulate data to demonstrate results, even though the reality is they are doing poorly.

Goal setting, when done well as an organization, is particularly useful for organizations to ensure they are focused on the same things, and that they are all working together in concert. This chapter focuses on organizational strategic goal setting, and provides a step-by-step guide for how to construct effective goals and how to work with them in your own organization.

WHAT ARE STRATEGIC GOALS

Strategic *goals* are distinct from strategic *direction* in that strategic direction provides a beacon of light to help aim the organization's efforts, while strategic goals provide specific areas to focus on, and a mechanism for measuring the organization's success. How long these goals last as a working guide depends a lot on the nature of your industry. In a rapidly changing industry like the computer industry, two years is probably a realistic time frame for one's strategic goals. In the insurance industry, which is relatively more stable, perhaps three to five years is more appropriate. Two-to-five-year goals are generally most appropriate to most organizations.

Not only do strategic goals provide the members of your organization with focus, but they also help to ensure that they are able to prioritize their activities on a daily basis. In most companies, people have more on their "things to do" list than they can possibly handle. The strategic goals of the company, however, tell them which items to put on their "priority A" list and which to put on their "priority B" list.

Finally, strategic goals can provide guidance on those most promising areas to create improvement efforts. In total-quality-oriented companies, for example, continuous improvement teams are typically formed to directly affect some aspect of the strategic goals. In this way, all total quality improvement efforts become meaningful and valuable, as opposed to trivial in nature.

FEATURES OF EFFECTIVE STRATEGIC GOALS

There are five principles to the creation of effective strategic goals. Together, these principles will provide you with an integrated roadmap for your organization. Based on my experience in working with organizations, strategic goals need to:

- be tied to and reinforce the strategic direction;
- be few in number so as to facilitate focus;
- be challenging in nature so as to stretch the organization to grow, either qualitatively or quantitatively;
- have clear measures attached to them so as to provide ample and regular feedback to the organization; and
- be collaboratively generated to ensure effective buy-in from all members of the organization.

Tying Strategic Goals to Strategic Direction. Above all, to be effective, an organization's strategic goals must be directly tied to the strategic direction. The strategic goals are the link between one's daily activities and the overall direction of the organization. For example, if one feature of your strategic direction is to be a leader in your field in the area of customer satisfaction, then one strategic goal might be "to increase our customer satisfaction index from 7.3 to 8.5 in the next 12 months." This goal, then, quantifies and makes concrete the strategic direction because it has embedded in it the specific target with which to measure success. While not always critical, having the measure quantified can add significantly to people's understanding of the strategic goal.

Strategic Goals Should Be Few in Number. Too often organizations have such a large number of goals that together they are almost useless. More often than not, these organizations have already learned that strategic goals are important, and hence, go overboard in their fervor. Here is an example of one organization's over-exuberant attempt at strategic goal setting.

The company was an accounting firm that by many standards was already one of the leaders in its area of expertise. After a period of slow growth and sluggish profits, it promoted one of its senior partners to the role of CEO. In his role, the new CEO did some very effective things to help provide focus and direction to the organization. He, along with others, developed a mission statement that challenged the organization to be the best in its geographic area. He articulated along with others a set of values that were meaningful and heartfelt. He assessed with others the environment they were in, both external and internal, and generated a strategic vision for the organization. This vision included the following statement (Figure 11–1).

All of this met with great interest and excitement from the rest of the organization and seemed to challenge and stimulate the organization towards greater accomplishment. The new CEO did not stop there, however. He had read in a number of books the importance of making strategic goals concrete, and so he took each of the features of their strategic vision and created a set of goals and actions associated with each of those goals (Figure 11–2).

Take a moment to think about what it would be like working in this organization. Picture yourself as a member of the accounting firm with more work than you can presently handle, and feeling burnt out from the huge amount of work that you have done in the past 12 months helping the firm to make a profit (these were the conditions under which these strategic goals were created). How would you react to all these goals?

STRATEGIC PLAN FOR SULLIVAN & HARGROVE
1993 — 1999

SECTION I: PURPOSE

This Plan expresses a vision of the Firm's future, providing strategies and goals for achievement of that vision.

It is a guide for preparation of plans of operation for the next few years. It is intended not as a point by point mandate, but as a framework for future decision making.

SECTION II: MISSION AND VALUES STATEMENT

1.   MISSION STATEMENT.

"Sullivan & Hargrove is committed to being the premier accounting firm practicing in New York City delivering excellent, efficient accounting services responsive to our clients' needs."

2.   VALUES STATEMENT.

We are committed to the achievement of our mission while adhering to these values:

(a)   Providing the highest quality accounting work, the most responsive service, and the optimum results for our clients.

(b)   Having the highest standards for integrity, and professionalism.

(c)   Working as a team — made up of diverse individuals with personal relationships characterized by respect, trust, affection, and loyalty — to promote the good of the Firm and its clients.

(d)   Being fairly compensated for our work efforts.

(e)   Placing needs of the Firm and the needs of our customers first.

(f)   Fostering opportunity for individual choice in balancing professional and personal life, without diluting our team commitment.

(g)   Being dedicated to the betterment of the accounting profession and New York City through active participation in professional, civic and charitable organizations, and selected pro bono work.

Figure 11-1. Example strategic vision.

While worthy of praise for his exuberance, the net result of all of his efforts was less than anticipated. Given their past history of putting together plans, yet not following through, these goals were not taken seriously. Part of why they were not taken seriously was that, taken as a whole, they were perceived by many as

1. **CLIENT SERVICE**

   Our Firm will place a high premium on satisfying our clients' needs. We will do this by actively seeking their thoughts, ideas and needs and integrating these needs into the fabric of our work. We will place the needs of our clients above all others, while retaining a practice that is of the utmost quality and excellence.

2. **QUALITY**

   The Firm will institute a process to continually improve the quality of service offered to clients and will have high quality personnel from top to bottom in the Firm's organization.

   (a)   <u>Goals:</u>

   (i)   Recruit and retain personnel who have a high desire for excellence and an intolerance for mediocrity.
   (ii) Maintain performance-based compensation systems.

3. **RENEWAL AND GROWTH**

   The Firm will be a constantly renewing and growing organization.

   (a)   <u>Goals:</u>

   (i)   Maintain our strength in the traditional areas of accounting that have caused and sustained our growth over the last thirty years.
   (ii) Expand our accounting services in areas of growing demand from present clients and potential areas from new clients.

4. **TEAMWORK**

   The Firm will continue to value a collegial work environment that fosters quality interaction, professional achievement and satisfaction.

   (a)   <u>Goals:</u>

   (i)   Maintain a supportive and satisfying place to work.
   (ii)   Teach that gratification from the practice of accounting comes from service to others, intellectual challenge, and professional dignity.
   (iii) Resolve all ethical issues in a manner that is consistent with the Firm's commitment to the highest standards of professionalism.
   (iv)   Treat everyone with dignity and respect.
   (v)   Foster our ability to work together toward a shared goal.
   (vi)   Reinforce and increase the productivity of all members of the team.

5. **EFFICIENCY**

   The Firm will function efficiently.

   (a)   <u>Goals:</u>

   (i)   Maximize the use of professional accountants' time by delegating administrative tasks to the support staff.
   (ii)   Organize to eliminate waste and maximize efficiency.
   (iii) Establish a presence in other markets to serve clients and export our expertise to selected new geographical areas where appropriate.

Figure 11-2. Example strategic goals.

unrealistic. Unfortunately, the culture of the firm was not one in which raising this directly and openly was seen as acceptable. So the partners signed off on the goals, but did not commit to them.

Interestingly, I have since learned that in spite of the

huge list of goals, the CEO did choose to focus on two of them. One of their goals was to strengthen their presence in alternative markets. Soon after establishing their strategic goals, they sought a merger with another accounting firm to do just that. Another of their goals, to foster retention of productive members while letting go of less productive ones, has begun to be addressed with some recent firings. This particular decision was met with an uproar by a number of partners. Many were surprised that the CEO carried through with his aims, for they did not take the strategic goals seriously. Now they do!

A good set of strategic goals is roughly four to five in number, tied directly to two or three features of the strategic direction. Remember, the purpose of having strategic goals is to provide you with focus. Any more than five or six will likely accomplish just the opposite. It is hard for people to remember more than six of these anyway, so I have found four to five to be a good ballpark figure.

Strategic Goals Should Be Challenging in Aim. Mihaly Csikszentmihali, noted psychologist and researcher on the factors that impact performance, recently came out with an intriguing book called *Flow: The Psychology of Optimal Experience.*[1] Flow is defined by the author as a state in which people achieve the highest levels of performance while at the same time experiencing the highest levels of satisfaction. This flow state is achieved when people are doing an activity that is meaningful to them, and that provides a challenge that matches their level of skills. This match, in turn, increases the likelihood that they will feel real accomplishment. If the

---

[1] Csikszentmihali, M. *Flow: The Psychology of Optional Experience*, Harper Collins, New York, 1990.

challenge is too high, they will experience anxiety. If the challenge is too low, they will either feel bored or successful, but without a real sense of accomplishment. His model for the flow state looks like the following (Figure 11–3).

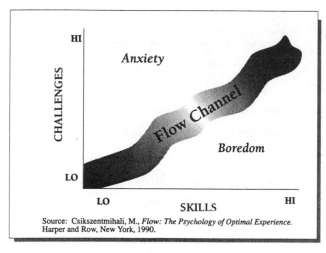

Source: Csikszentmihali, M., *Flow: The Psychology of Optimal Experience.* Harper and Row, New York, 1990.

Figure 11-3. The flow channel.

Organizations, just like individuals, have the possibility of achieving this state of flow. It requires, in part, that the organization create a set of strategic goals that, on the one hand, are challenging, while the other hand give the organization the opportunity to experience real success. Put simply, if the bar for a high jumper is set too high, he or she will not get over it and experience continued disappointment to the point of giving up. If it is set too low, he or she will succeed, yet feel no real sense of accomplishment. Hence, the optimum level is probably a bit beyond what most would consider a manageable risk. Adapting Czsikszentmihali's model,

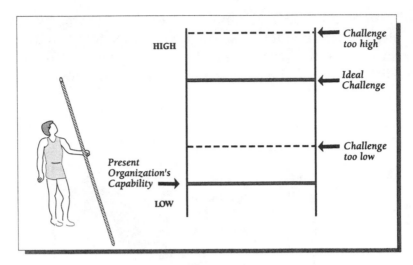

Figure 11-4. Optimal performance challenge.

for an organization, the optimal level looks something like that shown in Figure 11–4.

At the risk of confusing the reader, let me also point out that once in a while, seemingly outrageous strategic goals are exactly the best goals to have. When an organization is stuck, or needs to achieve a significant breakthrough in the market to succeed, an outrageous goal is sometimes called for. This is a goal that most everyone would consider almost impossible, yet if the organization achieved it, it would catapult the organization to new levels of effectiveness. President Kennedy's goal of having a man on the moon (and return) by the end of the 1960s was one such goal. While most scientists deemed it essentially impossible, he pushed on anyway and, as we all know, eventually succeeded. This target was a rallying cry for the country, around which great pride and satisfaction were generated.

Another example of a breakthrough goal was that of Roger Bannister who, in 1956, declared that he was going to break the four-minute mile. Before Bannister, no one had ever succeeded in running a mile in under four minutes. So many had tried and failed, in fact, that it was seen by many as humanly impossible and often referred to as the "invisible barrier." Undaunted, Roger Bannister decided he would do it, and after considerable training based on a meticulous scientific study of the dynamics of endurance and human performance, he eventually succeeded. After he broke this perceived barrier, numerous others rapidly followed suit. Nowadays, running the mile in under four minutes is almost commonplace among middle-distance competitors.

Strategic Goals Should Have Clear Measures. Over the years I have noticed an organizational phenomenon that is so pervasive that I have felt compelled to call it Merron's Axiom #1. Simply stated it reads: "In organizations, what you measure is what people focus on." While not a revelation by any stretch of the imagination, I am constantly astounded by the degree to which organizations miss this universal truth. For example, I often ask the following question early on my consulting work with clients: "What are the most critical things you must do to be successful in your business?" Typically, they answer with such things as:

- Be profitable
- Have low costs
- Have satisfied customers
- Produce a quality product
- Have enough volume, productivity, or some other thing that equates with the quantity of output

Then I ask, "How do you measure these things in your organization?" Typically, they come up with the quantity output measures and the profitability related measures immediately. Then I ask them how they measure customer satisfaction and the quality of the product. More often than not I get blank stares. Sometimes people will feel very uncomfortable with the recognition that some key factors in their success are not being measured, so they make up something like "Oh, we keep track of it," or "If we don't have any complaints, we know we're doing well." Salespeople will often say, "I keep track of my customers." When I ask them how, they will squirm and say, "I just know. It's part of my job."

What is also surprising to me sometimes is how little people know about what it means to measure something. They think measure means "to get information on," or "to keep track of in some way." Many people will define measures as "oh, they tell us when. . . ." or "when they complain, we know." These are not measures. Rather, they are forms of feedback. Important information, perhaps, but not measures.

A measure is like a ruler. Measures are recording devices that enable us to quantify phenomena. You know by a measure exactly how much something goes up or down. You can compare two different things with a measure and know which is bigger, smaller, faster, slower, worse, better. And you will know, with some high degree of confidence, by how much. Interestingly, people know what a measure is quite quickly regarding financial matters. They know exactly how profitable the company was last year, or by how much revenues increased in the last quarter. If you talk to the Sales or Marketing Department, they can also tell you which product yields the best operating margins, and which produces the most money in their pockets.

Yet when it comes to measuring such critical things as customer satisfaction, quality of product, employee satisfaction, or other "softer" features of the organization, many people get confused or lost. I believe this is due to the fact that few people know how to measure in quantifiable terms these softer aspects of their company. Yet these softer aspects are no less critical than any of the other areas. Measurement, in these softer areas, requires an ability to quantify people's feelings and impressions. Gathering this type of data may take a more sophisticated survey or questionnaire design, but it is eminently doable.

The importance of having an effective way to measure your progress cannot be overstated. The benefits of an effective measurement system are many.

1. It forces a disciplined approach to management. Good measurement systems force you to think about what is important to your success. It focuses attention and ensures people are working in the same direction.

2. It provides reliable information on what's working or not working in the organization. A good measurement system tracks the progress of an organization, thereby providing direct and immediate feedback.

3. It gives you valid information upon which to make decisions. Too often in business, decisions are based on hunch, conjecture, or strong bias. While there is an important place for intuition and educated guesswork, there is no place for stereotypic views, preformed and rigid biases, or unchallenged assumptions.

4. It tells you what you do well. By tracking progress and measuring results, you can, without hesitation, promote yourself honestly in the marketplace. Data from measures, particularly in areas of demonstrated strength, are critical to your sales and marketing force in helping them shape the way they communicate to others about your company.

5. It enables people in your organization to take pride in their progress. Too often people have no idea of the consequences of their efforts. Measures give direct and meaningful feedback to people, enabling them to learn and feel good about their efforts.[2]

Strategic Goals Should Be Collaboratively Generated. The importance of collaboration has been reinforced throughout this book, yet it needs particular emphasis here. Perhaps more important than anywhere else, the creation of strategic goals needs to be done in a collaborative fashion. How excited are you when someone says to you, "Here are your new goals, love them and live them!" Rarely do we buy into goals that others have set for us. In fact, more often than not, when someone gives us goals, it taps into the independent voice in all of us that says we are in control of our own destiny, and no one else is going to tell us what to do. Psychologists call this voice "counter-dependence" and it lives inside almost all healthy, normal, breathing human beings in Western society. Interestingly, this phenomenon is less obvious in Eastern cultures, but I suspect that at some level, perhaps in a more subtle way, it exists in all of us.

Hence, goal setting at the corporate or strategic level must tap into that part of us that wants to play a role in the creation of our own future direction and destiny. For strategic goal setting then, a collaborative approach is best. The Japanese, long noted for their ability to collaborate effectively, have developed just such an approach. It is sometimes called "catchball" and has as its

---

[2] I am indebted to Richard C. Whiteley, who, in his book, *the Customer Driven Organization: Moving From Talk to Action,* Addison Wesley Publishing Company, Reading MA, 1991, originally expressed many of the five ideas above.

main feature the idea that each level in the organization should participate in the creation of goals for their own area and for the next level above them. I will explain this process shortly.

HOW TO COLLABORATIVELY CREATE STRATEGIC GOALS

The best place to start to create strategic goals is with your strategic direction. The strategic direction, bolstered by a clear vision, provides clues and guidelines for what goals to create, and where to focus your attention. The process for creating these goals is shown in Figure 11–5, below.

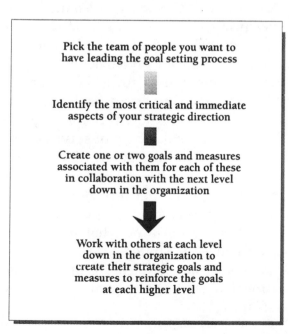

Figure 11-5. Steps to collaborative goal setting.

Pick the team to lead the goal-setting process. Generally speaking, the members of the top leadership of the organization are the appropriate members to create the strategic goals. Like the process of strategic direction setting, strategic goal setting needs to be a top-down process because charting the course and the direction of the organization is appropriately the responsibility of the top leadership of the organization.

Identify the most critical features of your strategic direction. To accomplish this, have the goal-setting team take a look at your vision and strategic direction and identify the features that are most immediate and most critical. In some cases this may take a lot of discussion, while in other cases, external forces and internal pressures will make it quite evident where to focus your attention.

Create one or two goals for each feature of the strategic direction. You can do this simply by asking the question, "What specifically does it mean to move toward this vision and accomplish the strategic direction?" Or you can ask, "what specifically do we need to accomplish in the next three years to move toward our strategic direction?" For example, if your strategic direction has something to do with being known as the highest-quality provider of your particular type of services, you might ask yourself, "What do we mean by highest quality?" or "How would we know if our services were of higher quality than those of another provider?" These sorts of questions will help you think concretely and specifically.

Once you have a sense of what it might mean to move forward in your strategic direction, create your strategic goals for each key feature of your vision and strategic direction. An effective goal statement will have three key features:

- It will identify what you want to improve or change.

- It will identify the direction in which you want to change.
- It will identify the measure or gauge you will use to determine your success.

Here are some examples of effective strategic goal statements:

- Our aim in the next three years it to achieve the highest customer-satisfaction rating in our industry.
- By 1994, we will become certified in ISO 9001 in all of our major product development divisions.
- We will reduce the cost of poor quality by 60 percent in the next 18 months.
- Within the next three years, we aim to reduce our product development cycle time by 30 percent without impairing the excellent quality of our products.

To create your strategic goals, use the table shown in Figure 11–6 as a guide. It will help focus your thinking in full and complete statements.

Be sure that you have a measure that indeed is a measure. Here are some example measures. They are measures because they clearly tell you not only up or down, but by how much.

- cycle time
- customer satisfaction rating
- employee satisfaction rating
- error rate
- response time
- cost of production
- turnover rate
- amount of rework
- return on investment
- profit margin

STRATEGIC DIRECTION	STRATEGIC GOALS	DESIRED DIRECTION	MEASURE
1.			
2.			

Figure 11-6. Strategic goal setting form.

As you create these goals, be sure they are meaningful to your customers. (You remember these people. They are the ones that keep you in business.) Here are some examples of what not to do (Figure 11–7).

While these examples may be humorous or seemingly preposterous, before you judge the people who wrote these too harshly, look at the standards that you have set for your own organization. Do they truly meet your customers' needs? If you are not sure, go out and ask your customers. I'll bet that you will be surprised with the answers you get.

Once you have come up with a small handful of strategic goals, it is time to test these with other people to be sure they are consistent with their sense of what goals the organization should have and to increase the eventual buy-in of these goals. To accomplish this buy-in, you need to play "catchball" with the goals. This

---

MAKE THE MEASURES MATTER

- One financial services company adopted a standard of responding to its customers within 14-21 days, although 60% of its customers expected a 7-day response.

- One utility company set a standard of meeting 92% of repair appointments even though by meeting that standard it would anger over 3,000 customers a month.

- One health insurance company evaluated managers on how fast they could turn around claims, ignoring the fact that customers don't care about speed if the payment is less than they expect and there is no explanation.

- Another health insurer labored to provide physicians with extra-fast turnaround, even though doctors only review their accounts receivable every 30 days.

Source: Davidow, W., and Uttal, B. *Total Customer Service.* Harper & Row Publishers, 1989.

Figure 11-7. Ineffective goals.

involves having each member on your leadership team meet with his or her direct reports and discuss each of the goals with them. Each member invites others to challenge, add to, delete, and change the goals.

Now have the leadership team meet with each other once more to take all the inputs from the next level down and discuss, dialogue, negotiate, etc. After all the critical inputs are considered they are either adopted or, if not adopted, a clear and compelling explanation for why not can be given that will satisfy the group or the individuals who had given the input. You now have an organization-wide set of broad strategic goals. A good gauge as to whether your process was effective would be if everyone involved signed their name to a document committing themselves to the successful achievement of these goals. While I don't suggest that you actually ask for signatures, this would be a litmus test of whether or not the chosen goals are the right ones for your organization and whether there is commitment to those goals.

Each level down does the same. Once you have a set of strategic goals you are committed to as the leadership of your organization, it is time to have this process cascade downward until all the members of the organization have their own sets of goals and are clear about how their goals fit with the larger strategic goals for the organization as a whole. In effect, this involves having the second tier in the organization take the strategic goals for the corporation and identify what their department or division's goals need to be to reinforce the company's goals. In some cases, a company strategic goal will not apply. In other cases, it is directly within the responsibility of that department to lead the charge in meeting this company-wide goal. Like the process of "catchball" above, this needs to be done in collaboration with each department head's direct reports.

Here is an example of what I mean. In one organization, the leadership of the company had identified the following strategic goals for itself:

To raise customer satisfaction levels from 7.8 to 9.0 by January 1993

Each division head, with his or her own direct reports, then took these goals and established the first draft of their strategic goals for their division. These managers in turn then took this draft to their direct reports, and through a dialogue, each division came to consensus on their goals.

Depending on the size of your organization, it may be appropriate to repeat the same steps at the next level down in the organization, until all key departments and divisions have a set of strategic goals and a sense of how everyone's goal fits with the overall aims of the company. This cascading approach to strategic goal set-ting has worked wonderfully well in many companies and it produces, often times for the very first time, a sense of clarity regarding the organization's direction, and how each person plays a role in the successful ac-complishment of that overall direction.

In summary then, Figure 11–8 shows an example of how the whole goal-setting process looks.

While not within the scope of this book, it should be noted that the process of strategic goal setting need not stop here. At this point, many companies identify specific areas for improvement to meet these targets. In many total-quality-oriented companies, for example, the leadership of the company uses these goals to iden-tify processes that need to be improved upon, processes that, when improved, will directly impact the accom-plishment of the strategic goals. Once these companies

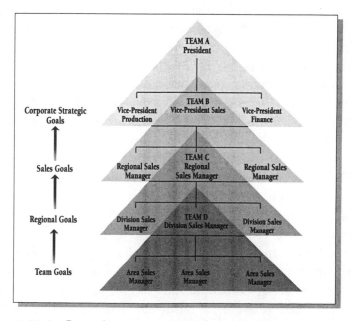

Figure 11-8. Cascading strategic goals.

have identified these processes, they set up continuous improvement teams to work on these processes. Over time, with many such teams working throughout the company, enormous improvement can occur over relatively short periods of time.

At Hewlett-Packard, for example, each year the CEO identifies its key corporate strategic goals. At HP these are referred to as Hoshin goals, named after the Japanese concept of systematic planning to execute strategic organizational breakthroughs. These goals flow naturally from their strategic direction, the process of which was described in chapter 10. In 1992, HP's Hoshin goals were to increase profits to prior robust levels and to improve processes in the areas of product-generation, people leadership, total quality management, information systems, and order fulfillment and delivery. In 1993, they were even more focused: profitability and order fulfillment. For each of these, Hewlett-Packard identifies how it will measure these objectives and asks each of its major divisions to identify what it will do to help the company meet these objectives. Each division, in turn, then sets up teams of people at all different levels to identify and execute ways to improve its operations to help HP meet these objectives. By connecting specific and focused improvement efforts to corporate strategic goals, HP has consistently been a leader in the business community.

The critical challenge, once the strategic goals are agreed and committed to, is to put them into effect. This, not suprisingly, is where the field of strategic planning falls short. Great ideas are useless if not implemented. For this, you will need a clear operational plan. While not within the scope of this book, let me say briefly that an operational plan would specify who does what, when, how, and what are the mechanisms by which we will track and monitor our progress. For a useful guide on this critical subject, I recommend an upcoming book entitled *Operational Planning* by Jack Knight, Bruce Dunn, and Pamela Adams.[3]

In short, strategic goal setting is not an exercise in an MBA student manual, but a practical, powerful method to achieve alignment throughout the company and direct one's forces to achieve demonstratable results. It is not an end in and of itself, however, for, like Hewlett-Packard, one must also create the means to achieve one's goals. The next chapter explores how developing an effective organizational structure is critical and then explains how to develop such a structure.

ARCHITECTING CHECKLIST

1. Effective strategic goals specific to the areas of focus for the organization in the next two to five years.

2. Strategic goals need to flow naturally from and effectively reinforce the organization's strategic direction and vision.

3. Strategic goals help make the direction of the organization specific and measurable.

4. Like other factors in the organization's architecture, strategic goals need to be collaboratively created and universally committed to.

5. Effective strategic goals need to be both challenging in nature and realistic in the eyes of the organization's members.

6. Strategic goals can provide the impetus and focus for improvement efforts throughout the organization.

---

[3] Knight, J., Dunn, B., and Adams, P., *Operational Planning: Moving from Strategy to Action* Roundtable Associates, to be released in 1994.

12

Structuring Your Organization for Optimal Success

We trained hard . . . but every time we were beginning to form up into teams, we would be reorganized . . . a wonderful method it can be of creating the illusion of progress while producing inefficiency and demoralization.

—Petronius Satyricon, first century A.D.[1]

Imagine for a moment that you are structuring your organization from scratch. What guidelines would you likely follow? Would you want to have many direct reports? How would you ensure effective communication flow? Where would the focus of power lie? How would the new structure ensure effective collaboration between business units? How would your organization respond to changing environmental conditions?

These are questions that have resulted in a whole area of study—that of organizational structure and de-

---

[1] Quoted by Bridges, W. *Surviving Corporate Transitions*, Doubleday & Company, 1988, p. 17.

sign. Answers to these kinds of questions determine the variety of ways you can design your organization's structure. In addition, within different organizational designs, decisions need to be made about how you structure different subparts of the organization in order to achieve the highest possible productivity and long-term effectiveness. Early research and practice have found that there are at least six structural factors that have an effect on organizational effectiveness:

1. The degree of decentralization

2. The degree of functional specialization

3. The amount of formalization

4. Span of control

5. Organizational size

6. Work unit size

These are, in effect, variables that you manipulate as you design an organizational structure. More recently, as with the principles outlined with this book, a great deal of attention has been placed on the importance of "fit" between an organization's structure and its mission, its customers, the culture of the organization, its strategy, its business environment, etc. As a result, new and creative organizational forms have emerged of late that seem to enhance performance as well as being more satisfying for people.

As a leader, you need to consider the above features of your organization's structure, and design it in a way that makes your organization most efficient and effective in the long run. This means in most cases that the structure needs to facilitate open communication, allow for efficient work processes, enable people to be more self-directing, and be adaptable to changing business conditions.

Creating such a structure is not an easy task. Indeed, mistakes are often made by highly experienced managers regarding how to structure their organization. Many managers tend to create too rigid a system of controls, mismanage the relationships between organizations, reorganize the structure when other changes are more appropriate, or reorganize so often that the employees lack a sense of stability. When considering the prospect of reorganizing, because of the long-term impact on the organization's well being, you need to avoid sloppiness or capriciousness, and enhance careful planning and swift execution.

Not only is extreme care and thoughtfulness important in the process of reorganizing, but it is also important not to make the decision too swiftly. Reorganization is too often viewed as *the solution* to problems that exist in the organization, such as poor information flow. While communication in general and information flow in particular is partly a consequence of the structural design of the organization, it is also a function of the attitudes people hold about the sharing of information. If information is seen as power, and if there is a tendency within your organization for people to be political in their orientation, then they will withhold information regardless of the nature of the structure. Reorganizing is not a panacea to cure whatever ails an organization. The structure is only one critical element of many that make the organization successful.

The first question you need to ask yourself before reorganizing is: "Is reorganization really needed in this case?" To help you answer this question, take a look at your own organization and choose the best response to the questions shown in Figure 12–1.

Do You Need To Reorganize?

1. To what extent does your organization adapt well to changing conditions in the industry?

1	2	3	4	5	6
not at all					to the greatest extent possible

2. Are important organizational tasks falling through the cracks?

1	2	3	4	5	6
not at all					to the greatest extent possible

3. Do people have easy access to others with whom they need to communicate and maintain contact?

1	2	3	4	5	6
not at all					to the greatest extent possible

4. Where groups are highly interdependent, do they have easy access to each other and do they work well together?

1	2	3	4	5	6
not at all					to the greatest extent possible

5. Are managers able to manage well the numbers of people they manage?

1	2	3	4	5	6
not at all					to the greatest extent possible

6. Is there ready access at all levels to key corporate information?

1	2	3	4	5	6
not at all					to the greatest extent possible

7. Do people feel challenged in their jobs?

1	2	3	4	5	6
not at all					to the greatest extent possible

8. Are people able to respond quickly and effectively to customers' needs?

1	2	3	4	5	6
not at all					to the greatest extent possible

Figure 12-1. Reorganization questionnaire.

If, for three or more of these questions, you circled "3" or less, it may be appropriate to restructure your organization. This decision should not be made lightly, however, for as the introductory quote implies, many problems are masked or worsened by inappropriate attempts to reorganize. One high-level executive, for example, felt very strongly that the marketing people in a given business unit did not work well with marketing people in other business units. On the basis of this, she decided to break up the existing business units and reorganize along more traditional functional lines. The result proved positive in the sense that marketing people worked well within the functional units, but relations between different functions went rapidly downhill afterwards.

In effect, she had the same problems as she had before, but then added a great deal of disruption as a result of all the changes. The error was in assuming that restructuring would "fix" the poor working relationships. Had she done a more careful analysis instead and looked at the organizational system as a whole, she would have seen that she could have created forums for marketing people to work together between business units, developed some shared goals in the marketing teams, and provided opportunities to share information between different product lines. This latter strategy would have developed cooperation between groups and avoided the pain that results from reorganization.

The second question you need to ask yourself is: What kind of structure will best enable my organization to be successful in the long run? Too often leaders of organizations answer this question by imbuing in organizations more bureaucracy. Bureaucracy in organization is hurting our competitive capabilities severely. In the course of my work with organizations, I have found, time and time again, a tendency on the part of managers to create layers of management as a way of ensuring they have control over the workers. I have found managers attempt to justify their roles with enormous paperwork, much of which adds little value. I have also found managers create fiefdoms out of some misguided notion that the size of one's organization is a reflection of one's self worth.

In one large company that I worked with, for example, there were numerous managers at the mid-levels who were known throughout the company as terrible managers, and who were considered by the labor union and management alike as the cause of severe distrust between labor and management, a distrust, I might add, that has lasted for over 15 years! Yet, in spite of overwhelming evidence that letting go of these managers and reorganizing in a more streamlined manner would aid considerably the organization as a whole, the top management of the company refused. They cited many reasons for their refusal, yet I could not help sensing throughout all their explanations that their greatest fear was that to let go of these managers or to move them into nonmanagement positions would signal to the rest of the organization, and the labor union in particular, that they were wrong in their judgment. In effect, the top management would rather be right (or have the illusion of being right), than have the organization operate effectively.

Such tendencies to hold on to bureaucracy or to create bureaucracy result in severe costs, not the least of which are slow and incomplete communication, enormous busy work, internal competition, perpetuated mistrust, and organizational immobilization in a time when rapid change is needed. In short, when you look to create a new structure, be wary of the tendency to create more bureaucracy, for this will likely be your own undoing.

DIFFERENT ORGANIZATIONAL STRUCTURES

Organization structure refers to the manner in which an organization puts together its human resources to best achieve its goals. It is the way the parts of the organization are divided up and related to each other. These patterns largely affect the level and quality of interaction, coordination between units, and efficiency of output. When reorganizing, one needs to first look broadly at what one's options are. In effect, you have five basic choices around which you can reorganize, plus a number of variations and adaptions around these five choices. You can organize:

- functionally
- by product, program, or project
- in the form of a matrix
- around particular customers and their needs
- around the work process or information flow

Within each of these choices, you still need to make decisions about span of control, how to divide up the labor, communication flow, and so on. But for now, to simplify the process, let's explore each of these choices in turn, and analyze their various strengths and weaknesses.

Traditional Functional Organization. In years past, the functional organization was what most people thought of when they thought of organizational structure (see Figure 12–2). It is characterized by:

- a clear division of labor between organizational functions
- centralized decision making where heads of each function make key decisions
- a single chain of command
- strong identity within functions
- functions that maximize their own goals

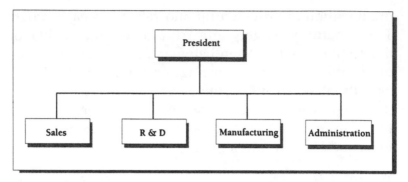

Figure 12-2. Typical functional organization.

The strengths of this traditional organizational structure tend to be:

1. Functions are often organized around professions where there are clearly determined standards of performance.

2. People within functions often talk the same language, thereby facilitating internal communication.

3. There is freedom within functions to specialize and develop specific competencies.

4. It tends to be relatively stable.

The weaknesses of this kind of organization tend to be:

1. Because the activities are specialized and people are strongly identified with their own functions, there can be greater conflict between the various functions.

2. Because decision making is focused at the top, few people see the big picture and decisions are, therefore, made more slowly.

3. The reinforcement of professionally focused units results in those units resisting change.

4. Because of the high emphasis on specialized knowledge, awareness and understanding about the other functions and of the organization as a whole is lacking.

5. It tends to be unresponsive to rapid changes in the marketplace.

Functional organizations tend to work best in situations where the company sells few products, or the product lines are technically similar, and in industry environments that are relatively stable.

Product-Driven Organizational Structure. The product-driven organization emphasizes a decentralized organization based on product or market segments, each managed by a general manager who is responsible for running the total business (see Figure 12–3). Each product, business unit, or division has its own dedicated functional resources, and is organized to respond quickly to changing conditions in each market. Large, highly diversified companies often organize in this way, particularly those whose product areas do not lend themselves well to cross-fertilization. Hewlett-Packard is one such organization that has effectively decentralized its businesses by focusing on different product lines and different product segments. One part of the company, for example, directs its attention to measurement systems while another on computer systems, while still a third is devoted to printing devices, and so on. At the same time, they all come together in an organization devoted to technological advancement.

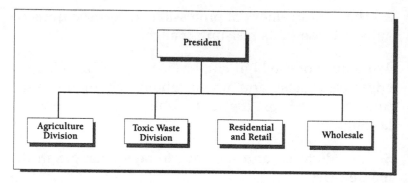

Figure 12-3. Typical product-driven organization.

In general, this kind of organization is characterized by:

1. strong identification with product lines or business units

2. a high degree of coordination between functions within units

3. minimal coordination between product lines

4. an emphasis on rapid product or service delivery

5. authority lying with heads of separate business units

6. complex communication flows

The strengths of the product-driven organizational structure tend to be:

1. Great flexibility within business units enables rapid responses to market changes.

2. Fewer conflicts between functional areas and greater integration within business units.

3. Employees tend to see the big picture and are not as singularly focused as in traditional functional organizations.

4. Opportunities exist for employees to learn different functional skills.

5. It can promote decentralized decision making.

6. It can bring people closer to the market needs.

The weaknesses of this type of organizational structure tend to be:

1. Coordination between business units is minimal, thereby reducing advantages of potential economies of scale.

2. Employees have difficulty staying on the cutting edge in their areas of expertise due to their greater focus on the whole and not on their professions.

3. Duplication of resources between business units often exists and competition between them can occur for scarce resources.

4. Since research and development is located within each existing product area, there is often little innovation beyond the present products.

The product-driven organization design is particularly well suited to highly changing markets and is most appropriate when the company serves multiple markets with multiple products. It tends to be less efficient in highly stable markets as economies of scale are lost.

Matrix Organization. In effect, a matrix organization is a hybrid of the two preceding organizational structures (see Figure 12–4). First introduced by the aerospace industry, it is characterized by a dual reporting structure.

Managers and employees are affiliated with both their functional areas and are part of a multifunctional team responsible for working on a particular project. Hence, people often report to two bosses, a functional manager and a product manager.

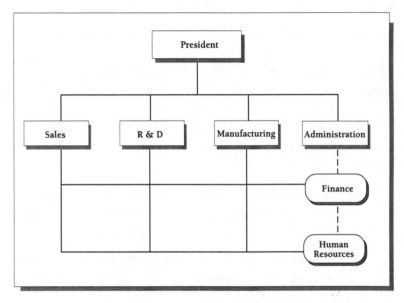

Figure 12-4. Example matrix organization.

The strengths of the matrix organization tend to be:

1. It provides maximum flexibility, and therefore responds well to changing environments.

2. It provides multiple career paths, enabling people to stay specialized in their profession, or to generalize by staying aligned with a product area.

3. It provides greater integration between both functions and business units, thereby reinforcing focus on the whole system.

Its weaknesses, however, make the matrix structure increasingly difficult to implement.

1. It often requires highly complicated and demanding coordination of activities.

2. Its structure tends to promote confusion, conflict, and ambiguity.

3. Groups have to continually negotiate conflicting resource requirements.

4. The great need for coordination requires members to engage in complex interactions and requires high communication skills.

In the 1970s and early 1980s, the matrix organization was viewed as the structure of the future for, although complex, it created more fluid organizational responses to changing environments. Over time, and after considerable experimentation with the matrix organization, experience has shown that its weaknesses have often outweighed its strengths. Its myriad of complications have caused Peters and Waterman, the authors of *In Search of Excellence*, to decry the value of the matrix structure. Nevertheless, many companies have used the matrix structure successfully to manage themselves in highly volatile industries such as the computer industry; and in the absence of any viable alternative, the matrix structure for some organizations has served the valuable purpose of challenging the traditional structures of the past.

Given its conflicting attributes of complexity and flexibility, the matrix structure is best suited for industries characterized by rapidly changing markets and in companies with multiple product lines or even families of products.

The Customer-Driven Structure. The customer-driven structure is a structure that brings different functions of the organization together and has them collaborating effectively in order to better meet particular sets of customers' needs (see Figure 12–5). This relatively new and emerging form of organization is becoming more and more popular as companies see that focusing their resources on customers needs not only gives them a competitive advantage, but also the ability to stay ahead of rising customer expectations.

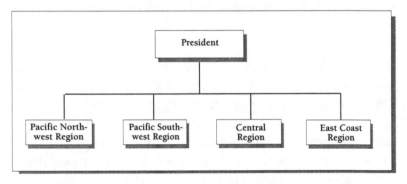

Figure 12-5. Example customer-driven organization.

Some large consulting firms are finding this kind of structure particularly effective to meet the unique needs of their customers. Some kinds of customers, for example, such as those in health care, require that their consultants and vendors understand the challenges they face in their industry—its regulatory environment, its language, as well as the unique needs of its customers.

Customer-driven organizations often organize either by customers in geographic areas, or by types of customers. All the functional features of the organization work together, often with a strong team orientation, to better understand and better serve their customers.

In general, this kind of organization is characterized by:

1. deep understanding of customers by population or segment.

2. high degree of coordination between functions within different customer-focused units.

3. minimal coordination between customer-focused units.

4. emphasis on responsiveness to customer problems and knowledge of changing customers' needs.

5. authority lies with heads of separate customer units.

6. complex communication flows.

The strengths of the customer-driven organizational design tend to be:

1. Great flexibility within business units enabling rapid response to market change

2. Fewer conflicts between functional areas and greater integration

3. Team members tend to see the big picture

4. High degree of responsiveness to customers

5. Greater understanding of customers' needs, yielding greater innovation

6. Can be more satisfying for people because of potential for high degree of teamwork

7. Opportunities for employees to learn different skills

The weaknesses of this organizational type tend to be:

1. Coordination between business units is minimal, thereby reducing advantages of potential economies of scale.

2. Employees have difficulty staying on the cutting edge in their areas of expertise due to greater focus on the whole and not on their professions.

3. Duplication of resources between business units.

4. Conflict between business units can often occur between them for scarce resources.

5. Requires a high degree of business knowledge on the part of the employees and a high degree of teamwork. (This is both a potential weakness and, if mastered, a great strength.)

Process-Driven Structure. The process-driven structure is one that is created to maximize efficiency and quality (see Figure 12–6). It is created by determining how the business processes should best flow and operate and then designing the structure around that flow.

The process-driven structure is an approach that is rapidly growing in popularity and has many advantages when compared to the method of structuring organizations based on a rigidly defined division of labor.

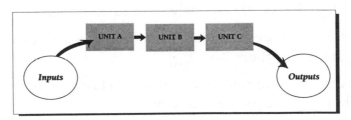

Figure 12-6. Typical process-driven structure.

It is based on the notion that organizational simplicity and natural work flow are key principles that guide organizational effectiveness. While not always the case, designing to best meet the process needs of the organization often requires challenging old assumptions about the process of production and designing from scratch. In this way, it can be an extraordinarily difficult approach to structuring the organization, yet enormously productive as well. According to Michael Hammer and James Champy, authors of *Reengineering the Corporation*, there are several recurring themes or characteristics of process-driven organizations:

1. Several jobs are combined into one.

2. Workers tend to make decisions in a flatter organizational system.

3. The steps in the process are performed in a natural order.

4. Processes have multiple versions, resulting in greater flexibility of response.

5. Work is performed where it makes most sense.

6. Checks and controls are reduced.[2]

The potential strengths of the process-driven structure are:

1. Greater efficiency in all aspects of operations

2. Greater satisfaction of workers due to their greater responsibilities

---

[2] Hammer, M., Champy, J. *Reengineering the Corporation: A Manifesto for Business Revolution*, Harper Business, New York, 1993.

3. Better ability to focus on process improvement

4. Greater ability to respond to unique customers' needs

5. Potential quantum leaps in performance

The potential weaknesses of this structure are:

1. It is often difficult to implement initially.

2. It requires a higher degree of skill on the part of workers (this can also be a tremendous strength).

3. It often means doing more with less people, which can cause hardship for individuals.

In practice, both the customer-driven structure and the process-driven structure are not structures at all, but principles upon which to guide structural design and decisions. These principles require organizations to let go of outdated ways of structuring their business and boldly seek alternatives that maximize efficiency, customer response, employee satisfaction, flexibility, and adaptability.

WHICH STRUCTURE TO CHOOSE

Generally, which structure to choose for your organization will be decided best by determining the organization's environment and the particular needs that come from that environment. For example, in highly stable environments where products change little over time and information is relatively certain, a functional organization seems best suited due to its overall efficiency. In a research group, where information is uncertain, standardized roles might limit creativity, and be incompatible with the flexibility of reporting relationships that researchers tend to prefer. In such an organization, a less formal, more integrating structure is appropriate. In a rapidly changing environment or where companies need to be extremely responsive to customers, such as those faced by marketing-driven organizations, a customer-driven organizational structure tends to be more effective.

While there are strengths and weaknesses to each organizational structure, the world is rapidly moving in the direction of being more and more complex and fluid. In such a world, the design principles that underlie both customer and process-driven structures are growing in emphasis as business success is becoming more and more dependent on an ability to understand customer's needs, respond to those needs in an efficient and effective manner, and improve one's ability to do both over time. In addition, in such a world, the ability to create relationships with other organizations is critical. No longer can an organization lock itself into one structure of employing a group of people and expect that changes will only require modifications. Strategic collaborations between organizations and networking between and among professions is becoming of paramount importance. No longer can any one organization successfully meet the needs of all of its customers. If it chooses and remains with an inflexible organizational structure, it will lock itself into a situation where the employee base may become obsolete in the future.

Organizations all over the world are seeing this situation coming about and establishing creative strategic alliances. One of the more graphic examples of this was demonstrated by Robert Reich in his outstanding book, *The Work of Nations*. In his book, he showed how, when you purchase a car from a U.S. manufacturer, you are really purchasing something that has been created from a huge number of strategic relationships all over the globe. Of the $10,000 you might have paid for a Pontiac Lemans in 1990, for example, $3000 of it went to South Korea for routine labor and assembly, $1750 went to Japan for advanced components such as engines and transaxels, $750 went to West Germany for styling and design, and so on (see Figure 12–7).[3]

$10,000 for Pontiac Lemans: 1990		
$ 3,000	South Korea	routine labor and assembly
$ 1,750	Japan	advanced components engines, transaxels, electronics
$ 750	West Germany	styling and design
$ 400	Taiwan, Singapore and Japan	small components
$ 250	Britain	advertising and marketing
$ 50	Ireland	data processing
$ 4,000	Detroit New York Washington, D.C.	strategists lawyers and bankers lobbyists

Source: Reich, R., *The Work of Nations*. Vintage Books, 1991, p. 113.

Figure 12-7. The global network.

Research on the subject of organizational structure also seems to suggest that today the most effective organizational structures are those that create opportunities for specialization and, at the same time, create ways to better integrate different functions.[4] Depending on the type of structure you choose, substructures may also need to be created to counterbalance the nature of the

---

[3] Reich, R., *The Work of Nations*, Alfred A. Knopf, New York, 1991, p. 113.
[4] Lawrence, P. and Lorsch, J., *Organization and Environment*, Graduate School of Business Administration, Harvard University, Boston, 1967.

superstructure. For example, in a highly specialized functional organization, one needs to create mechanisms and forums to allow for greater coordination between functions. In product-focused organizations, one needs to bring together people in the same functions now and then to support their professional identity, an identity that can get lost given the need to integrate cross-functionally. Finally, in matrix organizations where human systems can become overly complex, clear policies need to be created to counterbalance the chaos. Moreover, in matrix organizations, people need to be trained in managing diversity and change to help them manage more effectively within the more complex structure. In effect, then, no one structure works perfectly. They only work well to the extent that they balance the needs for specialization with the needs for integration in any given company.

As you consider alternative structures, it is important to keep in mind the long-term vision of your organization, as well the practical environmental factors that impact your effectiveness. Most importantly, for enduring success, you should think about the process of restructuring in terms of how to help your organization develop its strength and capability. The rest of this chapter provides a guide.

HOW TO DESIGN
YOUR ORGANIZATION'S STRUCTURE

In the field of organizational behavior, long dominated by a preoccupation with organization structure, it is curious to find that up until recently, there has been little literature on the process of how to change an organization's structure in order to make it more effective.

The following process is intended to provide guidelines for undertaking this venture, paying particular attention to the needs of the people who the structural change is intended to effect. This attention is crucial, for without it, people will likely both resist change and make the new structure every bit as ineffectual as the old one. With sufficient attention up front, the process promotes a more comprehensive understanding of your organization, and the differing perspectives and objectives your organizational members hold. At its best, the process will yield greater internal collaboration and permit a greater focus on the large picture, a result that presumably was in part the reason for the organizational change in the first place.

In brief, the phases of reorganizing your organization are as follows (Figure 12–8).

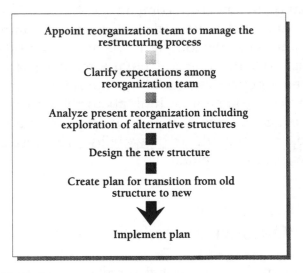

Figure 12-8. Steps to reorganizing.

APPOINTING A REORGANIZATION TEAM

Historically, most leaders of organizations have assumed that people are not capable of making decisions for the greater good of the organization. Many leaders fear that, if given the chance, others will make organizational recommendations that are self-serving. Consequently, most leaders of organizations have taken it upon themselves to make structural changes in the organization. If counsel is sought, they have traditionally turned to outside consultants who, they believe, will take a detached, unbiased view of the organization.

Based on this narrow and somewhat cynical view of human beings and their motivation, most leaders of organizations have traditionally made changes somewhat unilaterally, and hoped that the new structure would work out well. More often than not, the leader winds up paying the price of not involving others in the design process with their resistance, resentment, and passive/aggressive behavior. Other's behavior, then, reinforces the leader's original belief that employees are self-serving in their thinking, and therefore not capable of making structural changes in the organization for the greater good of all (see Figure 12–9).

Taking a participative approach to organizational design goes against conventional practice, yet it almost always produces far better results and greater commitment in the long run. Taking a participative approach, in which key people are included in the thinking through and implementation of a new organizational structure, requires the participants to expose their assumptions, clarify their objectives, and explore alternatives. It is a process that integrates different views and challenges the participants to focus on the organization

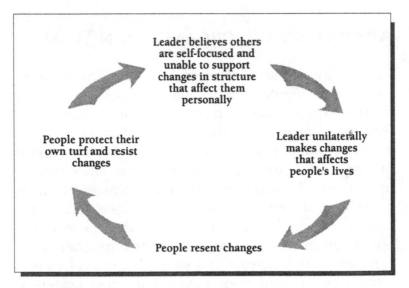

Leader believes others
are self-focused and
unable to support
changes in structure
that affect them
personally

People protect their
own turf and resist
changes

Leader unilaterally
makes changes
that affects
people's lives

People resent changes

Figure 12-9. Self-sealing cycle of belief.

as a whole as they make structural redesign recommendations.

To make the structural redesign process a collaborative one, you will need to create a reorganization team.
The purpose of the reorganization team is to ensure
that the organization's new structure is optimal, and to
anticipate organizational difficulties in the process of
change. In addition, the reorganization team can ensure
there is a relatively high degree of buy-in for the new
organizational structure on the part of others.

The best people to have on the team are the original
Design Team members, plus a handful of others who
have had experience in other major reorganization efforts. These people will be able to advise you and your
reorganization team of pitfalls that may occur in the
process of organizational restructuring, as well as help
you in coming up with the best new structure to suit
your present and near-term future needs.

It is important to be aware that the prospect of reorganization is often a foreboding one for organizational members. Relationships have been built up over time in the old structure and expectations have been established. These expectations may change, but in general, people are uncomfortable with change because of the potential loss that change portends. Hence, there will always be a tendency to resist change, and organizational performance during the period of change may suffer.

Anticipating these fears, and the ensuing potential resistance, many organizational leaders often withhold information to protect people from this feeling of threat and to protect themselves from the potential loss of productivity. This behavior is counterproductive: it only fuels the feelings of being threatened because what people fear the most is what they don't know.

The opposite response, to tell everyone everything, also has its risks. What if, in the middle of the process of analyzing the organization, you decide to keep the organization's structure almost the same as before. Is the associated disruption worth it? Probably not.

The best approach seems to be to let people know that a team is coming together to assess the effectiveness of the current organization and to look for areas to improve. If you decide to explore the possibility of reorganizing, let people know that they will have ample opportunity to express their concerns and to influence whatever choices are made, and that the intent of the team is to ensure the process of managing any changes will be smooth and effective. Communicate this to people in the organization, and then promise to keep people abreast of the progress of the team. This up-front approach to communication engenders trust, and minimizes the likelihood of anticipatory anxiety.

CLARIFICATION OF EXPECTATIONS

In your initial meeting with the reorganization team, begin the meeting, as always, by ensuring that everyone is on board and that everyone understands the nature of the team and its objectives. The objective of the team ought to be to analyze the effectiveness of the present structure and to discover and design the kind of structure that will best help the organization meet its future goals and accomplish its strategies.

The process of achieving these objectives can often take as much as six months to a year, depending on the size of your organization and the magnitude of the structural change that is needed. Members of the reorganization team may need to meet initially for a couple of weeks to become educated in the process of reorganization and their role in it, and as much as one-half to one day every week thereafter for many months until the process is complete. In larger organizations, it may require more time; in smaller organizations, less. Given the magnitude of the organizational effort involved, the team will need to be appraised in advance of what likely will be involved so that false expectations are not created.

It will be particularly important that ground rules be laid down for this team, for information can easily get out of hand, and sensitive issues can easily turn into heated discussions. In effect, when restructuring an organization, you are playing with people's lives. While you will need to step back as a team and coolly analyze the organization and the roles and relationships of the people within the current structure, the organization is much more than a bunch of boxes on an organizational chart. These are real people, whose careers and working relationships will be impacted by the change. To-gether, as a team, you will be making decisions that impact all these people, and yourselves. Establishing ground rules up front—such as honest communication, free exchange of ideas, a supportive environment within which to explore alternatives, and confidential-ity—will be critical.

Confidentiality about what gets discussed in the meetings is particularly critical. What if, for example, the group discusses a change that, in effect, will result in one person being promoted to head a new area in the organization. Let's imagine they explore who might be best suited for this role, that this information leaks out prematurely, and this person is made aware of the potential change and gets very excited about it. Let's also imagine that another person wanted that position and feels that they deserve it. What happens if you as a group later decided not to make the structural change. Both of these people will not only feel jerked around, but each will have built up resentment: one because he or she did not get the position, the other because he or she was in effect told they did not deserve the position as much as the other person. In either case, it is far more prudent to maintain confidentiality until the group has made its final decisions.

Having a facilitator guide these meetings will be par-ticularly helpful here, for highly sensitive issues and disagreements are almost sure to arise. Part of the role of the facilitator is to help the team keep to the ground rules and navigate the choppy waters that may from time to time surface.

Once you have set and clarified the ground rules, expectations, and challenges in front of the reorganiza-tion team, it is important to spend as much time as necessary educating members of the team on the process or reorganization, and its opportunities and pit-falls. Many members of the team may not have been through such a process, let alone led one, so education and training is critical. The content of the education should answer such questions as:

- What is structure and how does it influence organizational success?
- How does structure relate to other elements of an organization's architecture?
- How is the process of reorganization best led?
- What is their role in the process of reorganization?
- What is the purpose and aim of reorganizing?

In addition, some team-building activities will likely be valuable to begin to develop a strong sense of trust and teamwork among members.

ANALYSIS OF YOUR PRESENT ORGANIZATION

Designing a new organizational structure involves the assessment of one's current organization; an analysis of the fit between that organization, the emerging environment, and your strategic goals; and then finally the creation of a new, more effective structure. To elaborate, an appropriate structure effectively integrates each of four key features of organizational life: strategic direction and strategic goals, the business environment, the tasks and work processes, and the people (Figure 12–10).

Your understanding of these key features will be crucial in directing the creation of a new structure. To help you and your reorganization team think through the

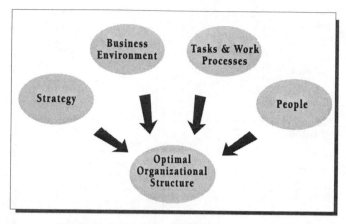

Figure 12-10. Factors influencing choice of the best organizational structure.

various factors that will impact the creation of a new structure, read through and answer as many of the following questions that seem relevant:

Strategy

1. What is the future strategic direction of your company?

2. How well does the present organizational structure help or hinder you in achieving the new strategic direction?

Business Environment

1. Describe your business environment in terms of its complexity and the degree of flexibility required to adapt to and respond to change. Where do you see your industry on the following graph in Figure 12–11?

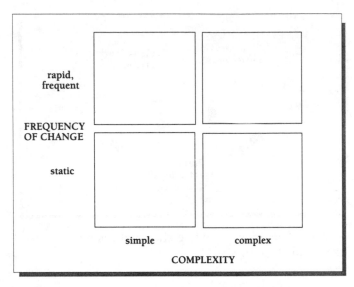

Figure 12-11. Different environmental conditions.

2. Describe the key demands or expectations that your customers place on your company below.

Demand 1 _____

Demand 2 _____

Demand 3 _____

Demand 4 _____

Demand 5 _____

Demand 6 _____

Demand 7 _____

3. How well do you presently respond to each of these requirements?

4. What kinds of changes are now occurring or will soon occur in your customers' expectations and how well are you presently organized to meet these changes?

5. What new technological developments are occurring in your industry and how will they impact on you?

6. What kinds of changes are occurring in the regulatory or legislative environment and how will the changes affect your business?

7. How are your competitors structuring their organizations? How does this help or hinder them in delivering their services/products?

8. What other features of the environment affect you, and what are their implications for an effective organizational design for your company?

9. What kinds of structures will best enable you to respond to your changing business environment?

Have each person on your reorganization team answer each of these questions separately. In a one- or two-day meeting, collect all their responses on flip charts, and come to consensus on as many of these as possible. The aim here is not to come to full agreement, but to get a sense of people's differing views and what factors are most important to consider.

On the basis of what comes out on the flip charts, construct a summary flip chart that identifies the five or six key factors that are affecting you and what those factors suggest in terms of an ideal organizational structure. Do not draw any conclusions yet, for you have assessed only two key features of the organization. Two more are still to come.

Work Processes

Continue the process of analysis by looking at your current work processes. The best way of looking at the way you currently manage or do work is as a flow, where there are inputs, internal processes, and outputs (Figure 12–12).

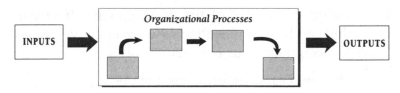

Figure 12-12. Work process diagram.

As you consider your work process, think first about what the key inputs are:

1. Who are your key suppliers?

2. How effective is your relationship with each supplier?

3. How does the present structure help or hinder you in those relationships?

4. What kind of structure will help improve that relationship?

Now think about your work processes. Your overall work process is made up of a set of activities that interrelate with one another in the form of a process. Years ago, people used to look at organizations purely in terms of functions, or in boxes of tasks. This simplistic approach tends to limit one's ability to look at the organization as a process. To help you look at your organization as a process, a flow chart is instructive.

A flow chart is a diagram of the sequential steps in a process. Flow charts typically show process inputs, activities, decision points, and outputs. Programmers and analysts have used flow charts for years to document the logic of computer programs. However, flow charts can also be extremely useful in analyzing the overall process by which an organization produces its products or delivers its services.

Flow charts are particularly useful to:

- Draw a picture of an existing or proposed process
- Identify process "bottlenecks" and source delays
- Identify unnecessary tasks
- Identify duplication of effort
- Identify tasks that can be automated
- Identify process complexity
- Serve as a training tool for new employees

In this case, we will use a flow chart to identify bottlenecks, unnecessary tasks, areas of duplication, and to discover opportunities to simplify the overall organization.

The best way to construct a flow chart is to interview the people performing each work process. This can be done in an individual or group setting. Often, people working in a given process are not aware of all of the steps in the process. Therefore, a group setting can be informative for all involved. Bear in mind that at this point you are not designing the optimal flow, but are describing how the work flow actually occurs. People may disagree on this, so do your best to arrive at a rough consensus.

There are many different flow chart symbols and styles. You can use the simplest ones for this particular situation, because you are looking for the overall features of the process and, at this point, are not interested in a microanalysis of each step in the work flow in your organization. For our purposes, have rectangles represent a step in the work process, a diamond for a yes/no decision, and an oval for a point in the flow indicating the beginning point in the process, the end point in process, or an interruption in the process. Here is how to create a flow chart, step by step.

Step One. Begin the flow chart at the top left-hand portion of the page. Create columns to represent each major function of the organization or each major unit. See, for example, Figure 12–13.

Step Two. Draw the chart in a vertical manner, keeping all the symbols the same distance from each other. Put the activities in the columns where the activity occurs Write your notations legibly and simply inside the flow chart symbol (Figure 12–14).

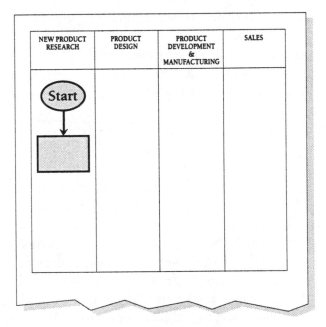

Figure 12-13. Columns of major functions.

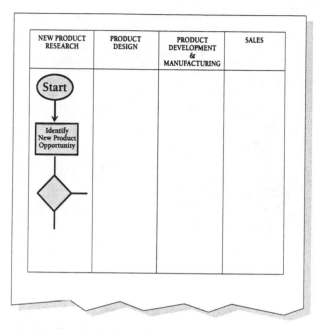

Figure 12-14. Symbols describing an activity or action and a decision point.

Step Three. Add arrows to show the direction of the work flow. Normal flow is down, or left to right. Decision symbols must have two flow lines coming out of them: one for yes, one for no. Alternative decisions are "maybe" or sometimes a decision will be "go to a, b, or c, depending on what occurred in a prior step." Use your judgment and some common sense in constructing the flow chart. Make up the proper pathway as you go. Be sure to remember that you are not describing the process as you would like it to be, but as it presently exists (Figure 12–15).

Step Four. At decision points that lead to an earlier point or where rework often occurs, draw the flow line to the left or right and upward (Figure 12–16).

At decision points that lead to a subsequent step,

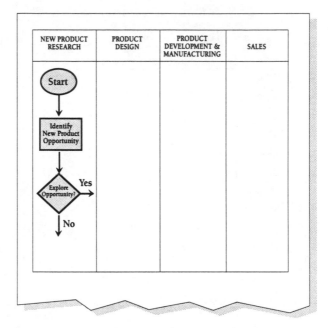

Figure 12-15. Arrows showing direction of work flow.

draw the flow line to the right or left and downward (Figure 12–17).

Based on your picture of the flow of your organization, discuss as a group where the flow breaks down or is ineffectual. To do this, use the following questions as a guide:

1. Where do errors typically occur in the process? Where is there (too much) rework?

2. Where is there redundancy or overlap that causes confusion?

3. Which steps seem to add little value to the customer? To the organization as a whole?

4. Where does the process get bogged down?

5. Where can steps be simplified?

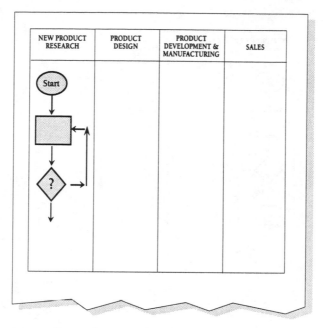

Figure 12-16. Rework example.

Based on this analysis, begin to think about a new flow for your process that will work more effectively. Consider ways to simplify the flow. Look closely at each key step in the process. Are there areas that do not add value to the customer? How can you reduce aspects of the process that do not add significant value? Play with it and create a flow for the process that minimizes the impact of breakdowns. In particular, what kind of flow will better meet your customers' needs? Create this new, more ideal flow diagram knowing you are not committing yourself to it. Do it as a group as a way of exploring alternatives.

Now look at your current structure. How does your present structure help or hinder your ability to manage this more effective flow or process? What changes or what new structure would facilitate a more efficient and effective work flow?

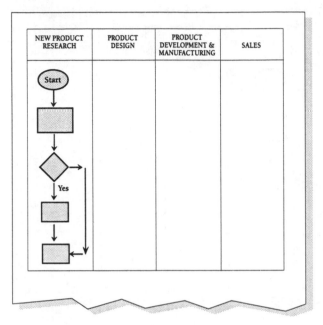

Figure 12-17. Movement to subsequent steps.

People

Organizations are not designed in a vacuum. People fill roles and relate to one another in those roles. It is important that you take into consideration the skill level of your people as you go about reorganizing. Do the people have the capabilities they need to manage a new structure? Where are they missing skill sets? What are the strengths of your people? Where can you best leverage those strengths? The answers to these questions are important to keep in mind as you develop your proposed new structure.

It is particularly important that you do not create a structure that is driven by the qualities, characteristics, and needs of individuals. Too often, organizations create structures at the top to suit the particular whims and desires of the individuals at the top. In these situations, the organizational structure will have little internal integrity, and people will be pushed into roles and relationships that are woefully inadequate to the task. One example of this is a company where I worked that hired a highly talented vice president responsible for marketing and sales. After a couple of years, he wanted to take on more responsibility and threatened to leave if this did not happen. Out of fear of losing his talents, the company put another part of the organization under his wing—product development. While there were some opportunities for synergy between the two functions, for most people the coupling of the two organizations did not make sense. He ended up leading both groups separately and at times trying to force team building to occur between the two functions. As a result, he gave only scant attention to each area and both lost focus and direction.

Hence, when you go about restructuring, you want to think of the skills, talents, and abilities of your work force as a whole, not those of the specific individuals.

Limiting Factors in the Design of New Structures. Before designing the organization and sometime during or after your analysis of strategy, business environment, processes, and people, it will be important to look at how your organization's culture impacts the choices you make about structure. You will likely find, for example, that people on the reorganization team have assumptions about what effective structures look like. These assumptions are often determined by the culture of the organization and can limit the choices they make for the structure. For example, people who manage in organizational cultures characterized by command and control often have difficulty letting go of their reliance on functional structures. It is important to be open to all kinds of forms of structure and not to let one's assumptions be a limiting factor.

At this point in the process of reorganization, what you will also need to fight against is the belief that you and other members of the team know more than others. People often have a strong tendency to limit their thinking out of a need to be right, or to have the right answer. This kind of thinking will impair your ability to consider creative and potentially fruitful alternatives.

To help challenge the members of the reorganization team to think openly and creatively, it may be valuable to seek input from others. In particular, look to your customers for ideas. They may have some excellent thoughts about how to structure your organization. Certainly they can tell you what works or doesn't work for them about your present structure. Also look at what other companies are doing in different industries. Benchmarking what they do can challenge you to consider alternatives that presently do not exist in your thinking. My business partners and I often seek input from valued clients about what other clients might consider as they make key decisions. We sometimes even have them talk with one another to extract ideas and stimulate creative thinking. You and others will likely find that there are options and approaches to structure available to you that you never dreamed would work. Not only do they work, but they work better than what you had considered.

DESIGNING YOUR NEW STRUCTURE

It is now time for you to put all of the above information together and design your new organizational structure. To design your organization, you will need to follow these steps (Figure 12–18).

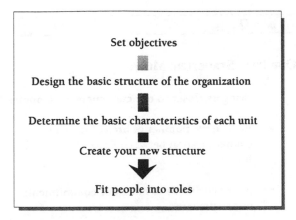

Figure 12-18. Steps to designing a new structure.

Step One: Set Objectives. To begin, it will be helpful to articulate the key objectives of the new design. To do this, take all of the information you gathered above and, using a flip chart in a group, write down the most important goals you want to achieve as a result of a new structure. This is not an abstract list of design principles, but a specific list that identifies the key points you want to cover in a new design. For example, one group condensed their analysis and on a flip chart put their restructuring goals (Figure 12–19).

Step Two: Design the Basic Overall Structure. Based on your list of objectives, the next important step is to think about the basic overall structure of the organization and where to put your organizational boundaries in the new design. Boundaries are where you put the dividing lines in your organization. In an organization chart, for example, the boxes represent groupings, the space between the boxes are the boundaries. The boundaries, in effect, define the boxes that make up the organization's structure (see Figure 12–20).

Boundaries are neither good nor bad. They just exist. They exist any time you define a group of people and

OUR NEW STRUCTURE MUST:

- Bring us closer to our customers geographically

- Reduce the number of breakdowns in communication between departments and function

- Better enable us to meet our commitments to our customers

- Improve and speed up the new product development process

- Cut down on corporate-level overhead and push more responsibility

- Put us in closer contact with our suppliers to include them in the process of production

- Reduce the need for quality inspection while at the same time increase the quality of our products

Figure 12-19. Example of goals for restructuring.

bring them together. Those who are part of that group are in, and those who are not are out. The stronger the group identity, the stronger the boundary. This principle is critical, for as soon as you create boundaries, you create the dynamics of "we" and "they." If not managed well, this "we/they" distinction can easily lead to counterproductive competition. If managed well, boundaries can serve to clarify areas of needed coordination and communication.

Louis Davis, an expert in organization redesign, argues that the most crucial single act in the design of an organization is where you place the internal boundaries. Boundary location, in his view, directly affects almost everything else in the organizational structure. It affects the units of the organization, influences what responsibilities are to be assigned, affects the flow of information, and impacts the nature of all of the relationships.[5]

There are no absolute rules for how to organize or where to place your boundaries. However, the follow-

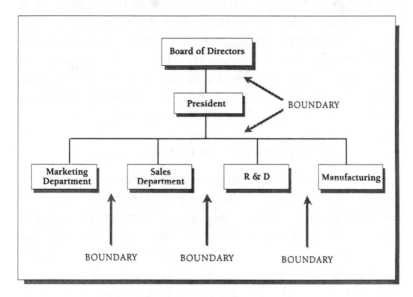

Figure 12-20. Where boundaries exist.

---

[5] Davis, L. E. "Guides to the Design and Redesign of Organizations," in Tannenbaum, R., Margulies, N., Massarik, F. and Associates, *Human Systems Development,* Jossey-Bass, San Francisco, 1985, p. 153.

ing principles are extremely useful in thinking about designing your new organizational structure.[6]

Principles for Designing Overall Basic Structure

1. Begin by focusing your attention on the primary nature of your business and use the five different models of organization structure as a guide. Build the basic structure and then move toward filling in the specific organizational parts.

2. Design your organization to have as few hierarchical levels as possible. Tall hierarchical structures are notorious for building bureaucratic impediments to effective communication. A. T. Kearny, Inc., a Chicago-based consulting firm, once studied the top 26 performing companies and compared them to 15 lesser-performing companies of similar size and product scope. They found that the top performers averaged 7.2 management levels while the poor performers averaged 11.1.[7]

These results are both powerful and telling. In the fast-moving world of today and tomorrow, sharing information and rapidly making and implementing decisions will continue to be a critical competitive advantage. Bureaucracies and hierarchies tend to inhibit information sharing and internal communication because of the tendency of people to manage by control, and not by commitment, and because of the tendency

---

[6] Many of these principles are highlighted in Davis, L. E. "Guides to the Design and Redesign of Organizations," in Tannenbaum, R., Margulies, N., Massarik, F. and Associates, *Human Systems Development*, Jossey-Bass, San Francisco, 1985, pp. 153–156, and Nadler, D., Gerstein, M., Shaw, R., and Associates, *Organizational Architecture: Designs for Changing Organizations*, Jossey-Bass, San Francisco, 1982, pp. 35–36.

[7] Peters, T. "Why Smaller Staffs Do Better," *The New York Times*, April 21, 1985, Section C, pp. 1, 14–15.

of people to protect their turf. Design your organization to limit these competitive killers—keep your hierarchy to a minimum.

3. In general, although by no means exclusively, a decentralized structure is better than a centralized one. Decentralized organizations put greater responsibility for results directly in the hands of the people leading the organizations. They also are more likely to be responsive to changing environments if you design the suborganizations to be closely aligned with customer sectors, product lines, or geographical concerns. IBM remained centralized for too long and paid the price. So did Digital Equipment Corporation. Hewlett-Packard just recently saw that a movement toward centralization was going to hurt them, and reinforced their commitment to remaining decentralized. As a result, their market capitalization is more two-thirds that of IBM (in 1990 it was one-tenth), and they posted robust earnings of $881 million on revenues of $16.4 billion for the fiscal year ending in October 1992.[8]

Similarly, General Electric has a policy of only staying in markets where their company can retain a first- or second-place market share. This requires each part of their business to stand on their own two feet. Such a policy, while not appropriate for all businesses (I'll take third place in some industries, thank you very much), it has helped GE stay strong in spite of its huge size.[9]

Related to the decentralization principle is the importance of chunking the organization into smaller, relatively autonomous units, each of which is self-

---

[8] Pitta, J., "It had to be done and we did it," *Forbes*, April 26, 1993, pp. 148–152.
[9] See Tichy, N. and Sherman, S., *Control Your Destiny or Someone Else Will*, Doubleday, New York, 1993.

contained. By doing so, you are helping the autonomous units maintain control over their own destiny.

David Nadler, one of the leading consultants in the
area of large-systems change, corroborates the above
and asserts that to be viable in today's rapidly changing
and complex business environment, businesses must
create organizational structures that are based on
smaller, interdependent systems and that are collaborative in nature. In a recent book, he and his associates
provide a clear and elegant model depicting the nature
of the business environment and the appropriate structures for that environment (Figure 12–21).

Based on the above guidelines, as a group decide
which principles or guidelines are most critical for your
organization. Keep in mind your objectives as you come
up with this list.

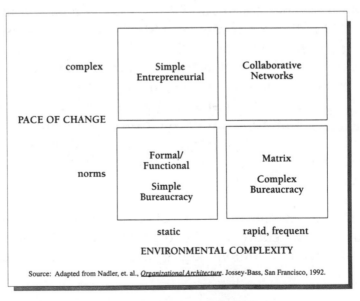

Figure 12-21. Appropriate structures for different
environments.

Step 3: Determine the Basic Characteristics of Each Unit (Divisions or Departments). As a group, discuss what is needed to comprise the basic units of your organization. As you discuss these, keep in mind your objectives and use the following principles as a guide.

Principles For Designing Units Within the Overall Structure

1. Since you are now entering into more specific areas of organizational structure, it would be valuable to seek the input of representative members of that area. Their lives will be affected by the changes you are exploring, so their input and commitment will be critical.

2. Identify the primary business unit of the organization. These could be work teams, project teams, groups that are focused on a particular customer, etc. For example, in traditional functionally designed organizations, the basic organizational unit is the function. For sales-driven organizations, organized to meet specific market needs, the basic organizational unit is the group that works together to develop and sell products or services to that market.

Have these units be the basic building blocks upon which to design your structure. To the fullest extent possible, these units should consist of a set of capabilities that permit the fulfillment of an entire segment of the work process, from start to finish. For example, if the primary work of the organization is to deliver a service to a particular set of customers, the unit should be comprised of a group of people capable of providing that entire service in full. How you define the unit determines all the other organizational boundaries and is very likely to be the single most crucial feature in the structure of your organization.

3. Design from the unit outward. Design the basic unit building block first, and then design the administrative and related staff functions around the unit. The administrative functions that surround the unit should be kept to a minimum.

4. To design a unit, take a typical unit and along with people who understand the unit, and whose input you respect, clarify its work process. Use your analysis above as a guide. Design the unit to best accomplish this process from both an efficiency standpoint and a human satisfaction standpoint. Designing of the work process that puts decisions in the hands of people directly developing or delivering the work is often best. In effect, what you are doing is designing work processes prior to designing the overall structure of the organization. Instead of building an organization around the division of labor and the creation of a hierarchy, analyze the steps in the work process and design as necessary to create subgroups based on natural boundaries and meaningful jobs for individuals and teams.

5. Whenever possible, have teams be the basic organization unit, not individuals. In other words, have teams be responsible for producing the product or delivering the service of your organization. Give these teams as much latitude as possible and work closely with them to clarify their goals and responsibilities as a team. Optimum team size is somewhere between five and fifteen. More than 20 is difficult to manage; fewer than four are easily disrupted by promotions, absenteeism, etc.

While I have intentionally stayed away from advocating strongly one approach over another and primarily focused on the process you use for making structural and related decisions, I do feel that for teams to operate most effectively, they should be as self-managing as possible and not traditionally supervised. Self-managed teams are becoming more and more popular as a way of organizing. They have the potential to be the most effective way to organize in many cases, but at the same time most difficult, for they require very different skills to manage and lead than ones most organizations are familiar with.

For self-managed teams to work, they need to have full control over the factors and processes that affect the outcome of their work. This includes having the information they need to make decisions. People in the teams should have multiple capabilities, and the teams' tasks should be defined with maximum flexibility and freedom. For the teams to work effectively, people in teams will need to be trained on how to be effective team members. Feedback mechanisms that measure the outcomes of each unit's work process need to be put in place to support the team's ability to manage itself, correct itself, and continuously improve.

Many managers in organizations oppose the idea of self-management for it raises their fears that they will not be needed. Contrary to their assumptions about self-managed teams, there is a critical role for managers in the organizations that utilize this approach. For example, in such organizations, managers can act as facilitators; they can and often do make important personnel-and budget-related decisions that are outside the scope of the team's charter; they can help provide effective integration with other departments and teams; and they can focus their attention on more strategic issues. Moreover, while creating such organizations there will likely be a transition period during which the manager's role will be a hybrid between the more traditional roles of management and the newer one.

It requires a significant movement from a direct-and-control orientation to a facilitate-and-guide orientation. Such a shift is not for everyone. Moreover, it requires training managers to adopt the skills and behaviors to successfully manage in the self-managed organization. While difficult to implement, requiring much time in planning and execution, the promise of greater results is, for many, well worth the effort.[10]

6. In general, organize to meet the needs of specific customer segments to ensure close connection and responsiveness to customers. Develop relatively self-contained units, able to anticipate and respond to these customers' needs.

Designing organizations in the above manner, while it goes against conventional wisdom that places boundaries around functions, often optimizes teamwork, internal coordination, flexibility and adaptability, long-term effectiveness, and human satisfaction.

Based on the above guidelines, write on flip charts two or three alternative designs of your basic units. For each of them, identify the potential strengths and weaknesses in terms of the most critical objectives for your new design. Out of this, a new unit structure will emerge that seems to best achieve your critical aims.

Step 4: Flesh Out the Design of Your New Structure. Once you have designed the basic overall structure and the units within that structure, design the support systems and related structures that will help the units do their

---

[10] For an excellent explanation of what self-managed teams are and how to create them, see Wellins, R.S., Byham, W.C., and Wilson, J. M. *Empowered Teams: Creating Self-Directed Work Groups That Improve Quality, Productivity, and Participation,* Jossey-Bass, San Francisco, 1991, and Fisher, K. *Leading Self-Directed Work Teams: A Guide to Developing New Team Leadership Skills,* McGraw-Hill, Inc., New York, 1993.

job. These include the staff functions like human resources, strategic planning, administrative support,
etc., the functions that help in planning, coordinating
information flow, and ensure effective communication
between units.

Create a management structure that fulfills the need
for coordination between units and high-level business decision making. Keep the executive and middle-
management functions to a minimum. Organizations
that have lean and efficient administrative and executive functions tend to have low overhead and higher
profits.

Write down on a flip chart this new structure with
boxes to represent key groups and/or individual roles,
and as a group flesh out the design. Between the various units, there may necessarily be variations. Discuss
these differences and come to tentative agreement
about the variations. Without becoming wedded to the
new structure, let it sit for a couple of days. See how it
feels. Ask the group to consider some questions over
these intervening days.

- Is there anything critical missing?
- Does it enable us to coordinate our efforts?
- Does it allow for innovation or expansion?
- Does it meet the needs of our customers?
- Does it allow for a balanced allocation of resources?
- Will it help us accomplish our strategic direction?
- Will all daily operational tasks be accomplished in
  this structure?
- What new problems will this new organizational
  structure create?

Consider whatever other questions come to mind,
such as those expressed earlier in the chapter. Share
your new ideas with others. Kick these ideas around.

Make revisions until you as a reorganization team feel good about your new design.

Step 5: Fit People into New Roles. Once you have a clear design in mind, it is now time to consider new reporting relationships and to fit people into their new roles. This is the point where people's sense of territoriality will likely come to the surface, so it is important to discuss and reaffirm with your reorganization team that this discussion must occur with the interests of the organization as a whole, with minimal politics or power plays. Discuss what you need to do as a group to best set the proper climate for this discussion and to maximize your effectiveness. *This step is critical!* Often people conducting this kind of discussion either trivialize people's feelings, or ignore the sensitive nature of the discussion, which only results in significant resentments and stalemates later.

Even more often, people make critical errors as to the qualities, characteristics, and qualifications of the people needed to fulfill leadership roles in the new structure. More often than not, if you are following the recommendations of this book, the qualities of your top management team will be critical. Finding the right mix of talent and weaving them into a team is a far more critical determinant of success than perhaps any other factor.[11]

Keeping in mind the importance of leadership qualities, such as openness, perseverance, communication skills, and vision, as a reorganization team fit people into the new structure as it makes most sense. Begin with the most obvious fits. Then fill in the blanks by

---

[11] Hambrick, D., "The Top Management Team: Key to Strategic Success," in *California Management Review*, Vol. 30, No. 1, 1987, p. 4.

discussing individual's strengths and weaknesses and their developmental opportunities. Ideally, you want to have most people in positions where they will be most effective right now. Changing an organizational structure is difficult enough without adding another complication of providing a lot of new career challenges. Nevertheless, if there are opportunities for new challenges that will not impair your ability to effectively implement the new organizational structure, it is worth considering these as you move forward.

At some point, you will likely reach an impasse, where you either do not know whether anyone is qualified, or two or more people seem equally suited for the role. Before you make a decision, agree as a group what the criteria are for effective decision making. For example, some of the criteria might be:

- Put the people in the role whose leadership style will most likely fit their role, and the people who will report to them.
- Minimize disruption by putting people who already have established relationships with others in the organization.

Having chosen these criteria, apply them in choosing who to put in what position. One way of doing this is through a selection matrix. The best way to do this is to put across the top of the matrix the criteria. If any of these criteria need to be weighed more heavily than others, agree on what the weighting should be. For example, if one criterion is twice as important as all the others, then give it a weighting of two and others a weighting of one. Put on the left-hand side of the matrix the names of the people you are considering for the position. Then, as a group, assign a number to represent to what extent each person meets the separate criteria. Assign a 1 if they do not meet the criteria well, a 2 if they meet it to some extent, and a 3 if they meet the criteria well. You may want to have all individuals in your reorganization team do this individually and then add up their totals in each box. This will produce a group score. Multiply the number by the weightings and add up the scores. The person who meets most of the criteria most fully (has the largest number) is the best person for the position (see Figure 12–22 as an example).

	KNOWLEDGE OF AREA X 2	FIT WITH PEOPLE	ABILITY TO DEAL WITH CUSTOMERS	LEADERSHIP ABILITIES	
	1 = low 2 = medium 3 = high	1 = low 2 = medium 3 = high	1 = low 2 = medium 3 = high	1 = low 2 = medium 3 = high	TOTALS
Jim	2.25 x 2 = 4.5	2.0	2.5	2.0	11.0
Sarah	2.5 x 2 = 5	2.75	2.5	2.5	12.75

Figure 12-22 Selection matrix.

This selection matrix is very useful for making a number of different decisions, and can be applied equally well to group decisions and individual decisions.

Once you begin fitting people into roles, you may find that there are more positions than people, or the opposite, more people than roles. Clearly there are a myriad of complex issues associated with this step, for it is the step that most affects people's daily working lives. Rather than explicate all of the issues and challenges of this step, I strongly urge the reader to seek guidance from their human resources representative for matters such as these. Have the human resources department represented on the reorganization team. If you do not have a human resources person as a guide, seek outside counsel. There are some legal as well as important human issues to take into consideration and decisions should not be made without the appropriate knowledge.

TRANSITION PLAN

You are now ready to plan the transition from the old structure to the new. A good way to do this is to ask your reorganization team to list all of the things you need to do in order to implement the new structure. Discuss with each other how you need to communicate the reorganization to everyone in the company. This discussion should include:

- A checklist of all people who need to be apprised of the change soon. These are people who will be directly or indirectly affected by the change.
- An agreement of when they need to know.
- A plan for how the change will be communicated, to whom, by whom, and by when.
- A clear agreement about how you as a group will ensure that everyone hears the news from the proper channels. You will want to minimize distortions and misunderstandings by managing the communication process as best as you possibly can.
- How to include the press in an appropriate manner (if relevant).

At this point you will need to discuss among your reorganization team in particular how you will handle particularly sensitive issues, such as the situation where two people are equally likely candidates for the same role, or where a person was previously a peer, but now reports directly to the former peer. It is best that each member of the reorganization team understands how to manage these sensitive communications and then discusses this approach with other key members who are involved in the reorganization. For example, if there is a person being put in a position of responsibility over others who were once peers, that person will need to be coached on how to balance their new authority with being as open and collaborative as possible with their new direct reports.

IMPLEMENTING YOUR PLAN

As long as you are implementing the plan, keep the reorganization team together, and keep meeting regularly to manage difficult periods during the implementation process. The difficulties that may arise are as wide and varied as there are people, so stay on top of the issues and deal with them as they arise. One of the most predictable difficulties will be in managing people's fears and concerns regarding "what is going to happen to me." The best way of managing these feelings is for you to keep the communications channels open. People's fears are exacerbated in a context of minimal information. The more open you are, and the more direct you are, the more these types of fears, as well as others, will be kept to a minimum.

You can almost inevitably expect that some people will feel victimized by the reorganization. They will undoubtedly feel they have had little control over their new roles or the changes in the structure around them. If you have done a good job of including them in the decision-making process, they will probably not feel this way to any considerable extent. Others who are being put into roles not of their choosing may feel resentment and anger. Be sure to be sensitive to these people's feelings. They will require your listening and understanding. One way of responding is by helping each person think about and begin to plan their new role. Have the managers begin to engage with these people in a collaborative manner. Give them opportunities to begin to shape their new role. Continue to be sensitive to their legitimate feelings of not being in control of their destiny.

What you do after the reorganization is as important as what you do before it and during it. There will likely continue to be a period of unrest after the reorganization as people learn their new roles and as the kinks in the new structure get worked out. To manage the process after the reorganization, consider the following suggestions to help get the organization back to running in smooth order:

- Follow up with your managers to find out what concerns came about during the process of reorganizing. Find out, in particular, if there were any glitches in the reorganization process, or any difficult employee transitions. Discuss with the individual managers how best to handle these situations.
- Invite each of the new teams in the new structure to clarify their mission and strategic objectives. Use this as an opportunity to create alignment within and between units in the new organization, and begin to establish a new sense of teamwork with the new units.

- Have each manager involved in the reorganization sit down with each of their new team members and have a candid conversation about their past performance and how to develop new performance objectives.
- After a period of time, perhaps six months, evaluate the new organization and make modifications as needed.

The principle to consider in all of the above recommendations is that reorganizations tend to disrupt the working lives of people. Whatever you can do to be sensitive to the experiences people are having as they implement the new structure, and to clarify and develop new processes within the new structure, will go a long way in helping to make the transition as smooth and painless as possible.

POTENTIAL TRAPS TO AVOID IN RESTRUCTURING

Reorganizing one's organization can often be viewed as a panacea to cure all ills. It is anything but this. As you can see from the description and analysis above, it is a difficult process that requires a great deal of care for you to be truly successful. All too often reorganization is used as a knee-jerk reaction to deepseated problems. Consider the following potential traps in the process of reorganizing and avoid them carefully:

Trap no. 1: Reorganizing as a way of solving unrelated problems. An extraordinary number of reorganizations occur as a way to avoid dealing directly with other specific problems. The most common situation occurs when a manager or an executive is not managing effectively. Rather than take him or her out of the management position and put in someone more qualified, organizations often remove units from the executive's domain, displace him or her from their natural place in the organization, and have the units report elsewhere. Another example of a poor use of reorganization is as a solution to alleviating personality clashes between managers of units that really need to relate well to one another. The expedient and frequently used solution is to split up both units. Both of these cases, and others like it, create enormous organizational disruption and inefficiency, all to save the discomfort of dealing directly with a problem that ought to have been managed head-on.

Trap no. 2: Let individuals' needs drive the reorganization. This is a corollary to Trap No. 1. Many times, executives or managers have particular needs that can be all too easily be fulfilled through reorganizing. When an executive, for example, wants more control or responsibility, and deserves it, the solution that organizations often devise is to give him or her a new unit or a new division. Now the executive has two perhaps unrelated divisions or departments reporting to him or her. This force-fitting rarely works and, for obvious reasons, is resented by others. More often than not, in such cases, the executive cannot do justice to leading both of the units simultaneously, and everyone feels slighted in the process.

There are numerous alternatives to such a situation. If an executive needs or wants additional responsibility, provide him or her with opportunities to move up to new positions, and experience different components of the business. Have the executive assume new roles, roles that naturally fit within the existing structure and that stretch the executive's knowledge. This will produce much less disruption, and at the same time, expand the executive's knowledge base and experience.

Trap no. 3: Using the reorganization as a method to "shake things up." After some period of time, many people start to get "antsy." They feel things are too staid, or that people are starting to get complacent. The solution? *Reorganize!* This solution, while it does shake things up, also creates unnecessary disruption. Organizational structures, when designed well, serve to help make the organization more responsive and efficient. If the structure does not serve this purpose, by all means, reorganize. If it does serve this purpose, leave it alone, and shake up other things. Move people to different positions. Give them exposure to different challenges. Develop new and more effective technical systems. Improve work processes. All of these kinds of steps shake things up in a positive and constructive manner.

Trap no. 4: Avoid reorganizing. Restructuring an organization is often a difficult and painful process. It raises anxieties about "what might happen to my job" and it requires people to make changes, some of which they might not welcome immediately. As a result, all too often organizations put off reorganizing until they really have to. While it is understandable to want to put them off, reorganizations are often necessary and highly desirable. If one's new strategy calls for new organizational capabilities and responsibilities, then do not hesitate to make the tough decision. If you put it off, like any other difficult decision that is avoided, you will only pay the price later.

Trap no. 5: Forgetting you are dealing with human beings. Too often we look at organizational systems and structures as boxes on a piece of paper. These boxes represent functions, and we believe that we can move them around like pieces on a chess board. We forget that these boxes and functions are actually groups of people, and the process of reorganization impacts their lives in significant ways. By making changes, we affect people's relationships, the process by which they do work, and the patterns they have grown accustomed to. More often than not, people worked hard to make their current relationships work, and to learn how to operate under the present system.

It is always amazing to me how, in the face of that knowledge, we don't give people the courtesy of involving them in the process of reorganizing in some way, and helping them to shape their new roles. Perhaps out of our own discomfort with the pain that we anticipate will ensue, or the resistance we expect, we do our best to shut out the human element of reorganizing. Yet the reality is that the human element is not only present, it is actual human beings we are impacting by the process of reorganizing. Were we to appreciate this fully, rather than to avoid the discomfort, we would go out of our way to treat people involved in this process in the way we would like to be treated: to be asked for our thoughts, to be given forewarning, to have our concerns listened to and respected. Doing this consciously and conscientiously will help the organization significantly in managing the reorganization process wisely, effectively and humanely.

ARCHITECTING CHECKLIST

1. Before you decide to reorganize your company, or any part of it, be sure you are not reorganizing in order to solve some other problem that has little to do with the organization's structure and design. The pain and anguish associated with reorganizing rarely is worth it.

2. There are a number of different organizational structures. Their viability and effectiveness depends on the business environment in which the organization resides.

3. Customer-and process-driven structures have a number of advantages in today's rapidly changing world.

4. Involve key people throughout your organization in the process of reorganizing. Contrary to many people's fears, including others in the process will likely yield greater results, and a more effective process in the long run.

5. Consider four factors as you determine your new structure: your vision and strategic direction, your business environment, your work processes, and your people.

6. There are three key phases in the process of reorganizing: the planning phase, the transition phase, and after the reorganization. Pay particular attention to the second and the third phases. Here you want to minimize the damage associated with the reorganization and maximize your organization's ability to perform effectively under the new structure.

7. When reorganizing, don't forget you are affecting people's lives, not boxes on a page.

13

The Case of Freddie Mac

. . . improving the quality of life by making the American dream of decent, accessible housing a reality.

In stark contrast to the experience of Wang Labs, the Federal Home Loan Mortgage Corporation has been a story of steady growth and enduring success. It was not an overnight success, but one born out of many years of establishing a strong foundation for the future. Cited in a recent issue of *Fortune* magazine as one of the most fiscally sound financial companies in the United States, it is also considered by those who work there as one of the most innovative. Its success has been built on a combination of careful strategic decision making and dedication to building a sustaining corporate culture.

Drawing from the experience of the Federal Home Loan Mortgage Corporation (often referred to as Freddie Mac), the purpose of this chapter is to provide a concrete example of what it means to design one's organizational architecture and what it involves.

WHAT IS FREDDIE MAC

Freddie Mac[1] is a stockholder-owned corporation chartered by the U.S. Congress in 1970 to increase the supply of money that mortgage lenders can make available to home buyers. It does this by buying mortgages from commercial banks, mortgage bankers, savings institutions, and credit unions, grouping them together in packages and selling them to investors, such as insurance companies and pension funds. How this works in practice represents an intricate interweaving of dynamics that together form the basis of a win–win situation. To understand this, let's first look at how the mortgage process operates.

When you or I go to a bank to borrow money for our house, the bank lends us money in the form of a mortgage at a predetermined interest rate. Contrary to what most people assume, most mortgage lenders do not hold on to this mortgage, but sell it to Freddie Mac or some other "secondary" mortgage lender. They do this in order to minimize their risk. As a nationwide lender, Freddie Mac is able to manage the interest-rate and default risks associated with loans.

Most banks, then, are go-betweens. They make decisions about whether to extend a loan for a house, and

---

[1] Much of the material in this chapter was derived from my interviews with Leland Brendsel, chairman of the board and CEO, and David Glenn, president and COO, as well as others in the company. It is also derived from my direct experience of Freddie Mac, having worked with them for three years in the late 1980s. I am deeply indebted to them for their generosity of time and support of this book. In addition, much of the factual and historical material was derived with permission from three sources published by Freddie Mac:
 A Citizen's Guide to the Secondary Mortgage Market
 What is Freddie Mac: 10 Frequently Asked Questions About Freddie Mac
 1992 Annual Report

they handle the administration of the loan. They then sell the mortgage to institutions in the secondary mortgage market, such as Freddie Mac. Freddie Mac, in turn, bundles these mortgages together in different forms of securities, guarantees the financial safety of the securities, and then sells these securities to investors who seek low-risk, solid return investments.

As a result of this efficient system for financing mortgages, banks and other lenders are able to provide loans at lower interest rates. It is estimated, for example, that mortgage rates are 25–50 basis points lower than they otherwise would be if Freddie Mac, Fannie Mae, and others in the secondary mortgage market were not in existence. In this way, housing is more affordable throughout the country. To understand how this evolved, let's look at a brief history of Freddie Mac.

A BRIEF HISTORY OF FREDDIE MAC

Freddie Mac was chartered in 1970 by Congress, with the assignment of creating a national secondary market for conventional home mortgages. Congress chartered Freddie Mac primarily to relieve the chronic regional mismatch between savings deposits and demand for mortgage credit. Its principal method was to purchase "conventional" mortgages, and its primary customers were to be thrift institutions. Through the early 1970s, Freddie Mac worked to overcome two obstacles: (1) the lack of uniform underwriting and documentation for mortgages, and (2) the lack of familiarity on the part of conventional mortgage lenders in selling their loans. To overcome the former, they developed standard legal documents, standard appraisal forms, and standard underwriting guidelines to be used by all lenders in every state in the union. To overcome the latter, they worked closely with lenders to help them get used to the notion of selling mortgages in the secondary market.

Since the 1970s, Freddie Mac has financed most of its mortgage purchases by selling mortgage-backed securities, beginning in 1971. During the 1980s, the secondary mortgage market grew considerably. The country was experiencing rapidly rising interest rates coupled with rising inflation. These two conditions posed significant risks to lenders, thereby dampening the housing market. Lenders responded by selling more loans and the concept of bundling and reselling mortgages, now the signature *modus operandi* of Freddie Mac, helped give the housing market the boost it needed.

By almost any standards, Freddie Mac has been enormously successful. Over the years, the number of conventional mortgage-backed securities issued by Freddie Mac has grown dramatically. Its stock has risen significantly over the past five years, and its shareholders have experienced an 81 percent increase in dividends per share from $.42 in 1988 to $.76 in 1992. During that period, Freddie Mac's primary capital base has more than doubled, while earnings per share and net income have risen consistently. In 1992, its net income was $622 million, up 12 percent from $555 reported in 1991, and up 63 percent from $381 million reported in 1988. As of 1993, Freddie Mac had over $4 billion in capital and reserves. The company's more than $450 billion in mortgage assets are backed by homes worth over $700 billion. Moreover, these numbers are growing every day.

DESIGNING A SUCCESSFUL ARCHITECTURE

Many might attribute Freddie Mac's success to the boon in the housing market coupled by the more recent increase in the number of refinanced mortgages. While those provided a strong market opportunity, it has been Freddie Mac's strong internal capabilities, combined with conservative fiscal management and effective strategic decisions, that have yielded strong results. Freddie Mac's exemplary performance can be attributed to a number of related factors, each of which together have conspired to form a strong architecture:

1. A series of cultural changes born out of a vision for an organization characterized by high teamwork, work satisfaction, and innovation.

2. Intelligent and far-reaching strategic decisions, the most significant of which was a change in governance of the institution in the late 1980s.

3. A recent focus on what Freddie Mac calls its "Relentless Pursuit of Quality."

4. Structural changes that have helped the company continue to be responsive to customers' needs despite its growth in size.

Cultural Changes at Freddie Mac. The effort to intentionally redesign the organization's architecture began in 1987 with a decision on the part of Leland Brendsel, then president and CEO, to strengthen the organization's culture. This decision was born out of Brendsel's realization that while the company was relatively successful, the executive team at the top did not work well together. In his words, "we didn't draw on each other, we didn't communicate well, and each individual area in the company would keep others out and only work in their own area . . . there was not enough cohesiveness."

To help strengthen teamwork, Brendsel brought in the services of a consulting firm called Human Factors, Inc. Human Factors, based in San Rafael, California, is a consulting firm dedicated to helping its client organizations strengthen their corporate cultures and achieve extraordinary levels of performance. It has had significant impact on a variety of companies including Silicon Graphics, Lotus Development Corporation, World-Corp, Inc., Canadian Tire Corporation, Ltd., and Polaroid.

To begin the team-building process, Human Factors took the top leadership team of eight executives on an off-site retreat for four days. The purpose of this retreat was to achieve a significant breakthrough in the quality, viability, and effectiveness of the executive team as a whole. To do this, Human Factors helped the executives at Freddie Mac explore such things as the degree to which they tended to compete with one another, their tendency to make politically driven decisions rather than those focused on optimizing the whole system, their leadership strengths and weaknesses, and ways to strengthen the sense of shared responsibility for the company as a whole.

The results of the executive team-building session were outstanding. At the end of the team-building session, the executives felt more unified than ever before. Moreover, using a process similar to the one described in Chapter 9, they left with a strong set of ground rules or agreements about how they would continue to work together as a team in the future. These agreements were to:

- Practice open, honest, direct, and timely communications
- Solicit, consider, and respond to other's input
- Accept ownership for all issues, conditions, and results
- Assume positive motivation
- Extend trust; empower others
- Recognize and learn from failures
- Support and acknowledge contributions of others
- Encourage development and well-being of our people
- Practice excellence; do the right things well
- Make decisions based on fairness
- Honor commitments
- Expand horizons; take risks, question the need, encourage innovation

At the end of the team-building session, each executive stood up and declared their personal commitment to the above agreements. Their commitment was so heartfelt that, to this day, the executive team reinforces these agreements in regular meetings and interactions with one another. Whenever anyone violates the agreement, another member will give them feedback and remind them of the agreement. In addition, the executives continue to meet occasionally with the sole purpose of revisiting the agreements to give and get feedback on the extent to which their daily behavior is consistent with them. These meetings are sometimes difficult. Each executive would readily admit that they have areas they need to improve. What distinguishes the executive team at Freddie Mac from others is not that they are perfect, but they work hard at growing, both individually and as a team.

On the basis of this positive outcome of the team-building session, the executive team decided to continue the process of strengthening their leadership capabilities by working with Human Factors to clarify their vision for the future. For this, Human Factors invited them to what they refer to as a strategic visioning program. The purpose of this program was to help Freddie Mac clarify its overall vision and direction of the company for the future. The session was held during February 1988 in an off-site retreat. During the session, the executive team at Freddie Mac put a lot of thought into its purpose as a company. After a great deal of soul searching, the executive team articulated its purpose as follows[2]:

> A shareholder-owned corporation, whose people are dedicated to improving the quality of life by making the American dream of decent, accessible housing a reality.

Almost without exception, the leaders of the company as well as many others throughout Freddie Mac point to this purpose as a source of meaning in their work. This is not just hype on the part of the company. It lives and breathes in all that they do. Witness their 1992 annual report. It begins on the front page with the statement shown in Figure 13–1.

In concert with this statement, interspersed throughout the annual report are stories and pictures of families who have benefited from Freddie Mac's efforts. Indeed half the report, signed by Leland Brendsel, now chairman and CEO, and David Glenn, president and COO, is taken up by these stories. The message is clear. While Freddie Mac's aims are lofty, they see the results in

---

[2] Freddie Mac calls this statement its mission.

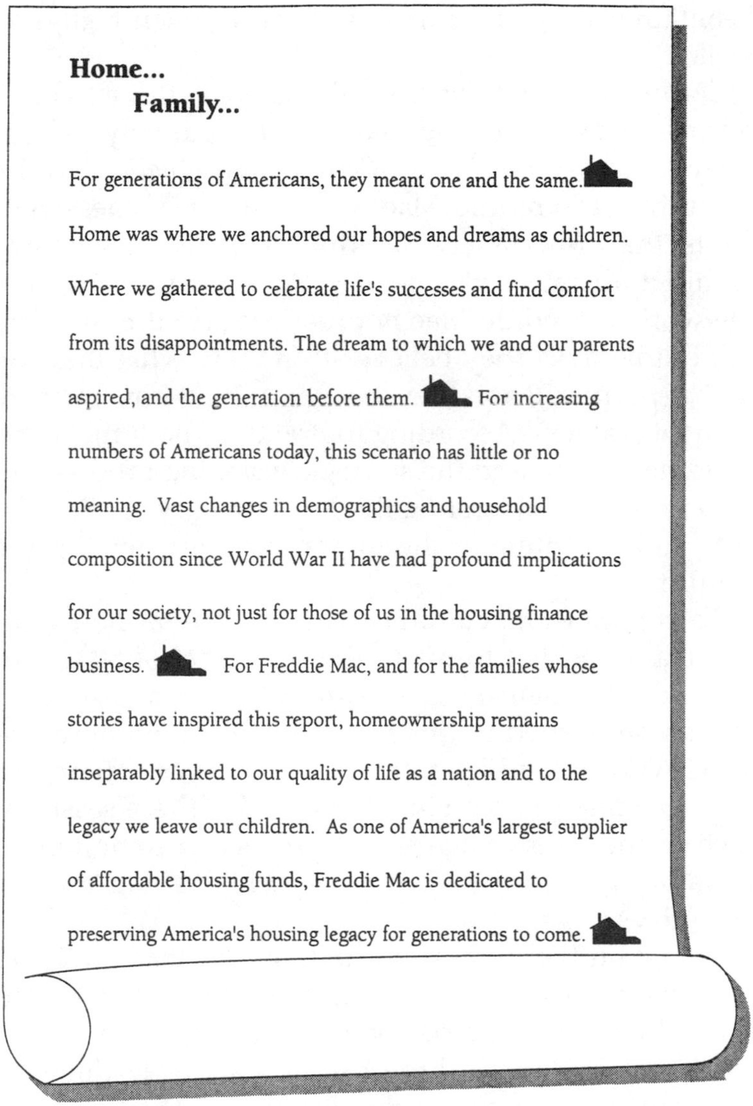

Home...
Family...

For generations of Americans, they meant one and the same. Home was where we anchored our hopes and dreams as children. Where we gathered to celebrate life's successes and find comfort from its disappointments. The dream to which we and our parents aspired, and the generation before them. For increasing numbers of Americans today, this scenario has little or no meaning. Vast changes in demographics and household composition since World War II have had profound implications for our society, not just for those of us in the housing finance business. For Freddie Mac, and for the families whose stories have inspired this report, homeownership remains inseparably linked to our quality of life as a nation and to the legacy we leave our children. As one of America's largest supplier of affordable housing funds, Freddie Mac is dedicated to preserving America's housing legacy for generations to come.

Figure 13-1. Freddie Mac's commitment to home and family.

benefiting not just human kind, but human beings as well.

During the strategic visioning retreat the executive team also explored and clarified its company values. They are: *Integrity*, *People*, *Service*, and *Quality*. To the executives at Freddie Mac, the focus on values highlights the importance that the company and people within it operate with integrity. As a result, many people work at Freddie Mac not just because it is successful, but because they believe strongly in what they are doing (purpose), and they feel good about how they are doing it (values). According to Brendsel, both the team-building session and the strategic visioning process had the effect of "accelerating the learning curve at Freddie Mac and heightening the importance of changing the culture."

To continue the cultural change process, the executive team decided to invite the next level of 50 executives to join them in the team-building process. This was accomplished in three four-day team-building sessions with executives from different areas. These too were extremely successful. At the end of these sessions, each of the 50 executives made the same commitment to values and to the team agreements as had the top executives.

Riding on the success of the first four team-building sessions, the executive team decided to invite all managers throughout the company to participate in a similar retreat so that all those responsible for leading the company can experience the quality and level of teamwork they had just experienced. For the next two years, groups of managers from different parts of the company participated in the team-building sessions.

These team-building sessions were patterned after the original session, and gave insight to all managers on ways they can improve as managers and leaders, and how they can work together as a team. While some sessions had more impact than others, as a whole, the positive effect on the company has been palpable. Many at Freddie Mac, even to this day, point to their experience in the team-building sessions as being a key point in their career and having heightened their ability to work with others and to lead their part of the organization. Many continue to give and get feedback on their leadership effectiveness, and continue to strive to work better with one another. The series of team buildings have served as a catalyst for creating a culture where developing their sense of team unity is an on-going, continuous process. Brendsel sums up his experience with Human Factors and the team-building process this way. "This work, to a great extent, provided insight into ourselves as individuals and our impact on others. Ultimately we have each gained a much greater acceptance that different people can have different approaches to the same thing and much greater teamwork throughout the company."

Changing the Strategic Direction. Since its inception, Freddie Mac has had two strategic foci that together have played a key role in its consistently positive performance. They are product innovation and risk management. Product innovation, in particular, has helped Freddie Mac successfully navigate through highly uncertain waters in the housing market. In the early and mid-1970s, the housing market was suffering from regional capital shortages. Freddie Mac responded by creating the first conventional, pass-through securities and sold them to Wall Street. In the early and mid-1980s, sharply rising interest rates forced lenders to sell far more loans and better package their loan portfolios. Freddie Mac again responded by issuing the first "multi-class" mortgage backed security they called the Collateralized Mortgage Obligation (CMO). These securities were designed to better satisfy investors and keep mortgage money flowing.

In the late 1980s and early 1990s, the market changed again, and Freddie Mac responded. A 1986 tax law brought the next stage in the evolution of CMOs, Real Estate Mortgage Investment Conduits or REMICs for short. Proof of the success of Freddie Mac's innovative creation of multiclass securities is that now most new conventional mortgages are financed with REMICs. REMICs give borrowers access to Wall Street and other financial markets around the world.

Product innovation has been important, but without a counterbalancing focus on risk management, the company could easily diffuse its energy. To Freddie Mac, risk management has to do with making only those decisions that have the highest likelihood of success. This has been critical because Freddie Mac's success is, in part, dependent on being viewed by their investors and customers alike as a solid and safe company. This requires that Freddie Mac set criteria for mortgage packages prior to purchase and evaluate financial risk in order to determine that its purchases will be sound investments for shareholders. Risk management is so critical to the strategic success of Freddie Mac that one of its key divisions is called Risk Management.

While the focus on risk management has been an important source of security for the company, it too has had a down side. Before the original executive team building session, the company was hampered in its ability to make key corporate-wide decisions due to an overemphasis on avoiding risks. For example, in the case of "special transactions," which required the company to make unique loan purchase decisions, it took up to 14 separate functions to sign off on a purchase decision. This resulted in a cumbersome decision-making process that wasn't responsive to either customer needs or timing requirements. Part of the problem was that in order to avoid a mistake, all 14 leaders of the functions focused their attention on finding something wrong. In so doing, they were missing opportunities to purchase loans that, if they were willing to take the risk, could have been fruitful. After the team-building sessions, the leaders at Freddie Mac recognized the need to change their decision-making process and move to one that supported more open-minded decision making.

While a focus on risk management coupled with innovation has helped the company manage effectively in the face of significant changes in its market, these alone have not caused the success Freddie Mac enjoys today. A more recent strategic decision to change the company's governance was perhaps even more critical.

Up until 1990, Freddie Mac was a quasi-government agency chartered by Congress and overseen by government officials. In 1990, a key change was made in its formal governance. This change was instigated in part by a feeling on the part of Brendsel and other key executives that for many years the relationship between the Board of Directors and the company was not as productive as they would like it to be.

The change in governance was initiated by Brendsel as far back as 1987, but took a few years to come to fruition. Up until the late 1980s, the Board of Directors consisted of three members of the Federal Home Loan Bank Board, each of whom were Presidential appointees. This Board changed with each new President and often much more frequently. Those who occupied the Board were naturally driven in part by whatever political climate existed at the time, and therefore by its very nature made it difficult for Freddie Mac to make long-term changes in its corporate direction. The difficulty in charting a clear and enduring course, combined with some strong differences of opinion between the Board and senior management about the company and its direction, led Brendsel and other executives to feel frustrated in their relationship with the Board. To deal with the core of this frustration, senior management began an intensive effort to work with the politically appointed Board members to remove trading restrictions on the company's stock. As David Glenn put it, "we knew that public ownership would create the right focus and environment for the company to maximize its potential. We also knew the Board would agree with this, even though it would ultimately lead to a change in Board membership and the company's governance."

Finally, after a long, hard series of negotiations with key entities including Board members, legislation in 1989 enabled the final step in the change in governance. This legislation was implemented in 1990. As a result, Freddie Mac's Board of Directors is now made up of 18 national leaders, only five of whom are political appointees. This new Board's challenge is to run an effective business as well as hold up their congressional-chartered responsibility. This change was brought about by having Freddie Mac become a stockholder-owned corporation with the first stockholder election occurring in February of 1990.

Why was this change in governance so critical to Freddie Mac's strategic direction and its success? It was more than a change in players and in the structure of the Board. It required a mental shift on the part of the leaders of the company. After the change, for better or worse, the leaders of Freddie Mac were now in control of their own destiny. On the plus side, they now were able to change their compensation levels and attract some of the finest people in the business community. They could also provide stock options as incentives. At the same time, standards of performance had to be raised in order to successfully compete in the business community. The change in governance also required a greater clarity of strategic focus. In the words of Leland Brendsel, "today we run our business for our shareholders. And every major business decision is run through a filter that requires us to ask ourselves how our actions affect owner value, how they protect our franchise and our competitive position, and how they prepare the corporation to profitably meet the current and emerging challenges facing the housing finance industry."[4]

Relentless Pursuit of Quality. While the experience of the team building throughout the company was enormously successful, the executive team and, in particular, David Glenn felt that the results were too intangible. While people throughout Freddie Mac tended to work better together as a result of the team-building process, bottom line results were not clearly evident. More than team building was needed to create the enduring results they desired. So in early 1991, the executive team started to develop a new vision and strategic direction for the future of the organization. Looking at its current environment and what it saw for the future, Freddie Mac refined its corporate vision to become a customer-focused business enterprise emphasizing execution and acting as a responsible force in addressing public issues. To develop this vision, they looked at some of the key changes that were occurring in the industry and the implications of these changes

---

[4] Drawn from speech given by Leland C. Brendsel on April 21, 1993, titled "Remarks delivered before the New York Society of Security Analysts."

on their business. To provide historical context, they also looked back by identifying four key eras in the secondary mortgage market from the time of inception of Freddie Mac (see Figure 13–2).

It was the clarification of this fourth era that served as the impetus for Freddie Mac's new focus on its "relentless pursuit of quality." Broadly, the relentless pursuit of quality is a far-reaching program designed to create a performance-based culture driven by the goal of understanding and meeting customer needs. Through the relentless pursuit of quality, the leadership of Freddie Mac has refined their vision for the company, re-emphasized its values, and established new strategies.

To accomplish this, David Glenn led the top executive team in articulating a number of long-term goals to guide the development of a performance-based culture. These goals included, but were not limited to, an aim

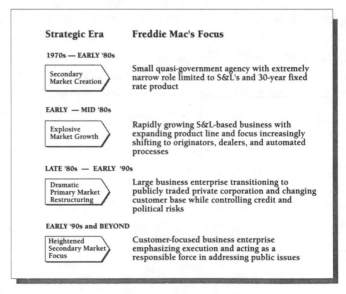

Figure 13-2. Freddie Mac's key strategic eras.

that every quality mortgage lender in every community will be a satisfied Freddie Mac customer, that Freddie Mac will be the acknowledged credit management leader in the residential mortgage finance industry, and that every Freddie Mac employee will be included in the effort to improve its processes. The latter was particularly critical given their strong cultural emphasis on the value of their people.

To involve everyone in its relentless pursuit of quality, Freddie Mac put together a day-long training program and rolled out the program level by level throughout the company. In the program, they explained the goals of the company, the strategic thinking behind those goals, the environment they saw the company in, and the response needed on the part of everyone. They also laid out how Fannie Mae had changed its business and the good work they were doing with their customers. In so doing, they raised everyone's expectations about what was needed of them. (Interestingly, during my interviews with them, both Leland Brendsel and David Glenn spoke about Fannie Mae in thankful terms. Rather than see Fannie Mae as competition they wished did not exist, they talked about the company in terms of having helped Freddie Mac become better.) They then asked participants of the training to analyze these issues and explore the meaning of these issues for their work. This proved to be critical for it required people to think as if they owned the business. According to Glenn, "it was probably the first time that people in the company understood what we were trying to accomplish, and what it would take to be successful in a competitive market."

After laying out the new vision for everyone in the company, the executive team put together a three- or four-year plan for executing the vision. Members of the top executive team guided the planning process and facilitated a series of discussions among senior executives. These meetings culminated in a strategic plan that had, as some of its key components, ways to strengthen Freddie Mac's management and control systems, and ways to improve its competitive position.

In addition to a clear strategic direction and multiyear corporate action plan, part of what resulted from these discussions was the recognition that the company needed to make some significant changes in the organization structure to become more responsive to a rapidly changing business environment. Perhaps even more importantly, what came out of the whole effort of its relentless pursuit of quality was a renewed sense of excitement, and a clear focus and direction.

Structural Changes. No different than any company, in the past few years Freddie Mac has had to find ways of increasing its productivity while at the same time managing its costs. To help accomplish this, two key decisions were made. The first was a change in the top leadership of the company. In late 1989, David Glenn was promoted from his role as chief financial officer to the role of chief operating officer, a newly created position. In March 1990, he was appointed president. These promotions were prompted by a discovery on the part of Leland Brendsel, then president and CEO, that in order to remain viable under the new governance structure, more attention would have to be placed on managing the external interfaces of the business. In addition, in a moment of self-reflection, Brendsel realized that he particularly enjoyed and was most effective in managing external relationships. David Glenn, on the other hand, was proving to be a savvy leader in linking business operations to customer needs and improving the company's performance.

By giving full reign of internal operations over to Glenn, to be successful, Glenn and Brendsel had to work extremely well together. This has not come without some work on both their parts. They do not always see eye to eye on key issues. But what they do have going for them, which is often lacking in key relationships such as these, is a commitment to raise issues openly and honestly and finding a solution to their differences. As a result of continued interaction, negotiation, and collaboration, they speak about each other with the utmost of respect and admiration.

The second key structural decision was to begin changing the overall structural design of the organization. This came directly as a result of Freddie Mac's recent focus on its relentless pursuit of quality. During their strategic discussions in 1991, the executive team began to realize that their structure, which was a typical functional structure, resulted in each division head operating as if they were a separate company. Such a structure promoted individual initiative rather than teamwork, and reinforced internal competition rather than cooperation. Moreover, in such a structure, the requirements for coordination fell too much on Brendsel and Glenn's shoulders. Instead, Freddie Mac sought to become a more customer-focused, streamlined organization. The first step in moving the company toward this aim was to create senior management teams called Integrated Business System Teams, or IBSTs for short. The purpose of the IBSTs is to help the company be more successful by clarifying, coordinating, and communicating priorities and direction of key processes and to build ownership and support for improving performance company-wide. These teams are made up of members from many of the different divisions and are designed to better manage processes that cut across organizational boundaries, establish appropriate performance standards for these processes, and monitor and assess their performance. In addition, through the

IBSTs, people throughout the company provide input to decision makers on key policies and decisions.

Recently, Freddie Mac has decided to go beyond the use of IBSTs to promote teamwork and has begun to reorganize a key part of their business along more process-driven lines. One of the IBSTs focuses on the security selling part of the business. The team is made up of people from twelve departments and five divisions, each of which play a key role in selling securities. The team has helped the company see that more than an IBST in this case is needed. As of late 1993, Freddie Mac is in the process of bringing separate operating groups into one division called dealer services. While it is premature to assess the success of such a change, it exemplifies Freddie Mac's willingness to let go of past structures and explore new ones.

THOUGHTS ABOUT FREDDIE MAC

Few successful companies the size of Freddie Mac make the dramatic changes that Freddie Mac has made and continues to make in a short period of time. Most, not surprisingly, rest on their laurels with the belief that if successful, why change? This is particularly true of companies in the financial services industry that can often be characterized by conservatism and an overemphasis on tradition. Freddie Mac has taken the road less traveled in their industry. They have actively and aggressively pursued changes, never satisfied with their current level of success. Such a stance is challenging for there is little impetus for change when one is successful. Perhaps that is why so few leaders of companies are able to make the kinds of changes needed to grow and develop in a rapidly changing environment.

Both Leland Brendsel and David Glenn are highly

articulate about why they have made the changes they have made, and the positive effect they have had. One gets the feeling that in talking with each of them, they combine a strong caring for the people at Freddie Mac and a strong focus on bottom-line results. They are both extraordinarily honest about themselves, their strengths and weaknesses, as well as some of the mistakes they have made over the years. At the same time, they are proud of what they have done, with good reason.

The changes at Freddie Mac have not come without their hardships, nor have they been made with a clear sense of the overall changes needed. Part of the changes described above were designed well in advance while others were incremental and responsive to immediate needs. For example, the need to change the culture and make it more collaborative and less bureaucratic had been stewing in Leland Brendsel's mind for many years. The decision to actually hire Human Factors was more immediate as they realized the need to change, but were not sure where to start. The key strategic decisions too were planned, like the change in corporate governance, and represent long-term efforts to shape the overall direction of the company, while some other changes were made in response to more immediate needs.

While the above discussion clearly highlights some of the more successful decisions Freddie Mac has made over the years, naturally it has not always been easy. Structural changes as well as a strong commitment to the emerging culture have caused the company to make personnel changes that have affected some people adversely and challenged others to adapt to changes. Moreover, not everyone in the company is satisfied with the results. To Freddie Mac's credit, it would be the first to admit it is not perfect. Its people, however, continue to aspire to live by their values and at the same time produce outstanding results.

Most importantly, the experience of Freddie Mac tells us that designing their organization's architecture is not a one-time event, nor is it necessarily a complete and planned intervention whose pieces can be anticipated well in advance. It is more a process of continuously improving the key elements of the organization's architecture over time, which together shape and reshape the organization's foundation for the future.

ARCHITECTING CHECKLIST

1. The beginning point of a successful architecting effort is the clarification of vision and the strengthening of the organizational culture.

2. By being unabashedly honest with themselves and by being deeply committed to their vision, Freddie Mac has been able to continually rearchitect itself during key phases in its life cycle.

3. The process of redesigning an organization's architecture is not always perfect, and is rarely immediate. It often takes years of hard work and needs to be constantly re-examined.

4. The process of redesigning one's organizational architecture takes courage. It often requires that the company examine some of its fundamental assumptions and explore alternatives that result in a discontinuous break from the past. Freddie Mac did this as it changed its governance, and now points to that and other changes as a key source of its success.

14

The Learning Organization

The most successful corporation of the 1990s will be something called the learning organization, a consummately adaptive enterprise.

—*Fortune* Magazine[1]

There is a scene from a movie, *Wargames*, which came out years ago, that is indelibly etched on my brain. In this fictional but all too realistic story, a young computer wizard accidentally accesses the U.S. military's master computer that is tied into our network of missiles with nuclear warheads. Thinking he is playing a computer game called "Global Thermonuclear War," he unwittingly sets off a series of simulated missile launchings from the former U.S.S.R. Unfortunately, the people running the computer room can't tell that it is only a simulation. They think it is real, and set the retaliatory computer program in motion and brace themselves for attack. Given how the computer

---

[1] B. Domain, *Fortune*, July 3, 1989, pp. 48–62.

has been programmed and its actual control over all the nuclear weapons throughout the U.S., when attacked, a process is set in motion to counterstrike automatically with actual weapons and the people in the war room are incapable of bypassing the system once it has started. They soon discover the young wizard's folly, but only after it is too late, and our warheads are about to be launched against an unsuspecting and completely innocent U.S.S.R. The young computer wizard and the original designer of the system are brought in to attempt to shut off the computer, but after a series of tries, they just can't seem to stop it. Just at the last minute, while the missiles with nuclear warheads are about to be launched, they figure out that the only way they can possibly stop the computer is for the computer to learn. Through a rapid-fire series of ideas, they decide to tell the computer to play a game of tic-tac-toe with itself. This is a game that is impossible for the computer to win. In so doing, they are in effect asking the computer to learn that like the tic-tac-toe game, Global Thermonuclear War is ultimately a "no-win" game.

The scene reaches a gripping climax where everyone in the war room is watching the computer and shouting, *"Learn, Learn, Learn."* Finally the computer figures out the utter senselessness of playing attack/counterattack with nuclear weapons and aborts its own program.

In many ways, I see this scene in the movie as a metaphor for our current businesses and our modern society. In effect, we must learn how to grow, adapt, and rapidly change or our organizations will perish, and our planet may as well. Yet, at the same time, we program our own organizations to avoid learning. We do this by creating structures that slow down decision making. We create policies and procedures that limit discretion and the ability to respond to unique situations. And we exemplify behaviors that reinforce the notion that we are closed to learning and to change. All of these things we do in order to have control over our systems, and all of them inhibit learning. This book suggests that there is an alternative—to design into our organizations new ways of operating that open up channels of communication, that actively promote change, that infuse in all the members of the organization a spirit of ownership, that create conditions of learning throughout the organization. Freddie Mac has done that well in the past few years and it is one of the key causes of its present success.

If you have already made changes in your organization as described previously in this book, you are well on your way to crafting an organizational architecture that will poise you for success far into the future. That's the good news. Well, here's the bad news. Your work has only just begun. The degree of rapid change in today's environment, coupled with the enormous and ever-increasing complexity of modern business life suggests that you can never rest on your laurels. You must continually seek ways of improving and learning over time. In other words, to truly succeed, you must create structures and conditions in your organization wherein learning is a lifelong event.

The importance of learning as a lifelong process was brought home to me early on in my adult life. I remember vividly an experience I had upon entering my doctoral program at Harvard University. This experience taught me that life is only a process, and in many ways we never arrive at our final destination.

It was September of 1981 and I had just been accepted into the Harvard Graduate School of Education as a doctoral student specializing in organization develop-

ment. I felt elated as I arrived at one of the most respected universities in the world. I felt as if I had
jumped through what I believed would be almost the
last hoop I would ever have to jump through in my
formal education, and I had been "accepted" at last.
And then a splash of reality hit me. I soon discovered
that some of the courses I had sought to take had limited seating capacity, and that I had to apply and be
interviewed in order to be allowed to take the courses.
This application process had emerged over time because the most popular courses were sought out by the
most people. As a consequence, in many courses there
were few seats available, and we all had to compete for
them. In effect, each of us interested in taking a specific
course had to be interviewed by the professor or teaching assistant to demonstrate our worthiness of being in
the course. Although I had been accepted in the doctoral program, I still had to apply for the courses!

After some initial frustration, I came to accept this
process, and with one exception, got into all of the
classes I sought. In many ways I became philosophical
about the whole experience, and have since seen this
particular experience as a metaphor for life. In life, you
never arrive completely. One is always (if one is open)
learning and growing. In fact, as I look back on each of
my past successes and failures, I see them now as only
steps on a never-ending stairstep of a life of learning.
During the moments I have truly accepted this fact, life
has been a wondrous journey. During the moments I
have fought this fact, life has been frustrating.

The life of the business world is no different. It is
changing right before our eyes. Long gone is the time
when we can expect workers to march to the orders of
managers and where simple organizational structures
will produce viable business results. In today's new and
ever-changing environment, the organization that will

endure and thrive is one that can anticipate changes and lead them. Such is the nature of organizations that learn. The learning organization as a model is not just something dreamed up in the minds of organizational theorists. It distinguishes those organizations that are successful over time from the ones that produce great results initially, but soon thereafter fizzle out. The ability of an organization to learn is perhaps the single most critical factor in creating a competitive advantage in today's business climate. It is also the most challenging one.

WHAT IS A LEARNING ORGANIZATION?

Because the concept of the learning organization is so new, we know very little about it. The concept was first introduced in book form by Chris Argyris and Donald Schon some 16 years ago. In their book, *Organizational Learning,* they described a learning organization as one that is capable of not only solving problems (single-loop learning), but also of increasing its ability to solve problems in the future (double-loop learning). An organization characterized by double-loop learning is an organization that learns how to learn, and can therefore reproduce success over time.[2]

More recently, Peter Senge, in *The Fifth Discipline,* condensed much of the research and experience of learning organizations to date to describe what he considered the five key features of a learning organization. To Senge, learning organizations and their members are characterized by the following qualities:

---

[2] C. Argyris and D. Schon, *Organizational Learning,* Addison Wesley, New York, 1978.

1. *A shared vision*—everyone in the organization is deeply committed to a clear vision of the future of the organization.

2. *Mental models*—An understanding of how our differing views of the world shape how we think and act, and an ability to meld these views into creative solutions to complex problems.

3. *Systems thinking*—an ability to see the bigger picture and how every part of the organization relates to all the other parts.

4. *Team effectiveness*—A strong spirit of teamwork that pervades all aspects of the organization.

5. *Personal mastery*—The process of learning about one's self in order to become more effective as an individual.[3]

While easy to describe in the abstract, these principles, or as Senge calls them, *disciplines*, are quite difficult to enact in practice. Part of the difficulty in learning what a learning organization is and how to become one is that the learning organization is generally an amorphous concept. Some think it is an organization that learns things. Others say that its members are constantly growing and learning. But the learning organization is more than that. It is a set of principles that, when followed, unleash the full potential of the organization and enable it to continuously learn and adapt over time.

To create such a learning organization, its leaders must place far more attention on creating the proper conditions for learning than on doing certain things.

---

[3] Senge, Peter. *The Fifth Discipline*, Doubleday Currency, New York, 1990.

Given a strong tendency in our society to take immediate action and to expect immediate results, attending to the contextual features of the organization is confusing to many, and not easy to adopt. To the few organizations that can be appropriately characterized as learning organizations,[4] learning is not an event, it is a process. It has to do with setting the proper climate or context within which people can learn and grow, and where the organization can continually adapt (see Figure 14–1).

Such a context requires attention to creating conditions in the organization where people welcome feedback, seek to discover the best solution to a given problem, welcome change, and take responsibility for

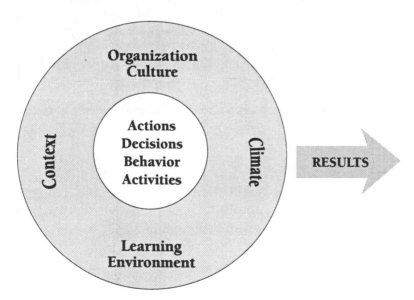

Figure 14-1. Actions exist within a larger context for learning.

---

[4] William Torbert in his book *Managing the Corporate Dream: Restructuring for long term success*, Dow Jones-Irwin, Homewood, Ill., 1987, suggests that roughly 3 percent of all organizations have truly reached a level where they are continuously learning or have learned how to learn.

LEARNING ORGANIZATION	STAGNANT ORGANIZATION
• People are open to and welcome feedback	• People closed to feedback
• People seek best solution	• People seek to be right, to win
• Collaborative mindset	• Competitive mindset
• Mistakes are opportunities to learn	• Mistakes are to be avoided
	• High risk avoidance
• High risk taking	
	• People tend to blame one another
• People take responsibility	
• Strong spirit of shared ownership	• Strong sense of dependence
	• Change is avoided
• Change is welcomed	
	• Overemphasis on immediate results
• Strong sense of purpose	

Figure 14-2. Differences between a learning organization and a stagnant organization.

the organization's results. Figure 14–2 shows some of the differences in climate and context that distinguish the learning organization for most others.

How To Create a Learning Organization

While the concept of a learning organization is difficult to grasp, how to create such an organization is even harder. Some say it has to do with creating structures in the organization where communication is fluid and key information is available to all. Some say it has to do with creating a shared vision, and creating commitment to that vision. Others say it has to do with aligning all the members around a set of strategic objectives. It actually requires all of those things, and a lot more.

In effect, it requires that you not only design your organization's architecture in ways described throughout this book, but you continually redesign your organization over time. This does not mean that you change the culture, the values, or the purpose of the organization, for those necessarily will likely endure. Rather, you consider adopting new strategies and new structures, and continually teach new skills in the spirit of continuous improvement.

The first step in doing this is to evaluate your design efforts to date, and explore ways of improving them. This step of evaluation is the last step in the process of designing change, and it is the first step toward redesigning. So many organizations that I am familiar with will take the trouble to diagnose the need for change, plan for change, implement those plans, but fail to test to see if their change efforts actually got them what they wanted. Our tendency to be self-protective would try to convince us that it is far better to be kept in the dark and assume that our efforts have worked than it is to gather data and discover that we have failed.

So we are inclined not to evaluate or seek feedback. Yet for true learning to occur, feedback is exactly what we need to discover how well we did, and then to readjust to improve our efforts. Learning is never easy, and is sometimes painful. But the road to long-term failure is strewn with organizations who avoided this last significant step in architecting their organization, and who consequently never learned from their mistakes.

Feedback can come in many forms. It can come in the form of financial results; the feelings and impressions that people have about the organization; the data collected in the service of organizational understanding. For our purposes, all of these are appropriate and useful. The hardest data to get, however, and perhaps the most critical, are the last of these. To get a sense of how well your design efforts have succeeded, go back to your original set of objectives that you created in chapter six. These objectives are the standards by which you can measure your success. If, for example, one of your objectives was to improve overall understanding and commitment to your strategic direction, then spend some time thinking about how you will measure this.

If you have followed the guidelines in this book, you will already have a sense of how to measure these objectives. Even better, you may already have a mechanism to actually measure your progress. This mechanism is key, for it provides you with valid data regarding the results of your efforts. If you are truly committed to change, then nothing less than a demonstrated, validated change will do, for you and for the rest of your company.

One example of how to go about determining the results of one's organizational efforts is an insurance company that I have been working with recently. Early on in their change process, they identified 12 different organizational areas that they felt needed improvement. These 12 areas include these items and others:

- understanding the company's mission, values, and strategic direction
- communication
- compensation and benefits
- computer technology
- empowerment
- the quality of working relationships
- leadership

On the basis of their 12 areas of interest, they developed a survey instrument designed to measure changes in these dimensions over time. At the beginning of the redesign efforts, they administered this survey to the whole company with the intent of creating a baseline measurement of the current state of the organization in terms of these 12 dimensions. The results are now in, and they show rather conclusively that indeed these are areas that need significant improvement. The most confronting aspect of the information, however, is the perceived low degree to which the company leaders live consistent with the company's new values, and their overall effectiveness as leaders.

A leadership team not committed to effective change might consider withholding this information and shying away from revealing the truth. This company did not, however, and to their credit, fed back to the organization completely and without reservation the results of the baseline data collection. Their feeling was, if we are truly committed to living our values of honesty and openness, then we must share this information with others. In doing so, they are choosing a path that will establish a strong foundation for the future, one built not on rhetoric, but on deeds.

THE LEADER OF THE FUTURE

Surprisingly few leaders of organizations make these kinds of choices. Those who do, however, often see the benefits of their choices. The benefits come from the kind of trust that develops in sharing information. The benefits come over time in the kind of people the organization attracts and retains. The benefits come in the form of learning.

In today's business climate, all too often, leaders of

organizations take the easy and quick path of immediate financial results, and forego the painful process of long-term learning. They make choices driven by pressures from their stockholders to produce immediate high returns on investment, and driven by societal expectations that focus on quick payback, and by their own definition of success, which is often focused on short-term financial results to the exclusion of long-term well-being. In addition, the leaders of today tend to be driven by models of the past that say leaders are strong, tough decision makers who do not make mistakes.

Successful leaders of significant and enduring organizational change take an alternative approach. They see their job as creating the context within which people learn. They focus far more on the kinds of factors that influence the creation of an effective, healthy organizational culture than on immediate results. They see their job as being a model of the values and behaviors they espouse. They create conditions where people can learn and grow and, from that growth, contribute to the future adaptability and long-term success of the organization well into the future. In addition, they motivate their middle managers to play a similar kind of leadership role in their own organizations (for leadership comparison see Figure 14–3).

Such a form of leadership is not the norm in today's business world. While we have learned as a society much about leadership in the past few years, we still have a long way to go to put into practice what we have learned. In today's businesses, more often than not, many leaders still view their job as that of decision maker rather than as a decision facilitator. Many leaders still hold the assumption that their job is to motivate others, rather than release the inherent motivation within people by creating systems, structures, and policies that maximize shared decision-making, individual and organizational growth, and continuous learning. Many leaders still see their job as adapting to change, rather than anticipating change and creating a vision for the future that leads the change. And many leaders still see their job as placating workers rather than creating conditions where all people experience ownership of and commitment to their work and their organization and to the business as a whole.

Leaders who take the alternative breakthrough approach seem to produce results that are way ahead of those created by traditional leaders. In Kotter and Hesketh's research, for example, the performance im-

	Current	Future/Breakthrough
RELATIONSHIP TO CUSTOMERS	*TOP MANAGEMENT* △ *CUSTOMERS*	*CUSTOMERS* ▽ *TOP MANAGEMENT*
WHERE KNOWLEDGE IS HELD AND WHERE DECISIONS GET MADE	At top	Throughout
LEADER'S ROLE	Direct, guide, and control	Establish direction Create environment to release energy Align organization
ASSUMPTION ABOUT PEOPLE	Leaders motivate others	Others are motivated Leader's job is to release motivation and inspire
AIM FOR ORGANIZATION	Adapt to change	Create the future
AIM FOR PEOPLE	Satisfaction	Ownership, commitment

Figure 14-3. Leadership designed for enduring success.

provements that accompanied these forms of leadership "ranged from good to extraordinary. More important, people well acquainted with these cases seem to agree almost universally that the firms involved were left better positioned for the future."[5]

CONCLUSION

Charles Darwin taught us, over a century ago, that the survival of all species on this planet can be described as survival of the fittest. Interestingly, this axiom has been distorted through the years to mean "survival of the strongest." But the tenor of his message was that survival of a species was a direct result of its ability to adapt to its environment. In its original meaning, "fittest" meant the best fit between the species and its environment. I believe the same is true of organizations. Their success is directly dependent on their ability to detect, anticipate, and respond to changes in the environment. When the environment changes, so must organizations. This is the true challenge of learning, and the ultimate challenge for organizations both now and in the future. When organizations adapt and rearchitect themselves as a result of their learning to learn, then and only then will they have the possibility of enduring success.

---

[5] Kotter, J. and Hesketh, J., *Corporate Culture and Performance*, Free Press, New York, 1992, p. 147.

Appendix A
XYZ Corporation Example Interview Questions

General Questions

1. What in your view are the major strengths of this organization?

2. What in your view are the major weaknesses of this organization?

Culture

3. Make believe this organization is a person. Describe this person to me.

4. What are the main rules around here that everyone has to follow?

5. If I were just starting out here and asked you what does it take to succeed here, what would you tell me?

6. On a scale of 1–10, where 1 is poor and 10 is excellent, how well do people work together in this organization?

Business Focus

7. How would you define your business? What business are you in?

8. Who are your major customers?

9. Who are your major competitors?

10. How do you define success in your organization?

11. What is your strategy to achieve success in your business?

12. To what extent are people in this company committed to that vision?

Vision

11. What is your vision for the future of this organization? What contribution do you want (the company) to be most known for?

12. To what extent are you moving toward your vision?

Appendix B
XYZ
Organizational
Questionnaire

GENERAL INSTRUCTIONS

This questionnaire contains a number of questions and statements about you, your job, and your feelings about XYZ Company as a whole. Through the questionnaire, we are inviting everyone at XYZ to give us their candid thoughts and feelings about XYZ. Please answer the questions based on your own experience at XYZ. Most of these questions ask that you circle one of several numbers on a scale. Please circle the number that best matches your feelings about the question.

Please note that the scale description may be different in different parts of the questionnaire. Some questions refer to your levels of satisfaction, while most others ask you how much you agree or disagree with a statement. Be sure to read the special instructions at the beginning of each section and mark your responses accordingly.

I. **The following information is needed to help us with the statistical analysis of this survey. This information will allow comparisons between different groups of associates. For each question below, indicate your answer by circling the letter on the scale to the right.**

1. What is your job classification? . . . . | a | b | c |

   (a) Associate
   (b) Technical Associate
   (c) Managing Associate

2. In which office of XYZ are you currently employed? . . . . | a | b | c | d | e |

   (a) Northwest Region   (d) Midwest Region
   (b) Southwest Region   (e) Home Office
   (c) Eastern Region

	Strongly Disagree	Disagree	Slightly Disagree	Neither Agree or Disagree	Slightly Agree	Agree	Strongly Agree

II. The following statements are about you and your job at XYZ. When answering, keep in mind your experiences in working here. Please circle the number that best represents how much you agree with each statement.

3. I am offered the training I need to be effective on my job   1   2   3   4   5   6   7

4. I am given freedom to make appropriate decisions to satisfy and serve XYZ's customers   1   2   3   4   5   6   7

5. When a problem comes up on my job, I am encouraged to take responsibility for solving it   1   2   3   4   5   6   7

6. I feel I have full freedom to make critical decisions in my job   1   2   3   4   5   6   7

7. I have a clear understanding of what is expected of me in this company   1   2   3   4   5   6   7

8. I am encouraged to take risks and be innovative in my work   1   2   3   4   5   6   7

	Strongly Disagree	Disagree	Slightly Disagree	Neither Agree or Disagree	Slightly Agree	Agree	Strongly Agree

III. The following statements are about XYZ as a company. When answering, keep in mind your experiences in working here. Please circle the number that best represents how much you agree with each statement.

Statement	SD	D	SlD	N	SlA	A	SA
9. People at XYZ are very responsive to customers when they have a problem or concern	1	2	3	4	5	6	7
10. Critical policies and procedures are regularly communicated and reinforced here at XYZ	1	2	3	4	5	6	7
11. I am regularly informed of changes in XYZ that affect me directly	1	2	3	4	5	6	7
12. Management at XYZ often keeps us in the dark about things we ought to know	1	2	3	4	5	6	7
13. XYZ does a good job of listening to its customers	1	2	3	4	5	6	7
14. When making decisions at XYZ, we take into consideration our customer's needs and expectations	1	2	3	4	5	6	7
15. When a change is needed in XYZ, we mobilize rapidly and take action	1	2	3	4	5	6	7
16. Critical information flows through this company in an efficient manner	1	2	3	4	5	6	7

	Strongly Disagree	Disagree	Slightly Disagree	Neither Agree or Disagree	Slightly Agree	Agree	Strongly Agree
17. Day to day work activities are sensibly organized	1	2	3	4	5	6	7
18. When we make a commitment to a customer, we keep it	1	2	3	4	5	6	7
19. XYZ does a good job of meeting its changing customers' needs	1	2	3	4	5	6	7
20. The way our work is organized helps us respond to our customers' needs	1	2	3	4	5	6	7
21. We respond to our customers' needs in a quick and timely manner	1	2	3	4	5	6	7
22. Regions or offices have full freedom to make their own decisions and shape their direction	1	2	3	4	5	6	7
23. Rules and regulations at XYZ get in the way of making decisions	1	2	3	4	5	6	7
24. Favoritism too often influences decisions at XYZ	1	2	3	4	5	6	7
25. We demonstrate care for our customers in all we do at XYZ	1	2	3	4	5	6	7
26. The way we are organized as a company hinders our ability to get things done	1	2	3	4	5	6	7

Appendix C
What to Consider
When Conducting
a Survey

WHEN CONDUCTING THE INTERVIEWS

Since the purpose of interviews is to obtain valid and accurate information about the thoughts, feelings, and opinions of your interviewees, it is important that the leadership of the organization does not administer the interview themselves. Experience shows that people will rarely give the leaders of an organization directly the kind of information they want. They will sometimes not be open about negative feelings, and they will often not talk directly about their concerns about the leadership team as a whole. In effect, if you or other members of the leadership team conduct the interviews, you run the risk of getting a white-washed version of what is really going on.

To conduct the interviews, it is often best to select

people, either in another part of the company, or outside the company. These people need to be skilled in research type interviews and know how to summarize the results for you.

Each interview should have:

1. An introduction—where the interviewer explains the purpose of the interview, what will happen with the results, and that information offered will be kept confidential.

2. Preliminary questions—where the interviewer gets facts about the person's job, responsibilities, and asks questions about organizational history.

3. Main questions—where the interviewer asks the most significant and critical questions that comprise the body of the organizational diagnosis.

4. Post-interview questions—where the interviewee is invited to ask questions of the interviewer and any concerns that were raised in the interview.

In addition to the above phases of the interview, the tone of each interview should have the following characteristics:

- Interviewer remains *neutral* and *nonevaluative*. All reactions to interviewee should be supportive and nonconfrontative, that is, accepting of the value of the person's point of view.
- Interview should be *voluntary* and results should be kept *confidential.*
- Both prepared questions and probing questions are important. The probing questions seek clarification of follow-up on important points raised by the interviewee. Leading questions are to be avoided.

• Answers should be written down as close to verbatim as possible.

How to Design
an Organizational Survey

As mentioned in chapter six, a key task in designing a survey is to determine the dimensions of the survey. The steps below expand upon the information provided in chapter six and give you a more detailed sense of how to proceed. It is important to note that there are numerous technical considerations in developing a survey. A full explanation of how to word the questions and how to construct a questionnaire is beyond the scope of this book. If you are serious about doing a study, I strongly recommend you work with someone who has considerable experience in designing and conducting organizational surveys to ensure you do not fall into the myriad of possible traps. The steps below, however, will give you a sense of the presence of creating a questionnaire.

Step One: Clarify the dimensions you want to survey. These are the broad categories of things you may want to get information on. They might include such things as:

- people's satisfaction with their job
- the effectiveness of managers in managing people
- the effectiveness of your performance management system
- the quality of information flow
- the degree to which people are clear about the strategic direction of the organization

- morale in the organization
- the effectiveness of the decision-making process

Use the information you generated from the interviews to guide and determine what dimensions to survey.

Step Two: Take each dimension and write a list of behaviors that seem to be examples of each one. For example, if one of your dimensions is the degree to which managers *empower employees,* ask yourself, what does that look like in actual behavior? Your answer might look something like the following:

Managers Empower Employees

- Ensure people who implement decisions are involved in making the decisions.
- Support risk taking by acknowledging and reinforcing risks even when a mistake is made as a result of the risk.
- Push decision making down to the lowest possible level.

In effect, for each dimension you want to survey, you are asking the question: What does this mean to us? How would I know if I had it? What types of behaviors would I see? The answers to these questions from the basis of constructing questions in the survey.

Step Three: Take the input above and construct questions for the survey. Be sure to use language like that in appendix B. These questions are worded in a way that is easy to read and understand. As you word questions, it is important they be worded in a way that ensures that each person interprets the question in the same way.

Step Four: Design the first draft of the questionnaire with full instructions and well-formatted questions.

Step Five: Conduct a pilot test of the survey by administering the survey to 8–20 people in the organization. After they take the survey, ask a number of questions to test the effectiveness of the survey, such as:

- How long did it take to fill it out? (15–30 minutes is an ideal range.)
- Were there questions that were unclear?
- Were there questions that you wish we had asked that we didn't?

In advance of this, go through the survey and identify questions that you think might be ambiguous or might produce differing interpretations of the question. Ask each person to tell you their interpretations of the question from different people. Take each question and ask the pilot survey taker to tell you how they interpreted the question. This way you will find out the extent to which the meaning people attached to the questions were the same as you had intended.

Step Six: Modify the questionnaire on the basis of the above input and either conduct another test if there were significant modifications, or have this be the final version.

How to Conduct a Survey
Using the Questionnaire

The following is a blow-by-blow explanation for how to conduct the survey.

There are three steps to conducting the survey:

1. Preparing your organization by informing people about the study.

2. Administering the survey.

3. Analyzing the results.

I will explore the first two in detail. See Chapter 6 for step three.

Preparing the organization. Since the organization will already be aware that you are in the process of seeking ways to strengthen the company as a whole, preparing the organization for a survey is relatively easy. It involves sending out a memo to everyone reminding them of the process that you have been going through as a company and informing them what the survey is intended to accomplish, how it will be conducted, and how the data will be used. In this case, assuming you have had ample meetings to discuss your growth and development efforts, a memo from the leader of the company should suffice.

Administering the Survey. In planning the survey administration, a number of decisions need to be made:

- When to administer the survey.
- Where to conduct the survey.
- How to distribute the surveys.
- Who administers the survey.

- How to collect the surveys to ensure confidentiality.

These questions need to be thought through prior to conducting the survey so that the survey goes smoothly and efficiently. Your actions need to reinforce the confidentiality of the study as well as its importance. The section below on administering the survey gives guidelines for the remaining questions. Once you have read the section below, get your Design Team together and discuss each of the above questions. Your answers to these questions provide the necessary planning for administering the survey.

Assuming you have already informed the organization about the survey and their involvement in it, you are now ready to administer the survey. You can do this after you have done the interviews, or simultaneously.

Survey administration should be planned with three overall aims in mind:

- to assure confidentiality
- to assure a high rate of return
- to assure valid results

This means that:

1. Everyone in the organization receives a copy of the survey with the least amount of confusion or inconvenience possible.

2. Participants have adequate time and proper conditions for completing their survey.

3. All completed surveys are returned.

4. The administration procedures make it clear that individual responses will not be seen by anyone except the survey researchers.

5. Someone other than management administer the surveys. It is important that management not be involved in administration as this may lead to the perception that a) employees are not free to give honest opinions, b) an individual's responses will be known to management, and c) the survey is not really going to be handled objectively.

To administer the survey, have the people responsible for administration go through the following steps:

> **Step One:** Pick a time to administer the survey. I think that the best time to administer the survey is during the week. If time is made available to employees during the workday, more people are likely to respond to the survey. Furthermore, this communicates to employees the importance and value you place on the organizational study. Pick a time when doing the survey will mimimally disrupt the workflow, yet have the greatest number of people available to take the survey.

> **Step Two:** Pick a place to administer the survey. For maximum results, surveys should be distributed, completed, and returned on-site. When people are allowed to take the survey home, they are less likely to return it. A good place to administer the survey is a central meeting place. This simplifies the distribution and collection of surveys. If a central meeting place is unavailable, have the survey administered for each department or unit in their own meeting room.

Step Three: Call the meeting to administer the survey.

Step Four: Introduce the survey, making sure the following key elements are covered.

- Directions are given for completing and returning the survey.
- There is an explanation of how confidentiality is ensured.
- People are told that their participation is voluntary; that they should skip any items they *choose* not to answer.
- That this is an opportunity to express their feelings and opinions frankly and freely
- When they will get feedback on the results of the survey.

Step Five: Establish a relaxed atmosphere in the room. Let people know this is not a test. There are no right or wrong answers. Provide coffee and donuts or whatever to make this informal. Be available to answer questions. Be sure there are sufficient supplies.

Step Six: Hand out the survey and ask people to fill it out.

Step Seven: When people are finished, have them place their survey in a plain, unmarked envelope which they seal. Place a box somewhere in the room. Be sure the box is sealed and that there is a slot on top for them to place their envelopes. Ask them to place their envelopes in the sealed box. All of this indicates to people that their responses will be handled with care and confidentiality. Send the box to a predetermined site outside the company where the survey data will be inputted into a computer and analyzed.

Step Eight: For people unavailable to take the survey on this day, send them a survey and ask them to complete it, seal it, and mail it to a predetermined data collection site. Enclose an addressed and stamped envelope for their convenience. Be sure you give them the same instructions, either verbally or written, as you did all the other people.

Appendix D
Excerpted Survey Results

The following summary identifies potential strengths and areas of needed improvement throughout XYZ as revealed in your responses to the recently administered organizational questionnaire. The numbers in parentheses are the average or mean scores for XYZ as a whole. The highest possible number is 7.0 and the lowest is 1.0. Anything above a 4.9 is considered a potential strength while anything below a 4.3 is considered a potential opportunity for further improvement.

POTENTIAL STRENGTHS

1. One surprise in the questionnaire results is how satisfied people seem to feel about benefits at XYZ. Many feel particularly good about the bank of days program (5.4) and the 401K savings plan (5.7) (see Figure D1).

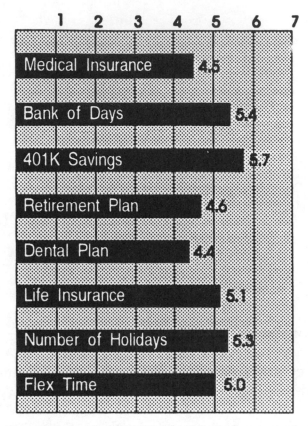

Figure D.1 Benefits/choices. How satisfied are you with the benefits offered in each of the above?

In addition, many feel XYZ is managing the process of administering benefits effectively (see Figure D2).

2. Quality and commitment to customer focus is strong overall (4.9); in particular, people at XYZ feel they are very responsive to customers when the customers have a problem (5.2), do a good job of listening to customers (5.0), take customers' needs into consideration when making decisions (5.1) and keep their commitments to customers (5.1).

   While our ability to focus on and satisfy our customers' needs seems strong, it is an area we can continue to improve in the future.

3. Strategic Direction is one of the stronger result areas in the company questionnaire (5.1). People seem to have a relatively clear and shared understanding of XYZ's strategic direction and support the company's focus on mission and values. In particular, they are excited about and committed to the mission (5.6), have a strong understanding of their role in the mission (5.5), are strongly committed to the values (5.9), and have a strong sense of pride in the company's values (5.9).

In addition, most of the people at XYZ are very familiar with the new mission and values. Roughly ⅔ have read about or heard about the Mission and Values many

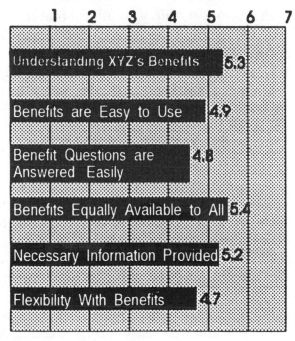

Figure D.2. Managing benefits.

times in the past six months are very familiar with it (see Figures D3 and D4).

4. The quality and availability of training seems to meet people's needs at XYZ relatively well. They feel encouraged by their managing associate to take time from their job for training (5.1), that training is available to be effective in their job (5.0), and that trainers are generally competent and effective (5.1).

5. The quality of leadership from our Managing Associates seems to be relatively high. In particular, Managing Associates tend to encourage open questioning of ideas (5.2). They welcome a variety of views and ideas (5.1). Managing Associates challenge people at XYZ to do high-quality work (5.6) and are open to new and creative ideas (5.1).

In addition, Managing Associates are perceived as behaving in an honest, fair, and ethical manner (5.2).

While relatively high compared to other areas surveyed in the questionnaire, the quality of leadership on the part of Managing Associates is an area that will continue to need attention and development in the future.

POTENTIAL OPPORTUNITY AREAS:

1. Generally, people at XYZ are not satisfied with the quality of technology available to them. The overall average or mean for questions related to Technology was 4.2. In particular, they are not satisfied with the equipment and technology (3.6), the data and information available to them to do their job (4.0), and the ability of the technology and equipment to help them respond to customers' needs and problems (4.0). Managing Associ-

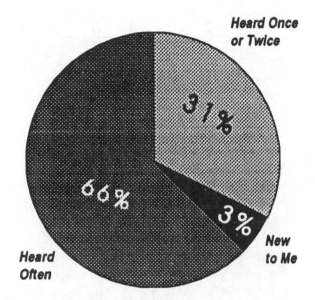

Figure D.3. Communication of mission.

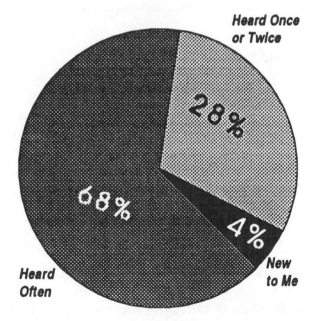

Figure D.4. Communication of values.

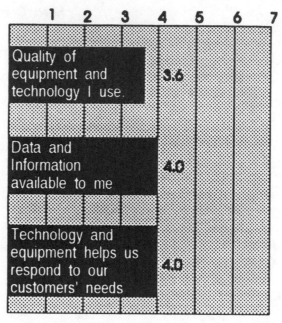

Figure D.5. Technology. How satisfied are you with the above?

ates in particular feel dissatisfied with these latter two areas (see Figure D5).

2. Communication at XYZ appears to be an area worthy of development. Overall, the average or mean for questions relating to communication is 4.2. In particular, many feel management keeps them in the dark about things they ought to know about (3.6). Many feel that critical information does not flow through XYZ in an efficient manner (3.6). Finally, many feel that sensitive information is not held in confidence (3.7).

3. In general, many feel that the executive officer's quality of leadership as a group, or in some cases as individuals, is an opportunity for development (4.2). In particular, many feel that the executive officers do not demonstrate an ability to establish trusting relation-

ships (4.0), they put too much focus on short-term issues (4.0), they do not encourage risk taking (4.0), and, when people have a complaint, many do not feel free to talk to them (3.8).

4. The organizational structure at the time of the questionnaire is seen as an area needing improvement (4.0). In particular, many feel XYZ does not mobilize rapidly to take action when change is needed (3.8), rules and regulations at XYZ get in the way of decision making (3.4) and the way XYZ is organized hinders our ability to get things done (3.7).

It should be noted that soon after the questionnaire

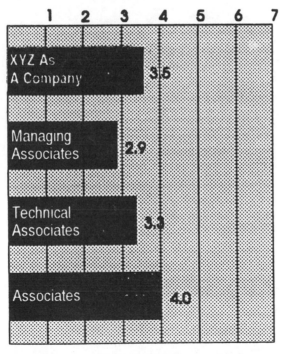

Figure D.6. Decision making. Regions or offices have full freedom to make their own decisions and shape their own direction.

was administered, a Product Management structure was introduced to improve many of the structural areas of concern.

5. In addition, there are a number of specific areas that emerged as opportunities for improvement.

    a. Many feel that offices do not have full freedom to make their own decisions or shape their own direction (3.5). This is felt most strongly by the Managing Associate population (2.9) (see Figure D6).

In addition, many feel that departments are not given freedom to make their own decisions and shape their direction (4.1).

Index

438